VISIBLE
LEARNING
FOR MATHEMATICS
GRADES K–12

VISIBLE LEARNING
FOR MATHEMATICS

What Works Best to Optimize Student Learning

GRADES K–12

JOHN HATTIE, DOUGLAS FISHER, AND NANCY FREY

WITH LINDA M. GOJAK, SARA DELANO MOORE, AND WILLIAM MELLMAN

Foreword by Diane J. Briars

FOR INFORMATION:

Corwin

A SAGE Company

2455 Teller Road

Thousand Oaks, California 91320

(800) 233-9936

www.corwin.com

SAGE Publications Ltd.

1 Oliver's Yard

55 City Road

London EC1Y 1SP

United Kingdom

SAGE Publications India Pvt. Ltd.

B 1/I 1 Mohan Cooperative Industrial Area

Mathura Road, New Delhi 110 044

India

SAGE Publications Asia-Pacific Pte. Ltd.

3 Church Street

#10-04 Samsung Hub

Singapore 049483

Acquisitions Editor: Erin Null

Editorial Development Manager: Julie Nemer

Editorial Assistant: Nicole Shade

Production Editor: Melanie Birdsall

Copy Editor: Liann Lech

Typesetter: C&M Digitals (P) Ltd.

Proofreader: Scott Oney

Indexer: Molly Hall

Cover Designer: Rose Storey

Marketing Managers: Rebecca Eaton and Margaret O'Connor

Printed in the United States of America

ISBN 978-1-5063-6294-6

This book is printed on acid-free paper.

SUSTAINABLE FORESTRY INITIATIVE

Certified Chain of Custody
Promoting Sustainable Forestry
www.sfiprogram.org
SFI-01268

SFI label applies to text stock

18 19 20 21 10 9 8 7

Contents

Visit the companion website at
http://resources.corwin.com/VL-mathematics
to access videos and downloadable versions
of all reproducibles.

List of Figures

Chapter 3. Mathematical Tasks and Talk That Guide Learning

Chapter 4. Surface Mathematics Learning Made Visible

Chapter 5. Deep Mathematics Learning Made Visible

Chapter 6. Making Mathematics Learning Visible Through Transfer Learning

Chapter 7. Assessment, Feedback, and Meeting the Needs of All Learners

List of Videos

Note From the Publisher: The authors have provided video and web content throughout the book that is available to you through QR codes. To read a QR code, you must have a smartphone or tablet with a camera. We recommend that you download a QR code reader app that is made specifically for your phone or tablet brand.

Videos may also be accessed at
http://resources.corwin.com/VL-mathematics

Chapter 4. Surface Mathematics Learning Made Visible

Chapter 5. Deep Mathematics Learning Made Visible

Chapter 6. Making Mathematics Learning Visible Through Transfer Learning

Chapter 7. Assessment, Feedback, and Meeting the Needs of All Learners

About the Teachers Featured in the Videos

Hilda Martinez is a kindergarten teacher at Zamorano Elementary School in the San Diego Unified School District in San Diego, CA. She has been teaching for eighteen years.

Zamorano Elementary School is in the San Diego Unified School District in San Diego, CA. The school has just over 1100 students comprised of 38 percent Hispanic, 26 percent Filipino, 19 percent African American, 10 percent multiethnic, 4 percent White, 1 percent Pacific Islander, 1 percent Indochinese, and 0.4 percent Asian. Approximately 30 percent of students are English Language Learners, and 74 percent are eligible for a free or reduced-price lunch.

Néstor Daniel Espinoza-Agraz is a third-grade teacher at the Excellence and Justice in Education (EJE) Academies Charter School in El Cajon, CA. He has been teaching for five years.

Excellence and Justice in Education (EJE) Academies Charter School is in El Cajon, CA. The school has just over 400 students composed of 86 percent Hispanic, 5.5 percent black or African American, 5.5 percent White, 1 percent American Indian or Alaska Native, 0.7 percent Asian, 0.5 percent Filipino, and 1.4 percent multiethnic. Approximately 62 percent of students are English Language Learners and 90 percent are eligible for a free or reduced-price lunch.

Lisa Forehand is a fifth-grade teacher at Dailard Elementary School in the San Diego Unified School District in San Diego, CA. She has been teaching for eighteen years.

Dailard Elementary School is in the San Diego Unified School District in San Diego, CA. The school has approximately 550 students composed of 61 percent White, 19 percent Hispanic, 10 percent Multiethnic, 3 percent African American, 2 percent Asian, 2 percent Filipino, and 3 percent Indochinese. Approximately 6 percent of students are English Language Learners, and 20 percent are eligible for a free or reduced-price lunch.

Steve Santana is a sixth-grade math teacher at Lewis Middle School in the San Diego Unified School District in San Diego, CA, and has been teaching for fourteen years.

Lewis Middle School is in the San Diego Unified School District in San Diego, CA. The school has just over 1,000 students composed of 33 percent White, 31 percent Hispanic, 13 percent Indochinese, 9 percent multiethnic, 7 percent African American, 3 percent Asian, 2 percent Filipino, 1 percent Native American, and 1 percent Pacific Islander. Seven percent of students are English Language Learners, and 48 percent are eligible for a free or reduced-price lunch.

Staci Benak is a seventh- and eighth-grade mathematics teacher at Health Sciences Middle School in San Diego, CA. She has been teaching for three years.

Health Sciences High & Middle College is in San Diego, CA, and educates 775 students in Grades 6–12. The school is focused on health and human services careers and the student population is 60 percent Latino/Hispanic, 20 percent African/African American, 14 percent White, and 6 percent Asian/Pacific Islander. More than 70 percent of the students qualify for free lunch, 15 percent

Joseph Assof is an eleventh- and twelfth-grade mathematics teacher at Health Sciences High & Middle College (HSHMC), a charter school in San Diego, CA. He has been teaching for three years.

Mindy Shacklett is Coordinator of Mathematics at the San Diego County Office of Education. She has been teaching for twenty-two years.

are identified as needing special education services, and 21 percent arc English Language Learners.

Foreword

Effective teaching is the non-negotiable core of any mathematics program. As mathematics educators, we continually strive to improve our teaching so that every child develops the mathematical proficiency needed to be prepared for his or her future. By *mathematical proficiency*, we mean the five interrelated strands of conceptual understanding, procedural fluency, strategic competence, adaptive reasoning, and productive disposition (National Research Council, 2001).

There is a plethora of "research-based" recommendations about instructional practices that we should employ to build students' proficiency, such as peer tutoring, using worthwhile tasks, building meta-cognitive capabilities, using manipulatives, project-based learning, direct instruction . . . the list goes on and on. But which practices have a strong research foundation? And which are likely to produce the most significant pay-off in terms of students' learning?

Several recent reports indicate considerable consensus about the essential elements of effective mathematics teaching based on mathematics education and cognitive science research over the past two decades. The National Council of Teachers of Mathematics' (NCTM) publication *Principles to Actions: Ensuring Mathematical Success for All* describes effective teaching as "teaching that engages students in meaningful learning through individual and collaborative experiences that promote their ability to make sense of mathematical ideas and reason mathematically" (NCTM, 2014, p. 5). It also identifies the following eight high-leverage teaching practices that support meaningful learning:

1. Establish mathematics goals to focus learning.
2. Implement tasks that promote reasoning and problem solving.
3. Use and connect mathematical representations.

4. Facilitate meaningful mathematical discourse.

5. Pose purposeful questions.

6. Build procedural fluency from conceptual understanding.

7. Support productive struggle in learning mathematics.

8. Elicit and use evidence of student thinking.

The 2012 National Research Council report *Education for Life and Work* identifies the following essential features of instruction that promotes students' acquisition of the 21st century competencies of "transferable knowledge, including content knowledge in a domain and knowledge of how, why, and when to apply this knowledge to answer questions and solve problems" (p. 6) in mathematics, science, and English/language arts:

- Engaging learners in challenging tasks, with supportive guidance and feedback

- Using multiple and varied representations of concepts and tasks

- Encouraging elaboration, questioning, and self-explanation

- Teaching with examples and cases

- Priming student motivation

- Using formative assessment

These features are strikingly similar to the NCTM effective teaching practices described above.

Consensus on these effective practices, while critically important, leaves open the questions of their relative effectiveness, the conditions in which they are most effective, and details of their implementation in the classroom. *Visible Learning for Mathematics* addresses these questions and more, which makes it an invaluable resource for mathematics educators at all levels.

First, *Visible Learning for Mathematics* extends John Hattie's original groundbreaking meta-analysis of educational practices in *Visible Learning* (2009) to specific mathematics teaching practices. The book goes beyond identifying research-based practices to providing the relative effect a teaching practice has on student learning—the effect size. For example, the second effective teaching practice calls for implementing tasks that promote reasoning and problem solving. In *Visible*

Learning for Mathematics, the authors describe how engaging students in problem-based learning by using tasks that require them to apply their prior knowledge and skills in new situations has a strong effect on student learning (effect size of 0.61). The authors emphasize the importance of selecting tasks that are appropriate, given students' prior knowledge and the learning goals for the lesson, and describe criteria for doing so.

High-quality instruction involves both implementing effective practices and eliminating ineffective practices. A second extremely valuable feature of *Visible Learning for Mathematics* is that it identifies ineffective practices, including ones that have face validity and are widely used, such as ability grouping in elementary grades (effect size of only 0.16) and stopping instruction prior to high-stakes testing to teach test-taking (test prep) (effect size of only 0.27). The authors then provide alternatives to these ineffective practices such as effective grouping strategies and distributed practice (effect size of 0.71) in place of test prep.

Further, the book situates highly effective teaching practices in three phases of learning—surface, deep, and transfer learning. It productively redefines "surface learning" as the phase in which students build initial conceptual understanding of a mathematical idea and learn related vocabulary and procedural skills. Unfortunately, many teachers stop here, which doesn't give students the complete picture. It is through the subsequent phases of deep and transfer learning that students begin connecting ideas, making generalizations, and applying their knowledge to new and novel situations.

This framework offers a precise way to consider when particular teaching practices most benefit students' learning, considering where students are in the learning process. For example, it recommends the kinds of mathematical tasks and talk that are likely to be most beneficial in each phase. It clarifies when and why practices like direct instruction or problem-based learning are most useful and effective and gives specific tools for implementing them. In short, it helps us know more specifically what to do, when, and why to achieve maximum impact in our classrooms. The authors illustrate this through the use of vignettes and concrete tools that show readers how to incorporate particular practices into one's teaching. The supplemental videos offer classroom-based models of what these practices look and sound like for each phase of learning across the K–12 spectrum, along with teachers' personal reflections on how they incorporate these practices into day-to-day instruction.

Finally, the book is designed to support individual and collaborative professional learning. We know teachers are more effective when they're working together. The reflection and discussion questions at the end of each chapter give teachers an opportunity to digest the book a chapter at a time, considering and discussing how what they're learning can be applied in their own situations. It is an extremely valuable extension of the ideas in *Principles to Actions* in that it supports taking action. And while the book is written for teachers, it will surely be an equally valuable resource for all mathematics educators, including leaders, administrators, and teacher educators.

In short, with its focus on true student-centered teaching, this book brings all the research together into a coherent and precise structure that can guide our practice, making the learning visible both to our students and to us. It's a must-read. I highly recommend it.

—Diane J. Briars
Past President (2014–2016)
National Council of Teachers of Mathematics

About the Authors

Dr. John Hattie has been Professor of Education and Director of the Melbourne Education Research Institute at the University of Melbourne, Australia, since March 2011. He was previously Professor of Education at the University of Auckland, University of North Carolina, and University of Western Australia. His research interests are based on applying measurement models to education problems. He is president of the International Test Commission, served as adviser to various Ministers, chaired the NZ performance-based research fund, and in the last Queen's Birthday awards was made "Order of Merit for New Zealand" for services to education. He is a cricket umpire and coach, enjoys being a dad to his young men, is besotted with his dogs, and moved with his wife as she attained a promotion to Melbourne. Learn more about his research at www.corwin.com/visiblelearning.

Douglas Fisher, PhD, is Professor of Educational Leadership at San Diego State University and a teacher leader at Health Sciences High & Middle College. He holds a master's degree in public health with an emphasis in research methods and biostatistics and a doctoral degree in multicultural education. He has been an early intervention teacher, elementary teacher, health educator, and administrator in California.

Nancy Frey, PhD, is Professor of Educational Leadership at San Diego State University. The recipient of the 2016 Thought Leader Award in Adolescent Literacy from the International Literacy Association, she is also a teacher-leader at Health Sciences High & Middle College and a credentialed special educator and administrator in California.

Linda M. Gojak, MEd, is a past president of the National Council of Teachers of Mathematics. At Hawken School in Lyndhurst, Ohio, Linda chaired the K–8 mathematics department and taught Grades 4–8 mathematics. In her work as director of the Center for Mathematics and Science Education, Teaching, and Technology (CMSETT) at John Carroll University, she planned and facilitated professional development for K–12 mathematics teachers. Linda has been actively involved in professional organizations including the Mathematical Sciences Education Board, the Conference Board of the Mathematical Sciences, the Council of Presidential Awardees in Mathematics, and the MathCounts Board of Directors. She has served as president of the National Council of Supervisors of Mathematics and president of the Ohio Council of Teachers of Mathematics. Among her recognitions are the Presidential Award for Excellence in Mathematics and Science Teaching and the Christofferson-Fawcett Award for lifetime contribution to mathematics education.

Sara Delano Moore, PhD, is an independent educational consultant at SDM Learning. A fourth-generation educator, she focuses on helping teachers and students understand mathematics as a coherent and connected discipline through the power of deep understanding and multiple representations for learning. Her interests include building conceptual understanding of mathematics to support procedural fluency and applications, incorporating engaging and high-quality literature into mathematics and science instruction, and connecting mathematics with engineering design in meaningful ways. Sara has worked as a classroom teacher of mathematics and science in the elementary and middle grades, a mathematics teacher educator, Director of the Center for Middle School Academic Achievement for the Commonwealth of Kentucky, and Director of Mathematics & Science at ETA hand2mind.

William Mellman, EdD, has been a math and science teacher, vice principal, instructional leader, and program director who oversaw the mathematics department at Health Sciences High & Middle College, which he turned into an exemplar that other school districts and teachers strive to emulate. He currently serves as an elementary school principal in National City, CA, where he has significantly raised student achievement.

Acknowledgments

Corwin gratefully acknowledges the contributions of the following reviewers:

Kristen Acquarelli
Consultant; Former Director
 of Elementary Mathematics
 Teachers Development Group
West Linn, OR

Ellen Asregadoo
Elementary Teacher
New York City Department
 of Education
New York, NY

JoAnn Hiatt
Mathematics Teacher
Belton High School
Belton, MO

Karen Kersey
Elementary Teacher
Kanawha County Schools
St. Albans, WV

Lyneille Meza
Director of Data and Assessment;
 Former Math Teacher
Denton ISD
Denton, TX

Nanci N. Smith
Education Consultant
Classrooms Educational
 Consulting
Cave Creek, AZ

David Weiss
Principal
Westgate Elementary School
Lakewood, CO

Preface

We believe that everyone can and should learn mathematics. We believe that numbers and the mathematics we use to make sense of them are amazing and beautiful. Some of the ways people have experienced mathematics instruction didn't invite them into that beautiful space. If you love numbers and the way you were taught mathematics, this book is for you. It will help you extend and validate your teaching repertoire. But if you dislike mathematics because of how you were taught, this book is also for you because it will provide you with ideas for improving students' learning and perhaps improve your own understanding along the way. This book is about teaching ideas in ways that propel students into the beauty, logic, usefulness, and joy of mathematics.

Why Learn Mathematics?

Mathematics knowledge is one of the significant gatekeepers in modern society. Demonstrating understanding of mathematics in high school opens doors to college. Passing college mathematics classes increases the likelihood that a student will actually earn a degree. Most of us know that people who do better in school, and who attend school for a longer portion of their lives, go on to live longer, healthier, happier lives. Unfortunately, those who don't do well in mathematics often get locked out of these benefits (Stinson, 2004). It may be stating the obvious, but we will say it anyway: People who understand mathematics have a higher quality of life.

According to *Forbes* magazine, the top ten highest earning college degrees are computer engineering, economics, electrical engineering, computer science, mechanical engineering, finance, mathematics, civil engineering, political science, and marketing. These degrees have one thing in common—mathematics. Another service aimed at helping young people choose a college major, www.payscale.com, found that the top forty-eight highest paying college majors are mathematics related. The lack of adults with high levels of mathematical understanding consistently makes mathematics teaching positions among the most difficult to staff (Ingersoll, 2011).

The recognition of mathematics as a gatekeeper dates at least as far back as Plato's *Republic*. Plato (1996) argued that, although mathematics was important for all people who take part in everyday transactions, the study of math would take some from "Hades to the halls of the gods" (p. 215). But Plato, like many of his contemporaries, believed that mathematics education should be reserved for those that were "naturally skilled in calculation."

Plato's analysis of mathematics as a determinant of one's future success is still very much true. We now know that his assertion that mathematics should be reserved for those "naturally skilled in calculation" is absolutely false. This argument has been used for centuries to keep traditionally underrepresented groups, including females and students who live in poverty, out of high-level mathematics classes (Stinson, 2004) and, in turn, out of the top and middle of our economic structure. But neurological and brain studies have contributed to educational research, showing that all but a small group of students with significant cognitive disabilities are capable of success in high-level mathematics courses given the right instruction and resources (Boaler, 2015). Suggesting that groups of students won't be good at mathematics isn't only harmful, it's inaccurate. But, as Boaler notes, to be successful, students must receive high-quality instruction.

A major problem among many math teachers and students is that they believe they have to be talented or smart to successfully undertake mathematics. But if you review the biographies of great mathematicians, the common denominator is that they knew how to struggle. They knew that it was not exceptional talent that enabled success but the ability to persist; to enjoy the struggle; to see the growth of their learning as a function of seeking help and listening to others solve problems; and to try, try again (Lin-Siegler, Ahn, Chen, Fang, & Luna-Lucero, 2016).

Aspects of Mathematics Instruction That Works

There is an ongoing debate about what makes for good mathematics instruction, and how similar or different good mathematics instruction is to instruction in other disciplines such as English language arts, science, or history. The traditional approach to mathematics teaching has been one of explicitly teaching procedures and algorithms first, and then allowing students to build fluency through a lot of repeated practice. This is often thought of as "show-and-tell" or "drill-and-kill" mathematics, and is sometimes (wrongly) labeled as "direct instruction." Our definition of direct instruction includes much more than showing and telling students how to perform the computational skills they are learning. In Chapter 4, you will see an argument that there is a role for this expanded definition of direct instruction. In that chapter, we'll discuss when and how direct instruction might show up appropriately in a lesson, and the type of learning for which it is most effective.

Some researchers have argued that most children perform better in mathematics and can apply it more successfully to real-life situations when they first wrestle with a rich problem, make meaning of an idea and build conceptual understanding through a problem-solving process, consolidate that understanding by learning the associated procedures and skills, and then apply that understanding to real-life situations. Some people might label this as "inquiry-based" or "problem-based" instruction.

We believe that the story is not so black-and-white. Depending on the learning goals, and where students are in their learning progression, there is a balance of methods that makes for high-impact instruction and effective learning. In fact, in the United States, one of the three instructional shifts called for by the Common Core and other state standards for mathematics is a focus on **rigor**, which is defined as a balance among conceptual understanding, procedural skills and fluency, and application with *equal* intensity (National Governors Association Center for Best Practices & Council of Chief State School Officers, 2010).

While researchers and experts work to achieve consensus about quality instruction, teachers have to design and deliver instructional experiences for students. That's why we wrote this book. We know that there is "no 'one way' to teach mathematics" (National Council of Teachers of Mathematics [NCTM], 2000, p. 18). There are common threads and research-based principles that define high-quality mathematics instruction, as well as common thinking about what defines poor mathematics instruction. To our thinking, mathematics instruction—like any good instruction—must be intentionally designed and

> Direct instruction includes much more than showing and telling students how to perform the computational skills they are learning.

> Mathematical **rigor** is an instructional shift that calls for a balance among conceptual understanding, procedural skills and fluency, and application.

carefully orchestrated in the classroom, and should always focus on impacting student learning. We believe that mathematics teaching is most powerful when it starts with appropriately challenging learning intentions and success criteria. Teachers need to be clear on where their students are, where they need to go, and what the achievement of learning milestones looks like. We also believe that good mathematics learning is rooted in discourse and collaboration—both with teachers and among peers—and is orchestrated around appropriately challenging tasks. We think students should be doing more of the thinking and talking than the teacher. Finally, we believe that students deserve to own their learning. They must be partners in understanding with metacognition (thinking about their own thinking) and evaluating where they are going, how they are doing, and where to go next. These beliefs are reinforced by what the National Council of Teachers of Mathematics (2014, p. 10) has defined as the eight effective Mathematics Teaching Practices:

- Establishing mathematics goals to focus learning
- Implementing tasks that promote reasoning and problem solving
- Using and connecting mathematical representations
- Facilitating meaningful mathematical discourse
- Posing purposeful questions
- Building procedural fluency from conceptual understanding
- Supporting productive struggle in learning mathematics
- Eliciting and using evidence of student learning

Mobilizing the *Visible Learning* Evidence

Our hope is that this book will help to guide you as you plan your mathematics instruction. We outline specific actions that, when used in concert, strategically, and at the appropriate times based on learners' needs, will help students build their mathematical confidence and competence. The difference between this book and others is that we draw on the extensive research base John Hattie first developed and published in *Visible Learning* (2009) and has extended since then (e.g., 2012). The recommendations we make in this book are those that we believe hold the most power, because they stem from the research analysis that John has done, representing more than 300 million students. These recommendations are also supported by specific studies that mathematics education researchers have done over the past fifteen years, which will be referenced throughout this book.

For teachers unfamiliar with *Visible Learning*, we'd like to take a moment to explain. The *Visible Learning* database is composed of more than 1200 meta-analyses, with more than 70,000 studies and 300 million students. That's big data when it comes to education. In fact, some have claimed it's the largest educational research database amassed to date. To make sense of so much data, John focused his work on synthesizing meta-analyses. A meta-analysis is a statistical tool for combining findings from different studies with the goal of identifying patterns that can inform practice. In other words, they are studies of studies. The tool that is used to aggregate the information is an effect size. An effect size is the magnitude, or size, of a given effect. Effect size information helps readers understand the impact in more measurable terms. For example, imagine a study in which teaching students mathematics while having them chew gum resulted in statistically significant findings ($p < 0.01$, for example). People might buy stock in gum companies, and a new teaching fad would be born.

But then suppose, upon deeper reading, you learned that the gum-chewing students had a 0.03-month gain over the control group, an effect size pretty close to zero. You also learn that the sample size was very large, and the results were statistically significant because of that even though the impact was not very valuable. Would you still buy gum and have students chew away? Probably not (and we made this example up, anyway).

Understanding the effect size lets us know how powerful a given influence is in changing achievement, or how much bang you get for your buck. Some things are hard to implement and have very little impact. Other things are easy to implement and still have limited impact. We search for things that have a greater impact, some of which will be harder to implement and some of which will be easier to implement. When you're deciding what to implement to impact students' mathematical learning, wouldn't you like to know what the effect size is? Then you can decide if it's worth the effort. John was able to demonstrate that influences, strategies, actions, and so on with an effect

THE BAROMETER FOR THE INFLUENCE OF TEACHING TEST-TAKING

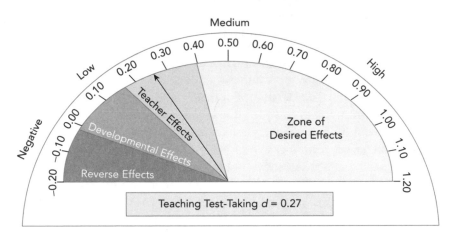

Source: Adapted from Hattie (2012).

Figure P.1

size greater than 0.40 allow students to learn at an appropriate rate, meaning a year of growth for a year in school. Before this level was established, teachers and researchers did not have a way to determine an acceptable threshold, and thus weak practices, often with studies that were statistically significant, continued.

Let's take two real examples.

First, let's consider teaching test-taking. There have been many efforts to review or reteach or coach students to do better on tests, such as the SAT or state accountability assessments. To help people understand effect sizes, John created a barometer so that information could be presented visually. The barometer for teaching test-taking can be found in Figure P.1. As you can see, the effect size is 0.27, well below the zone of desired effects of 0.40. This is based on 10 meta-analyses, with 267 studies, and a total population of 15,772. Although it's appealing to want to teach students the test before they take it, the evidence suggests that there are more effective ways for impacting students' learning.

THE BAROMETER FOR THE INFLUENCE OF CLASSROOM DISCUSSION

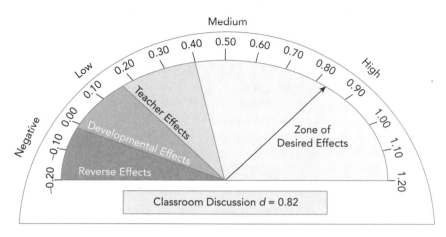

Classroom Discussion $d = 0.82$

Source: Adapted from Hattie (2012).

Second, let's consider increasing classroom discourse (synonymous with classroom discussion or dialogue). Students would be invited to talk with their peers in collaborative groups, working to solve complex and rich tasks. The students would not be ability grouped, but rather grouped by the teacher intentionally to ensure that there is academic diversity in each group as well as language support and varying degrees of interest and motivation. As can be seen in the barometer in Figure P.2, the effect size of classroom dialogue, or what we prefer to call discourse, is 0.82, well above our threshold, and likely to result in two years of learning gains for a year of schooling. Note that instructional practice aligns with the NCTM effective mathematics teaching practice of *facilitating meaningful mathematical discourse* as well as the Common Core Standards for Mathematical Practice (MP) of expecting students to *construct viable arguments and critique the reasoning of others* (MP 3). Other state and national standards list this practice as *mathematical communication* or *communication and interpretation* (see Appendix C). As a teacher, you would be wise to focus your energy on building classroom discourse rather than attempting to teach test-taking.

EFFECT SIZE
FOR CLASSROOM
DISCUSSION = 0.82

You'll find a complete list of the Standards for Mathematical Practice (MPs), a side-by-side chart of international mathematics practice or process standards, and Mathematics Teaching Practices in Appendixes B, C, and D of this book, respectively.

The Structure of *Visible Learning for Mathematics*

In the first chapter of this book, we focus on the methods John used to create *Visible Learning*. We explore in greater depth the concepts of meta-analysis and effect sizes. We also define and begin to discuss the importance of surface, deep, and transfer learning, including the impact of various instructional moves on each type of learning. The claim is that in all subjects, students have to develop surface-level understanding if they are ever going to go deep. In this book, it's important to note that we do not define surface-level learning as superficial learning of procedures and algorithms. Rather, we define it as the initial development of conceptual understanding, procedural skills, and vocabulary of a new topic. Deep learning is when students begin to make connections among conceptual ideas, and practice and apply procedural skills with greater fluency. It's when they plan, investigate, elaborate on their conceptual understandings, and begin to make generalizations based on their experiences. And we know that deep learning can facilitate transfer—the ability to more independently apply deeply understood concepts and skills to new and novel situations—which has been our goal all along. For mathematics especially, this is a framing device we have found useful for making decisions about *how* and *when* as a teacher you engage in certain tasks, questioning techniques, and teaching strategies to facilitate each level of learning. We will continue to refer to these phases of learning throughout the rest of the book.

In the second chapter, we explore the importance of teacher clarity, which has a strong effect size. In this chapter, we focus on learning intentions and success criteria because that is where teachers start, asking themselves, "What do my students need to learn today, and how will I know if they learned it?" Without a clear path, learning is left to chance. We want to be sure that teachers and students know what they are learning and what success looks like.

In Chapter 3, we will share our thinking about mathematical tasks that require different levels of cognitive demand and discuss what kinds of tasks are appropriate to use within different learning phases, depending on the learning intentions and success criteria defined. This chapter will offer some examples of the kinds of questions that teachers should ask to encourage rich mathematical discourse.

Chapters 4 through 6 discuss three phases of learning—surface, deep, and transfer—and discuss how the learning intentions (i.e., the instructional goals) of any lesson need to be a combination or balance of these phases of learning (Hattie, 2012). Chapter 4 will address the surface phase of learning in detail. Note that surface learning does not mean superficial learning. Rather, surface learning is a time when students initially are exposed to concepts, skills, and strategies. Surface learning is critical, because it provides a foundation on which to build as students are asked to think more deeply. Also, sometimes—but not always—there tends to be more teacher input during surface learning.

In Chapter 5, we define deep learning as a period when students consolidate their understanding and apply and extend some surface learning knowledge to support deeper conceptual understanding. Strategies for helping students to develop deep learning are included in this chapter with examples of how both small group and whole class discourse support deep learning. We think of this as a "sweet spot" that will often take up more instructional time, but can be accomplished only when students have the requisite knowledge to go deeper.

In Chapter 6, you will read about transfer learning as the point at which students take their consolidated knowledge and skills and apply what they know to new scenarios and different contexts. It is also a time when students are able to think more metacognitively, reflecting on their own learning and understanding.

A key point that we will make repeatedly is that teachers must know their students well and understand the impact that they have on their students. In planning lessons, teachers need to be empowered to choose the tasks and approaches that will maximize that impact. Mismatching a task or a pedagogical approach with the nature of learning expected will not create the desired impact. *What* and *when* are equally important when it comes to instruction that has an impact on learning. Approaches that facilitate students' surface-level learning do not work equally well for deep learning, and vice versa. Matching the right approach with the appropriate phase of learning is the critical lesson to be learned.

In Chapters 4 through 6, we also explore more deeply the *what*, *when*, and *how* to give you a clearer picture of how to orchestrate your class based on your learners' needs and your explicit learning intentions, in order to achieve maximum impact. In these chapters, we will dive more

Surface-level learning does not mean superficial learning.

deeply into the kinds of tasks, discussion and questioning techniques, and pedagogical strategies that are appropriate to each phase of learning.

It's important to point out, too, that learning is not linear. It is recursive. You should feel empowered to understand where in the cycle of learning your students are so that you can strategically select and employ the right tasks and strategies at the right time, based on where individual learners are in the surface-deep-transfer cycle on any given topic of study.

In the final chapter of this book, we focus more deeply on the role of continual assessment to help your learners answer the questions "Where am I?" "How am I doing?" and "Where to next?" We discuss some of the needs around differentiating instruction and response to intervention to help teachers ensure that they're meeting the needs of *all* learners, and point you toward resources where you can explore those topics in more depth. You'll also find several appendixes at the end of this book that cover (a) Hattie's full list of interventions with their effect sizes; (b) a list of Common Core Standards for Mathematical Practice (MPs) and what they mean in terms of what teachers do and what students do; (c) a non-exhaustive, side-by-side list of other state and international mathematical practice or process standards; (d) a list of NCTM's eight effective Mathematics Teaching Practices and what they mean in terms of what teachers do and what students do; and (e) a list of resources and websites we recommend to help you make mathematics learning visible.

This book includes a number of features that we hope will help you adopt and implement the practices outlined. For example, we include QR codes and links to videos. In these videos, you'll meet teachers and hear their perspectives about teaching mathematics. You'll also visit their classrooms. In addition, we include effect sizes in the margins for easy reference. We also include a number of teaching tips and definitions of terminology in the margins as well as a number of reproducible forms and tools that you can use in your classroom. These forms will be downloadable from our companion website at **http://resources.corwin.com/ VL-mathematics.**

Why This Book Now?

There is a reason there are six authors on this book. No one person can be *the* expert on learning, and we, as authors, come from a variety of teaching backgrounds across disciplines. We bring together a depth of experience, research, and perspectives that have helped us stretch our own thinking and challenge assumptions. We have worked to pool our knowledge and understanding about excellent instruction, recognize that there are subtle differences about what works when, and offer our best guidance as supported by research from both Hattie's meta-analyses and some of the excellent research that comes directly from the mathematics education community. Rather than being confined to labels of "researchers" or "literacy people" or "math people," we like to think of ourselves as "education people." We have worked together to share with you the what, when, and how of teaching practices that evidence shows work best for student learning in mathematics.

Finally, we feel that teaching begins with a promise. Robyn Jackson, an expert teacher and leader, suggests that teachers make promises to students. Her promises are included in Figure P.3. on the following page. Are these promises that you hope to make to your students? If so, this book will help.

PROMISES TO STUDENTS

1. I promise to pay attention to who you are and respect the currencies you bring with you to the classroom.

2. I promise to keep out of your way so that you can take on the work of learning and enjoy the fruits of learning for yourself.

3. I promise to provide you with a physically and psychologically safe learning environment.

4. I promise to listen to the feedback you give me verbally, non-verbally, and in your work, and use this feedback to do a better job of meeting your needs.

5. I promise to keep trying until together, we figure out the best way to help you learn.

6. I promise to do all that I can to set you up to succeed.

7. I promise to help you learn from your mistakes and show you how to get better at learning.

8. I promise to carefully choose the work I give you so that it clearly increases your understanding and proficiency and doesn't encumber you with meaningless rote exercises that do little to help you learn.

9. I promise to provide you with challenging and engaging instruction that stretches you to within but at the outer limits of your ability. In this way, I will help you grow as a learner.

10. I promise to learn alongside you.

Source: Robyn Jackson (2015). Used with permission.

Figure P.3

MAKE LEARNING VISIBLE IN MATHEMATICS

1

2 + 2 = 4.

It just adds up, right? But think about how you know that two plus two equals four. Did you memorize the answer from a flashcard? Did someone tell you that and then expect that you accept it as truth? Did you discover the answer while engaged in a relevant task? Were you asked to explore a concept, and when you grasped the concept, someone provided you with labels for the ideas? In all likelihood, it was a combination of these things that led you to come to understand the concept of the number two, the possibility of combining like items, and the idea that the sum is a result of these combinations. Over time, you were able to consider an unknown term such as *x* in the equation *2 + x = 4* and master increasingly complex ideas that are based on algebraic thinking. Your learning became visible to you, your teachers, and your family.

And that's what this book is about—making learning visible. By visible learning, we mean several things. First and foremost, students and teachers should be able to see and document learning. Teachers should understand the impact that they, and their actions, have on students. Students should also see evidence of their own progress toward their learning goals. Visible learning helps teachers identify attributes and influences that work. Visible learning also helps teachers better understand their impact on student learning, and helps students become their own teachers. In this way, both teachers and students become lifelong learners and develop a love for learning. Importantly, this is not a book about visible teaching. We do, of course, provide evidence for various teacher moves, but our goal is not to make teaching visible but rather the *learning* visible. Before we explore the research behind visible learning, let's consider the ways in which you may have been taught mathematics. We need to accept and understand that high-quality learning may require that we discard ineffective pedagogy that we may have experienced as learners of mathematics.

Forgetting the Past

Do you remember the *Men in Black* movies? The agents who are protecting the universe have neuralyzers, which erase memories. They use them to erase encounters with intergalactic aliens so that people on planet Earth are kept in the dark about threats to their world. We wish we had that little flashy thing. If we did, we'd erase teachers' memories of some of the ways they were taught mathematics when they were younger. And we'd replace those memories with intentional instruction, punctuated with collaborative learning opportunities, rich discussions about mathematical concepts, excitement over persisting through complex problem solving, and the application of ideas to situations and problems that matter. We don't mean to offend anyone, but we have all suffered through some pretty bad mathematics instruction in our lives. Nancy remembers piles of worksheets. Her third-grade teacher had math packets that she distributed the first of each month. Students had specific calculation-driven problems that they had to do every night, page after page of practicing computation with little or no context. A significant amount of class time was spent reviewing the homework, irrespective of whether or not students got the problem wrong or right. In fact, when she asked if they could skip the problems everyone completed correctly, she was invited to have a meeting with the teacher and the principal.

In algebra, Doug's teacher required that specifically assigned students write out one of their completed homework problems on the chalkboard while the teacher publicly commended or criticized people. Doug wasn't academically prepared for entry-level algebra, so he hid outside the classroom until the teacher ran out of problems each day. (He took the tardies rather than show everyone he didn't understand the homework.) When this ritual was completed, the teacher explained the next section of the textbook while students took notes. The teacher wrote on an overhead projector with rollers on each side, winding away, page after page. Doug learned to copy quickly into his Cornell notes since the teacher often accidentally erased much of what he wrote because of his left-hand hook writing style. When finished with this, students were directed to complete the assigned odd-numbered problems from the back of the book in a silent classroom. Any problems not completed during class time automatically became homework. Doug copied from his friend Rob on the bus ride home each day but failed every test. This spectator sport version of algebra did not work for students who did not already know the content. Doug's learning wasn't visible to himself, or to his teacher.

If you're worrying about Doug, after failing algebra in ninth grade, he then had a teacher who was passionate about her students' learning. She modeled her thinking every day. She structured collaborative group tasks and assigned problems that were relevant and interesting. Doug eventually went on to earn a master's degree in bio-statistics.

John did okay in mathematics and enjoyed the routines, but if offered, he would have dropped mathematics at the first chance given. But his school made all students enroll in mathematics right to the last year of high school. It was in this last year that he met Mr. Tomlinson—rather strict, a little forbidding, but dedicated to the notion that every one of his students should share his passion for mathematics. He gave his students the end-of-the-year high-stakes exam at the start of the year to show them where they needed to learn. Though the whole class failed, Mr. Tomlinson was able to say, "This is the standard required, and I am going to get you all to this bar." Throughout the year, Mr. Tomlinson persistently engaged his students in how to think in mathematics, working on spotting similarities and differences in mathematical problems so they did not automatically make the same mistakes every time. This teacher certainly saw something in John that John did not see in himself. John ended up with a minor in statistics and major in psychometrics as part of his doctoral program.

These memories of unfortunate mathematics instruction need to be erased by *Men in Black* Agent K using his neuralyzer, as we know that one of the significant impacts on the way teachers teach is how they were taught. We want to focus on the good examples—the teachers we remember who guided our understanding and love of mathematics.

We've already asked you to forget the less-than-effective learning experiences you've had, so we feel comfortable asking you one more thing. Forget about prescriptive curricula, scripted lesson plans, and worksheets. Learning isn't linear; it's recursive. Prescriptive curriculum isn't matched to students' instructional needs. Sometimes students know more than the curriculum allows for, and other times they need a lot of scaffolding and support to develop deep understanding and skills. As we will discuss later in this book, it's really about determining the impact that teachers have on students and making adjustments to ensure that the impact is as significant as possible.

A major flaw of highly scripted lessons is that they don't allow teachers to respond with joy to the errors students make. Yes, joy. Errors help teachers understand students' thinking and address it. Errors should be celebrated because they provide an opportunity for instruction, and thus learning. As Michael Jordan noted in his Nike ad, "I've missed more than 9,000 shots in my career. I've lost almost 300 games. 26 times, I've been trusted to take the game winning shot and missed. I've failed over and over and over again in my life. And that is why I succeed."

Linda remembers playing a logic game using attribute blocks with her students. The beginning of the game required that students listen carefully to the ideas of others and draw some conclusions as to whether those ideas were correct or accurate. At one point, she commented to an incorrect response, "That's a really important mistake. I hope you all heard it!" The reaction of almost every student was a look of surprise. It was as if the students were thinking, "Have you lost your mind? The goal in math is to get it right!" That response made a real impact on Linda's teaching moves in terms of recognizing how important it is for students to understand they learn and develop understanding from making mistakes (and, in fact, she still says that to this day!). The very best mathematicians wallow in the enjoyment of struggling with mathematical ideas, and this should be among the aims of math teachers—to help students enjoy the struggle of mathematics.

When students don't make errors, it's probably because they already know the content and didn't really need the lesson. We didn't say throw away textbooks. They are a resource that can be useful. Use them wisely, and make adjustments as you deem necessary to respond to the needs of your students. Remember, it is your students, not the curriculum writers, who direct the learning in your classroom.

What Makes for Good Instruction?

When we talk about high-quality instruction, we're always asked the chicken-and-egg question: "Which comes first?" Should a mathematics lesson start with teacher-led instruction or with students attempting to solve problems on their own? Our answer: it depends. It depends on the learning intention. It depends on the expectations. It depends on students' background knowledge. It depends on students' cognitive, social, and emotional development and readiness. It depends where you are going next (and there needs to be a next). And it depends on the day. Some days, lessons start with collaborative tasks. Other days, lessons are more effective when students have an opportunity to talk about their thinking with the entire class or see worked examples. And still other days, it's more effective to ask students to work individually. Much of teaching is dependent on responding to student data in real time, and each teacher has his or her own strengths and personality that shine through in the best lessons. Great teachers are much like jazz musicians, both deliberately setting the stage and then improvising. Great teachers have plans yet respond to student learning and needs in real time.

But even the most recognized performers had to learn techniques before applying them. Jazz musicians have to understand standards of music, even if they choose to break the rules. Similarly, great teachers need to know the tools of their craft before they can create the most effective lessons. Enter *Visible Learning*.

The Evidence Base

The starting point for our exploration of learning mathematics is John's books, *Visible Learning* (2009) and *Visible Learning for Teachers* (2012). At the time these books were published, his work was based on more than 800 meta-analyses conducted by researchers all over the world, which included more than 50,000 individual studies that included more than 250 million students. It has been claimed to be the most comprehensive review of educational research ever conducted. And the thing is, it's still going on. At the time of this writing, the database included 1200 meta-analyses, with more than 70,000 studies and 300 million students. A lot of data, right? But the story underlying the data is the critical matter; and it has not changed since the first book in 2009.

Meta-Analyses

Before we explore the findings, we should discuss the idea of a meta-analysis because it is the basic building block for the recommendations in this book. At its root, a **meta-analysis** is a statistical tool for combining findings from different studies with the goal of identifying patterns that can inform practice. It's the old preponderance of evidence that we're looking for, because individual studies have a hard time making a compelling case for change. But a meta-analysis synthesizes what is currently known about a given topic and can result in strong recommendations about the impact or effect of a specific practice. For example, there was competing evidence about periodontitis (inflammation of the tissue around the teeth) and whether or not it is associated with increased risk of coronary heart disease. The published evidence contained some conflicts, and recommendations about treatment were piecemeal. A meta-analysis of five prospective studies with 86,092 patients suggested that individuals with periodontitis had a 1.14 times higher risk of developing coronary heart disease than the controls (Bahekar, Singh, Saha,

> Errors help teachers understand students' thinking and·address it. . . . They provide an opportunity for instruction, and thus learning.

> A **meta-analysis** is a statistical tool for combining findings from different studies with the goal of identifying patterns that can inform practice.

Molnar, & Arora, 2007). The result of the meta-analysis was a set of clear recommendations for treatment of periodontitis, such as the use of scaling and root planing (SRP), or deep cleaning of the teeth, as initial treatment. The evidence suggests that this has the potential of significantly reducing the incidence of heart disease. While this book is not about health care or business, we hope that the value of meta-analyses in changing practice is clear.

The statistical approach for conducting meta-analyses is beyond the scope of this book, but it is important to note that this tool allows researchers to identify trends across many different studies and their participants.

Effect Sizes

The meta-analyses were used to calculate effect sizes for each practice. You might remember from your statistics class that studies report statistical significance. Researchers make the case that something "worked" when chance is reduced to 5 percent (as in $p < 0.05$) or 1 percent (as in $p < 0.01$). What they really mean is that the probability of seeing the outcome found as the result of chance events is very small, less than 5 percent or less than 1 percent. One way to increase the likelihood that statistical significance is reached is to increase the number of people in the study, also known as sample size. We're not saying that researchers inflate the size of the research group to obtain significant findings. We are saying that simply because something is statistically significant doesn't mean that it's worth implementing. For example, if the sample size was 1,000 participants, then a correlation only needs to exceed 0.044 to be considered "statistically significant," meaning the results are due to factors other than chance; if 10,000 are sampled, then a correlation of 0.014 is needed, or if 100,000 are sampled, then a correlation of 0.004 is sufficient to show a nonchance relationship. Yes, you can be confident that these values are greater than zero, but are they of any practical value? That's where effect size comes in.

Say, for example, that a digital app was found to be statistically significant in changing students' learning in geometry. Sounds good, you say to yourself, and you consider purchasing or adopting it. But then you learn that it increased students' performance by only three right answers for every twenty-five choices (and the research team had data from 9,000 students). If it were free and easy to implement this change, it might be worth it to have students get a tiny bit better as users of geometric knowledge. But if it were time-consuming, difficult, or expensive, you

Video 1.1
What Is Visible Learning for Mathematics?

http://resources.corwin.com/ VL-mathematics

To read a QR code, you must have a smartphone or tablet with a camera. We recommend that you download a QR code reader app that is made specifically for your phone or tablet brand.

Effect size represents the magnitude of the impact that a given approach has.

EFFECT SIZE
FOR SELF-
VERBALIZATION
AND SELF-
QUESTIONING
= 0.64

should ask yourself if it's worth it to go to all of this trouble for such a small gain. That's **effect size**—it represents the magnitude of the impact that a given approach has.

Visible Learning provides readers with effect sizes for many influences under investigation. As an example, self-verbalization and self-questioning—students thinking and talking about their own learning progress—has a reasonably strong effect size at 0.64 (we'll talk more about what the effect size number tells us in the next section). The effect sizes can be ranked from those with the highest impact to those with the lowest. But that doesn't mean that teachers should just take the top ten or twenty and try to implement them immediately. Rather, as we will discuss later in this book, some of the highly useful practices are more effective when focused on surface learning (initial acquisition of knowledge) while others work better for deep learning (consolidation of knowledge) and still others work to encourage transfer (application to new and novel situations).

Noticing What Does and Does Not Work

If you attend any conference or read just about any professional journal, not to mention subscribe to blogs or visit Pinterest, you'll get the sense that everything works. Yet educators have much to learn from practices that do not work. In fact, we would argue that learning from what doesn't work, and not repeating those mistakes, is a valuable use of time. To determine what doesn't work, we turn our attention to effect sizes again. Effect sizes can be negative or positive, and they scale from low to high. Intuitively, an effect size of 0.60 is better than an effect size of 0.20. Intuitively, we should welcome any effect that is greater than zero, as zero means "no growth," and clearly any negative effect size means a negative growth. If only it was this simple.

An **influence** is an instructional strategy, idea, or tool we use in schools.

It turns out that about 95 percent or more of the **influences** (instructional strategies, ideas, or tools) that we use in schools have a positive effect; that is, the effect size of nearly everything we do is greater than zero. This helps explain why so many people can argue "with evidence" that their pet project works. If you set the bar at showing any growth above zero, it is indeed hard to find programs and practices that don't work. As described in *Visible Learning* (2009), we have to reject the starting point of zero. Students naturally mature and develop over the course of a year, and thus actions, activities, and interventions that teachers use should *extend learning beyond what a student can achieve by simply attending school for a year.*

This is why John set the bar of acceptability higher—at the average of all the influences he compiled—from the home, parents, schools, teachers, curricula, and teaching strategies. This average was 0.40, and John called it the "**hinge point**." He then undertook studying the underlying attributes that would explain why those influences higher than 0.40 had such a positive impact compared with those lower than 0.40. His findings were the impetus for the *Visible Learning* story. We expect, at minimum, students' learning to progress a full year for every year that they are in school. And we hope that students gain more than that. Ensuring this level of growth requires a relentless focus on learning rather than on teaching.

Borrowing from *Visible Learning*, the **barometer of influence** and hinge point are effective in explaining what we focus on in this book and why. Here's an example of how this might play out in learning mathematics. Let's focus on volunteer tutors, which some have argued could be used to address the basic skills needs that some students have in mathematics. In essence, students are taught by volunteers, often parents or university students, and this instruction focuses on topics such as adding fractions, long division, or some other skill. Importantly, we are not advocating for skills-based instruction, but rather using this example to highlight the use of effect sizes. As with much of the educational research, there are studies that contradict other studies. For example, Scott (2007) described an experiment in engaging parents as volunteers to boost mathematics learning. She suggests that the effort was worthwhile but does not provide information on the impact it had in terms of learning that exceeded one year. Similarly, Carmody and Wood (2009) describe a volunteer tutoring program, this time with college seniors tutoring their younger peers in college mathematics classes. They report that their effort was generally well received, but do not provide information about the impact that it had on students' learning. That's where the meta-analyses and effect size data can teach us. The barometer and hinge point for volunteer tutors are presented in Figure 1.1. Note that this approach rests in the zone of "teacher effects," which is below the level of desired effects but better than reverse effects. Our focus in *Visible Learning for Mathematics* is on actions that fall inside the *zone of desired effects*, which is 0.40 and above. When actions are in the range of 0.40 and above, the data suggest that the effort extends beyond that which was expected from attending school for a year.

Hinge point is the average point at which we can consider that something is working enough for a student to gain one year's growth for a year of schooling.

The **barometer of influence** is a visual scale that can help us understand where an influence falls in terms of relative effect size.

EFFECT SIZE
FOR VOLUNTEER
TUTORS = 0.26

THE BAROMETER FOR THE INFLUENCE OF VOLUNTEER TUTORS

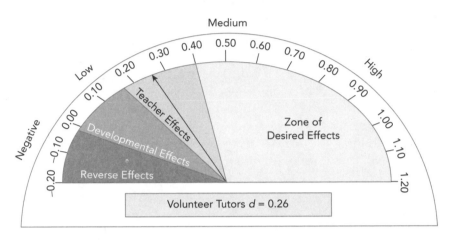

Source: Adapted from Hattie (2012).

Figure 1.1

EFFECT SIZE FOR SIMULATIONS = 0.33

Caution: That doesn't mean that everything below 0.40 effect size is not worthy of attention. Hattie (2012) points out that the hinge point of 0.40 is not absolute. In actuality, each influence does have its own hinge point; therefore the hinge point of 0.40 is simply a good starting point for discussion about the nuances, variability, quality of the studies, and other factors that give an influence a particular effect size. It's just not black-and-white, and there are likely some useful approaches for teaching and learning that are not above this average. For example, drama and arts programs have an effect size of 0.35, almost ensuring that students gain a year's worth of achievement for a year of education. We are not suggesting that drama and art be removed from the curriculum. In fact, artistic expression and aesthetic understanding may be valuable in and of themselves.

It is also important to realize that some of the aggregate scores mask situations in which specific actions can be strategically used to improve students' understanding. Simulations are a good case. The effect size of simulations is 0.33, below the threshold that we established. But what if simulations were really effective in deepening understanding, but not as useful when used for surface learning? (See Chapters 4 and 5 for more on surface and deep learning.) In this case, the strategic deployment of simulations could be important. There are situations like this that we will review in this book as we focus on the balance and sequencing of surface learning compared with deep learning or transfer learning. For now, let's turn our attention to actions that teachers can take to improve student learning. We'll start by directly addressing a major debate in mathematics education: direct instruction compared with dialogic approaches.

Direct and Dialogic Approaches to Teaching and Learning

Debates about the teaching of mathematics have raged for decades. In general, the debate centers on the role of direct instruction versus dialogic instruction, with some teachers and researchers advocating for one or the other. Proponents of both models of instruction have similar goals—student mastery of mathematics. But they differ in the ways in which learning opportunities are organized within the context of a lesson. According to Munter, Stein, and Smith (2015b):

> In the direct instruction model, when students have the prerequisite conceptual and procedural knowledge, they will learn from (a) watching clear, complete demonstrations of how to solve problems, with accompanying explanations and accurate definitions; (b) practicing similar problems sequenced according to difficulty; and (c) receiving immediate, corrective feedback. Whereas in the dialogic model, students must (a) actively engage in new mathematics, persevering to solve novel problems; (b) participate in a discourse of conjecture, explanation, and argumentation; (c) engage in generalization and abstraction, developing efficient problem-solving strategies and relating their ideas to conventional procedures; and to achieve fluency with these skills, (d) engage in some amount of practice. (p. 6)

As the authors note, there are several similarities and some important differences between these two competing models. In terms of similarities, both focus on students' conceptual understanding and procedural fluency. In other words, students have to know the *why* and *how* of mathematics.

Neither model advocates that students simply memorize formulas and procedures. As the National Council of Teachers of Mathematics (2014) states, procedural fluency is built on a foundation of conceptual understanding. Students need to develop strategic reasoning and problem solving. To accomplish this, both models suggest that (1) mathematics instruction be carefully designed around rigorous mathematical tasks, (2) students' reasoning is monitored, and (3) students are provided ample opportunities for skill- and application-based practice.

Munter, Stein, and Smith (2015b) also identify a number of differences between the two models, namely in the types of tasks students are invited to complete, the role of classroom discourse, collaborative learning, and the role of feedback. Figure 1.2 contains their list of similarities and differences. Importantly, these researchers also recognize that teachers use aspects of each model. As they note, "teachers in dialogic classrooms may very well demonstrate some procedures, just as students in a direct instruction classroom may very well engage in project-based activities" (p. 9). They argue that the purposes for using different aspects of each model may vary, and the outcomes may be different, but note that "high-quality instruction must include the identification of both instructional practices and the underlying rationales for employing those practices" (p. 9).

We agree that direct instruction should not be thought of as "spray-and-pray" didactic show-and-tell transmission of knowledge. Neither direct nor dialogical instruction should be confused with "lots of talking" or didactic approaches. John (Hattie, 2009) defines **direct instruction** in a way that conveys an intentional, well-planned, and student-centered guided approach to teaching. "In a nutshell, the teacher decides the learning intentions and success criteria, makes them transparent to the students, demonstrates them by modeling, evaluates if they understand what they have been told by checking for understanding, and re-tells them what they have been told by tying it all together with closure" (p. 206).

When thinking of direct instruction in this way, the effect size is 0.59. Dialogic instruction also has a high effect size of 0.82. This doesn't mean that teachers should always choose one approach over another. It should never be an either/or situation. The bigger conversation, and purpose of this book, is to show how teachers can choose the right approach at the right time to ensure learning, and how both dialogic and direct approaches have a role to play throughout the learning process, but in different ways.

> **Direct instruction** is when the teacher decides the learning intentions and success criteria, makes them transparent to the students, demonstrates them by modeling, evaluates if they understand what they have been told by checking for understanding, and re-tells them what they have been told by tying it all together with closure.

> EFFECT SIZE FOR DIRECT INSTRUCTION = 0.59

> EFFECT SIZE FOR CLASSROOM DISCUSSION = 0.82

COMPARING DIRECT AND DIALOGIC INSTRUCTION

Dialogic Instruction	Distinction	Direct Instruction
Fundamental to both knowing and learning mathematics. Students need opportunities in both small-group and whole-class settings to talk about their thinking, questions, and arguments.	The importance and role of **talk**	Most important during the guided practice phase, when students are required to explain to the teacher how they have solved problems in order to ensure they are encoding new knowledge.
Provides a venue for more talking and listening than is available in a totally teacher-led lesson. Students should have regular opportunities to work on and talk about solving problems in collaboration with peers.	The importance of and role of **group work**	An optional component of a lesson; when employed, it should follow guided practice on problem solving, focus primarily on verifying that the procedures that have just been demonstrated work, and provide additional practice opportunities.
Dictated by both disciplinary and developmental (i.e., building new knowledge from prior knowledge) progressions.	The **sequencing of topics**	Dictated primarily by a disciplinary progression (i.e., prerequisites determined by the structure of mathematics).
Two main types of tasks are important: (1) tasks that initiate students to new ideas and deepen their understanding of concepts (and to which they do not have an immediate solution), and (2) tasks that help them become more competent with what they already know (with type 2 generally not preceding type 1 and both engaging students in reasoning).	The nature and ordering of **instructional tasks**	Students should be given opportunities to use and build on what they have just seen the teacher demonstrate by practicing similar problems, sequenced by difficulty. Tasks afford opportunities to develop the ability to adapt a procedure to fit a novel situation as well as to discriminate between classes of problems (the more varied practice students do, the more adaptability they will develop).
Students should be given time to wrestle with tasks that involve big ideas, without teachers interfering to correct their work. After this, feedback can come in small-group or whole-class settings; the purpose is not merely correcting misconceptions, but advancing students' growing intellectual authority about how to judge the correctness of one's own and others' reasoning.	The nature, timing, source, and purpose of **feedback**	Students should receive immediate feedback from the teacher regarding how their strategies need to be corrected (rather than emphasizing that mistakes have been made). In addition to one-to-one feedback, when multiple students have a particular misconception, teachers should bring the issue to the entire class's attention in order to correct the misconception for all.

(Continued)

Dialogic Instruction	Distinction	Direct Instruction
Students' learning pathways are emergent. Students should make, refine, and explore conjectures on the basis of evidence and use a variety of reasoning and proof techniques to confirm or disprove those conjectures (CCSS-M-SMP 3), asking questions that drive instruction and lead to new investigations.	The emphasis on **creativity**	Students' learning pathways are predetermined and carefully designed for. To "make conjectures and build a logical progression of statements to explore the truth of their conjectures" (CCSS-M-SMP 3) is limited to trying solution strategies for solving a problem posed to them.
Students' thinking and activity are consistent sources of ideas of which to make deliberate use: by flexibly following students' reasoning, the teacher can build on their initial thinking to move toward important ideas of the discipline.	The purpose of **diagnosing student thinking**	Through efficient instructional design and close monitoring (or interviewing), the teacher should diagnose the cause of errors (often a missing prerequisite skill) and intervene on exactly the component of the strategy that likely caused the error.
Students participate in the defining process, with the teacher ensuring that definitions are mathematically sound and formalized at the appropriate time for students' current understanding.	The introduction and role of **definitions**	At the outset of learning a new topic, students should be provided an accurate definition of relevant concepts.
Representations are used not just for illustrating mathematical ideas, but also for thinking with. Representations are created in the moment to support/afford shared attention to specific pieces of the problem space and how they interconnect.	The nature and role of **representations**	Representations are used to illustrate mathematical ideas (e.g., introducing an area model for multi-digit multiplication after teaching the algorithm), not to think with or to anchor problem-solving conversations.

Source: Munter, Stein, and Smith (2015b). Used with permission.

Figure 1.2

Precision teaching is about knowing *what* strategies to implement *when* for maximum impact.

Many readers of *Visible Learning* (Hattie, 2009) attend to the details about effect sizes and measuring one's impact (important, to be sure), but fewer may notice that this body of research points to *when* it works as well as *what* works. Knowing *what* strategies to implement *when* for maximum impact is what we think of as **precision teaching**.

The Balance of Surface, Deep, and Transfer Learning

As mentioned in the preface, it's useful when planning for precision teaching to think of the nature of learning in the categories of surface, deep, and transfer. It is a framing device for making decisions about *how* and *when* you engage in certain tasks, questioning techniques, and teaching strategies. The most powerful model for understanding these three categories is the SOLO (structure of observed learning outcomes) model developed by Biggs and Collis (1982). In this model, there are four levels, termed "unistructural," "multi-structural," "relational," and "extended abstract." Simply put, this means "an idea" and "many ideas" (which together are surface), and "relating ideas" and "extending ideas" (which together signify deep). Transfer is when students take their learning and use it in new situations. Figure 1.3 shows two examples of the SOLO model for mathematics.

One key to effective teaching is to design clear learning intentions and success criteria (which we'll discuss in Chapter 2), which include a combination of surface, deep, and transfer learning, with the exact combination depending on the decision of the teacher, based on how the lesson fits into the curriculum, how long- or short-term the learning intentions are, and the complexity of the desired learning. Also, we recognize that learning is not an event, it is a process. It would be convenient to say that surface, deep, and transfer learning always occur in that order, or that surface learning should happen at the beginning of a unit and transfer at the end. In truth, these three kinds of learning spiral around one another across an ever-widening plane. Also, we want to be clear that because learning does not fall into a linear and repeating pattern—and is different for different students—we are in no way suggesting a specific order or scaffold of methods. In education, we spend a great deal of time debating particular methods of teaching and the pros and cons of certain strategies and their progression as applied to different content areas. The bottom line is that there are many phases to learning, and there is no one way or one set of understandings that unravels the processes of learning. Our attention is better placed on the effect we, as teachers, have on student learning. Sometimes that means we need multiple strategies, and, more often, many students need different teaching strategies from those that they have been getting (Hattie, 2012). Before further discussing how these phases of learning interweave, let's dive into what each one means in terms of mathematics.

> **Teaching Takeaway**
>
> The issue should not be direct versus dialogic but rather the right approach at the right time to ensure learning.

THE SOLO MODEL APPLIED TO MATHEMATICS

Learning Intentions		Success Criteria
SOLO 1: Represent and solve problems involving addition and subtraction.		
Uni-/Multi-Structural	Know basic facts for addition and subtraction.	I know my sums to twenty in both addition and subtraction.
	Represent addition and subtraction using multiple models (manipulatives, number lines, bar diagrams, etc.).	I can show my thinking using manipulatives and pictures.
Relational	Understand the meaning of addition or subtraction by modeling what is happening in a contextual situation (Carpenter, Fennema, Franke, Levi, & Empson, 2014).	When I read a word problem, I can describe what is happening and use addition or subtraction to find a solution.
	Recognize when either addition or subtraction is used to solve problems in different situations.	
Extended Abstract	Use addition and subtraction to solve problems in a variety of situations.	I can use what I know about addition and subtraction contexts to figure out how to use addition and subtraction to solve problems beyond those I solve in class.
SOLO 2: Reason with shapes and their attributes.		
Uni-/Multi-Structural	Know the definitions and key attributes for shapes.	I can identify and name the attributes of shapes.
Relational	Recognize relationships among shapes.	I can explain how two shapes are related to each other.
Extended Abstract	Classify two-dimensional shapes based on properties.	I can create a diagram to show how different quadrilaterals are related to each other.

Source: Adapted from Biggs and Collis (1982).

This figure and a blank template are available for download at **http://resources.corwin.com/VL-mathematics**

Figure 1.3

Surface Learning

In mathematics, we can think of **surface learning** as having two parts. First, it is initial learning of concepts and skills. When content is new, all of us have a limited understanding. That doesn't mean we're not working on complex problems; it's just that the depth of thinking isn't there yet. Whether a student is exposed to a new idea or information through an initial exploration or some form of structured teacher-led instruction (or perhaps a combination of the two), it is the introductory level of learning—the initiation to, and early understanding of, new ideas that begins with developing conceptual understanding—and at the right time, the explicit introduction of the labels and procedures that help give the concepts some structure. Let us be clear: surface learning is not shallow learning. It is not about rote skills and meaningless algorithms. It is not prioritizing "superficial" learning or low-level skills over higher order skills. It should not be mistaken for engaging in procedures that have no grounding in conceptual understanding. Second, surface learning of concepts and skills goes beyond just an introductory point; students need the time and space to begin to consolidate their new learning. It is through this early consolidation that they can begin to retrieve information efficiently, so that they make room for more complex problem solving. For example, counting is an early skill, and one that necessarily relies initially on memorization and rehearsal. Very young children learn how to recite numbers in the correct order, and in the same developmental space are also learning the one-to-one correspondence needed to count objects. In formal algebra, surface learning may focus on notation and conventions. While the operations students are using are familiar, the notation is different. Multiplication between a coefficient and a variable is noted as $3x$, which means 3 times x. Throughout schooling, there are introductions to new skills, concepts, and procedures that, over time, should become increasingly easier for the learner to retrieve.

Importantly, through developing surface learning, students can take action to develop initial conceptual understanding, build mathematical habits of mind, hone their strategic thinking, and begin to develop fluency in skills. For example, surface learning strategies can be used to help students begin developing their metacognitive skills (thinking about their thinking). Alternatively, surface learning strategies can be used to provide students with labels (vocabulary) for the concepts they have discovered or explored. In addition, surface learning strategies can be used to address students' misconceptions and errors.

Surface learning is the initiation to new ideas. It begins with development of conceptual understanding, and then, at the right time, labels and procedures are explicitly introduced to give structure to concepts.

Surface learning is not shallow learning. It is not about rote skills and meaningless algorithms.

One challenge with surface learning is that there is often an overreliance on it, and we must think of the goal of mathematics instruction as being much more than surface learning. When learning stalls at the surface level, students do not have opportunities to connect conceptual understandings about one topic to other topics, and then to apply their understandings to more complex or real-world situations. That is, after all, one of the goals of learning and doing mathematics. Surface learning gives students the toolbox they need to build something. In mathematics, this toolbox includes a variety of representations (e.g., knowing about various manipulatives and visuals like number lines or bar diagrams) and problem-solving strategies (e.g., how to create an organized list or work with a simpler case), as well as mastering the notation and conventions of mathematics. But a true craftsman has not only a repertoire of tools, but also the knowledge of which tools are best suited for the task at hand. Making those decisions is where **deep learning** comes to the forefront, and, as teachers, we should always focus on moving students forward from surface to deep learning.

Deep Learning

The deep phase of learning provides students with opportunities to consolidate their understanding of mathematical concepts and procedures and make deeper connections among ideas. Often, this is accomplished when students work collaboratively with their peers, use academic language, and interact in richer ways with ideas and information.

Mrs. Graham started the school year for her fourth graders working with factors and multiples, connecting this work to previous third-grade experiences with arrays as models for multiplication, and extending these ideas to understanding prime and composite numbers. Students started by building and describing rectangular arrays for numbers from 1 to 50 (some students continued on to 100) and then discussed their answers to a variety of questions that developed the idea of prime and composite numbers. Class discussion incorporated mathematical vocabulary so it became a natural part of the student conversations (surface learning). The next day, students played a game called Factor Game (http://www.tc.pbs.org/teachers/mathline/lessonplans/pdf/msmp/factor.pdf) in which an understanding of primes and composites was crucial to developing strategies to win (deep learning is now occurring). However, the story doesn't end there. In March, students were beginning to study

Deep learning is about consolidating understanding of mathematical concepts and procedures and making connections among ideas.

area and perimeter of rectangles. Following an initial exploration, several students approached Mrs. Graham to comment, "This is just like what we did last September when we were building arrays and finding primes and composites!" Talk about making connections!

As you can see, students move to deep learning when they plan, investigate, and elaborate on their conceptual understandings, and then begin to make generalizations. This is not about rote learning of rules or procedures. It is about students taking the surface knowledge (which includes conceptual understanding) and, through the intentional instruction designed by the teacher, seeing how their conceptual understanding links to more efficient and flexible ways of thinking about the concept. In Mrs. Graham's class, students began by developing surface knowledge of factors and multiples using concrete models and connected that to primes and composites. Mrs. Graham's use of the Factor Game provided students a way to apply their surface knowledge to developing strategies to win a game . . . deep knowledge. A teacher who nurtures strategic thinking and action throughout the year will nurture students who know when to use surface knowledge and when deep knowledge is needed.

We need to balance our expectations with our reality. This means more explicit alignment between what teachers claim success looks like, how the tasks students are assigned align with these claims about success, and how success is measured by end-of-course assessments or assignments. It is not a matter of all surface or all deep. It is a matter of being clear about when surface and when deep is truly required.

Consider this example from algebra. A deep learning aspect of algebra comes when students explore functions—in particular, the meaning of the slope of a line. Surface knowledge focuses on understanding the term mx in the slope-intercept ($y = mx + b$) form to mean m copies of the variable x. Deep learning requires students to understand and show that this term represented visually is the steepness or flatness of the slope of a line and the rate of change of the variables. Such learning might come from working collaboratively to explore a group of functions represented in multiple ways (equations, tables of values, and graphs) and make inferences about the slope in each representation. At this point, students are connecting their conceptual knowledge of ratio to their surface knowledge of algebraic notation and the process of graphing. This is deep learning in action.

Students move to deep learning when they plan, investigate, and elaborate on their conceptual understandings, and then begin to make generalizations.

Transfer Learning

The ultimate goal, and one that is hard to realize, is transfer. Learning demands that students be able to apply—or transfer—their knowledge, skills, and strategies to new tasks and new situations. That transfer is so difficult to attain is one of our closely kept secrets—so often we pronounce that students can transfer, but the processes of teaching them this skill are too often not discussed, and we'll visit that in Chapter 6.

Transfer is both a goal of learning and also a mechanism for propelling learning. Transfer as a goal means that teachers want students to begin to take the reins of their own learning, think metacognitively, and apply what they know to a variety of real-world contexts. When students reach this level, learning has been accomplished.

Nancy once heard a mathematics teacher say that transfer is what happens when students do math without someone telling them to do math. It's when they reach into their toolbox and decide what tools to employ to solve new and complex problems on their own.

For example, transfer learning happens when students look at data from a science or engineering task that requires them to make sense of a linear function and its slope. They will use their surface knowledge of notation and convention, along with their deep understanding of slope as a ratio, to solve a challenge around designing an electrical circuit using materials with a variety of properties. Ohm's law ($V = iR$, where V represents voltage, i represents the current, and R represents resistance) is the linear function that relates the relevant aspects of the circuit, and students will use their mathematics knowledge in finding their solution.

One of the concerns is that students (often those who struggle) attempt to transfer *without* detecting similarities and differences between concepts and situations, and the transfer does not work (and they see this as evidence that they are dumb). Memorizing facts, passing tests, and moving on to the next grade level or course is not the true purpose of school, although sadly, many students think it is. School is a time to apprentice students into the act of becoming their own teachers. We want them to be self-directed, have the dispositions needed to formulate their own questions, and possess the tools to pursue them. In other words, as students' learning becomes visible to them, we want it to become the catalyst for continued learning, whether the teacher is present or not. However, we don't leave these things to chance. Close association between a previously learned task and a novel situation is necessary for promoting transfer of learning. Therefore, we teach with intention, making sure that

> **Transfer** is the phase of learning in which students take the reins of their own learning and are able to apply their thinking to new contexts and situations.

students acquire and consolidate the needed skills, processes, and meta-cognitive awareness that make self-directed learning possible.

One of the struggles in teaching mathematics is to determine how much to tell students versus how to support students as they engage in productive struggle on their own, and when to know which is the right step to take. Let's take a look at helping elementary-age children build a toolbox of problem-solving strategies. Linda once attended a workshop for teachers that opened a whole new world of problem-solving strategies to use when solving nonroutine or open-ended problems. She was excited to take these problems back to her students and give them the opportunities to solve rich problems that involved some higher order thinking—that is, solving problems that involve much more than simple calculations. After some careful planning, she started a Monday class with her fifth graders by presenting the following problem.

> Mrs. Thompson, the school cook, is making pancakes for the special fifth-grade breakfast. She needs 49 pounds of flour. She can buy flour in 3-pound bags and 5-pound bags. She only uses full bags of flour. How can she get the exact amount of flour she needs?

Having never solved this type of problem before, the students rebelled. Choruses of "I don't know what they want me to do!" rang out across the classroom. "But they said in this workshop that kids could do this!" Linda thought.

Refusing to give in to the students' lament that the work was too hard, Linda decided that she needed to go about this differently. She resolved to spend each Monday introducing a specific strategy, presenting a problem to employ that strategy for students to solve together, and discuss their thinking. This was followed by an independent "problem of the week" for students to solve. After introducing all of the strategies (surface learning) and following up with independent applications of those strategies for students (deep learning), students continued to work independently or in small groups to solve a variety of open-ended problems on their own using strategies of their choice (transfer learning). Later that year, a group of girls approached Linda asking why she had saved all of the easy problems for the end of the year. That's transfer!

It's important to note that within the context of a year, a unit, or even a single lesson, there can be evidence of all three types of learning, and

THE RELATIONSHIP BETWEEN SURFACE, DEEP, AND TRANSFER LEARNING IN MATHEMATICS

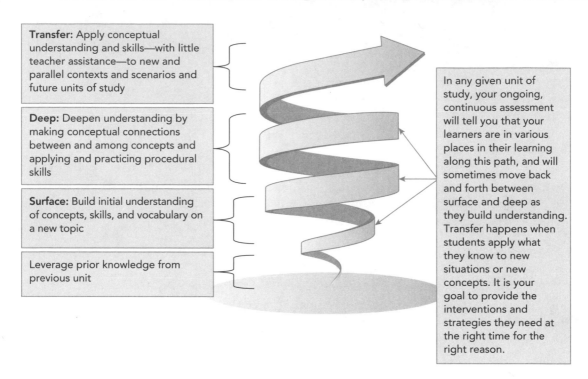

Transfer: Apply conceptual understanding and skills—with little teacher assistance—to new and parallel contexts and scenarios and future units of study

Deep: Deepen understanding by making conceptual connections between and among concepts and applying and practicing procedural skills

Surface: Build initial understanding of concepts, skills, and vocabulary on a new topic

Leverage prior knowledge from previous unit

In any given unit of study, your ongoing, continuous assessment will tell you that your learners are in various places in their learning along this path, and will sometimes move back and forth between surface and deep as they build understanding. Transfer happens when students apply what they know to new situations or new concepts. It is your goal to provide the interventions and strategies they need at the right time for the right reason.

Source: Spiral image copyright © iStock/EssentialsCollection/83158933.

Figure 1.4

that students can sometimes move among various kinds of learning depending on where they are as individual learners. Figure 1.4 describes the relationship between surface, deep, and transfer learning.

Surface, Deep, and Transfer Learning Working in Concert

As mentioned before, when it comes to the surface, deep, and transfer phases of learning, knowing *what* strategies to implement *when* for maximum impact on learning is key. How, then, should we define learning, since learning is our goal? John defines it as

> the process of developing sufficient surface knowledge to then move to deeper understanding such that one can appropriately transfer this learning to new tasks and situations.

Learning has to start with fundamental conceptual understanding, skills, and vocabulary. You have to know *something* before you can do something with it. Then, with appropriate instruction about how to relate and extend ideas, surface learning transforms into deep learning. Deep learning is an important foundation for students to then apply what they've learned in new and novel situations, which happens at the transfer phase. And tying all of this together is clarity about learning outcomes and success criteria, on the part of both teachers and students. If students know where they are going and how they'll know when they get there, they are better able to set their own expectations, self-monitor, and predict or self-report their own achievement. All of these phases can be present within the body of a single lesson or multiday or multiweek unit, as well as extend across the course of a school year.

Conclusion

Teachers have choices. As a teacher, you can unintentionally use instructional routines and procedures that don't work, or don't work for the intended purpose. Or you can choose to focus on *learning*, embrace the evidence, update your classrooms, and impact student learning in wildly positive ways. You can consider the nature of the phases of surface, deep, and transfer learning and concentrate on more precisely and strategically organizing your lessons and orchestrating your classrooms by harnessing the power of activities that are in the zone of desired effects—above a 0.40 hinge point. Understanding the phases of learning by examining the evidence will help you to make instructional choices that positively impact student learning in your classroom.

The following chapters are meant to help you design lessons and appropriately employ instructional moves that honor students' need to develop their surface understanding of a topic, help you extend the depth of their mathematical learning, and help them transfer their

Video 1.2
Balancing Surface, Deep, and Transfer Learning

http://resources.corwin.com/ VL-mathematics

EFFECT SIZE FOR STUDENT SELF-MONITORING = **0.45**

EFFECT SIZE FOR SELF-REPORTED GRADES/STUDENT EXPECTATIONS = **1.44** learning to new tasks and projects. The journey starts when you turn the page and delve into the topic that matters most—establishing learning intentions and success criteria. Let's start the journey of making mathematics learning visible for students.

Reflection and Discussion Questions

1. Think about the instructional strategies you use most often. Which do you believe are most effective? What evidence do you have for their impact? Save these notes so you can see how the evidence in this book supports or challenges your thinking about effective practices.

2. Identify one important mathematics topic that you teach. Think about your goals for this topic in terms of the SOLO model discussed in this chapter. Do your learning intentions and success criteria lean more toward surface (uni- and multi-structural) or deep (relational and extended abstract)? Are they balanced across the two?

3. A key element of transfer learning is thinking about opportunities for students to move their learning from math class, to use their knowledge to solve their own problems. Think about the important mathematical ideas you teach. For each one, begin to list situations that might encourage transfer of learning. These might be applications in another subject area or situations in real life where the mathematics is important.

MAKING LEARNING VISIBLE STARTS WITH TEACHER CLARITY

2

Early in Will's second year of teaching middle school, after learning about the importance of routines and procedures, he felt sure that he finally had his classroom running smoothly. His teaching pattern was this: students would come in and get their notebooks, open a textbook from the middle of their tables, and do the warm-up on the assigned page. When they finished the warm-up, they would be introduced to the daily objective—a "students will be able to" or SWBAT—and then Will would explain the math before students got started on the problem set from the textbook that usually consisted of practice exercises on that skill. When two thirds or so of the students had finished (some with Will's individualized help), the class would go over the questions together and students would have the opportunity to change their answers to the correct ones. Then he'd assign homework, and the bell would ring. Although Will's students were relatively well behaved and seemed busy, they weren't learning as much as they deserved to. Like many novice teachers, Will valued compliance over learning. Here are five reasons why true learning was limited:

- Will's students didn't know what they were supposed to learn, or why they were supposed to learn it. So, they were less likely to learn it, or even to want to learn it.

- Even if Will's students did decide to memorize his objective from the SWBAT on the board, and even if they understood what it meant, at the end of the lesson they wouldn't know whether or not they had learned it.

- Will's students didn't really benefit from Will's expertise.

- Will's students didn't have a sense of where this learning would lead, or how it connected to what they had already learned.

- Will's students never learned how to manage their own learning.

As we begin this journey of visible learning, let's think about the importance of teacher clarity. Teacher clarity involves the instructional moves a teacher makes that begin with carefully planning a lesson and making the learning intentions for that lesson or unit clear to herself and her students. It extends to consistently evaluating where students are in the learning process and describing the success criteria on which students can assess their own progress and on which the teacher bases her evaluation of a student's progress with a mathematical idea or concept. What was lacking in Will's early teaching experiences was clarity!

Will went on to drastically improve his teaching when he read about and applied some key ideas, and his early struggles made him more effective in coaching and leading other teachers to success in their classrooms later on. A major step in this journey was when he examined the way he planned his lessons.

A starting place for lesson planning is the **learning intention**, or the statement of what students are expected to learn from the lesson. The learning intention for a given lesson, and the ability to communicate it clearly to students such that they can use it to gauge their progress, is foundational in the learning sciences. Stated simply, when one knows what the target is, there is an increased likelihood that the target will be achieved. Knowing one's learning destination is crucial for mathematics students.

If learning intentions serve as one bookend for learning, the other bookend consists of the criteria used to measure success. How do you know whether your students are successful at learning what you wanted them to? How do *they* know whether they're successful? How can they know whether or not they've met the intended learning intentions, or whether they're making progress toward doing so? With success criteria. **Success criteria** are statements that describe what success looks like when the learning goal is reached. They are specific, concrete, and measurable. In this chapter, we will focus on the importance of knowing and communicating learning intentions and success criteria to students. When success criteria are communicated clearly, and teachers and students are actively looking for evidence of learning, learners understand the importance of the lesson. Even better, strategic use of learning intentions and success criteria promote student self-reflection and metacognition—that is, thinking about their own thinking. These are two essential yet often overlooked lesson outcomes. For students, this means knowing what they are expected to learn (learning intentions) and what the learning goal looks like when they have learned it (success criteria), having an idea of the route or strategies that will help them get there, and knowing what to do when they don't know what to do (Bransford, Brown, & Cocking, 2000).

As we noted in the previous chapter, Hattie (2009) underwent the enormous task of studying and consolidating more research on quality teaching and learning than had ever been amassed before. After completing this monumental feat, John realized that the single most important thing teachers can do is to *know their impact on student learning*.

Learning intentions describe what teachers want students to learn.

Success criteria are specific, concrete, measurable statements that describe what success looks like when the learning goal is reached.

EFFECT SIZE FOR METACOGNITIVE STRATEGIES = 0.69

Strategic use of learning intentions and success criteria promote student self-reflection and metacognition.

Teacher clarity is clarity of organization, explanation, instruction, and assessment that is seen by the students.

EFFECT SIZE FOR TEACHER CLARITY = **0.75**

Teachers need to be aware of the effect they have on their students (Hattie, 2009). Thus, teachers have to assess students' understanding. To determine if learning occurred, teachers first use preassessments to identify baselines in understanding and performance.

Taken together, learning intentions, success criteria, preassessments, and checking for understanding contribute to **teacher clarity**. Fendick (1990) defined teacher clarity as "a measure of the clarity of communication between teachers and students—in both directions" (p. 10) and further described it across four dimensions:

1. *Clarity of organization* such that structured lessons include links to the objectives and outcomes of learning.

2. *Clarity of explanation* such that explanations are accurate and comprehensible to students.

3. *Clarity of examples and guided practice* such that the examples are illustrative and illuminating, and students gradually move to independence, making "quick and accurate progress without help" (p. 10). Guided practice refers to the guidance teachers provide as they make strategic decisions about the right type of practice for each student throughout instruction.

4. *Clarity of assessment of student learning* such that the teacher is regularly seeking out and acting upon the feedback he or she receives from students, especially through their verbal and written responses.

Learning Intentions for Mathematics

Effective teachers know where their students are in the learning cycle and design their instruction to foster learning. As we mentioned in Chapter 1, learning intentions can include a combination of surface, deep, and/or transfer learning, with the exact combination dependent on what kinds of choices a teacher makes based on where her learners are and where she wants them to go. A teacher who fails to identify where her students are in their mathematical learning is likely to undershoot or overshoot expectations for them. In mathematics and science, it is more often the latter, and there's a term for it: the expert blind spot (Nathan & Petrosino, 2003). This is the condition created when a teacher knows the content well, but fails to recognize the fits and starts of students as they attempt to learn new concepts. This can often happen in mathematics when students have learned a procedure but do not know the meaning of the calculation they've done. Our algebra example in Chapter 1 included a discussion on the meaning of slope as an example of deep learning. A teacher with an expert blind spot might mistake the fact that students can identify or calculate the slope without understanding of what it means and how to interpret its value. "But I taught it! Why don't they get it?" is the lament of anyone who has possessed an expert blind spot. That's why it is essential to align the right instructional practices at the right time in the learning cycle. Kolb (1984) defines the learning cycle as having four elements: concrete experience, reflective observation of that experience, abstract conceptualization (based on the experience and reflection), and active experimentation (applying the new learning to daily life). Different strategies support learning at each phase in this cycle. The first three elements of the learning cycle will incorporate surface and deep learning, while the active experimentation phase is about transfer. The daily learning intentions that are communicated by the teacher are an end product of her careful planning, as she determines the type of expected learning (surface, deep, or transfer) and how to implement instruction for that type of learning. The success criteria provide a means for students and the teacher to gauge progress toward learning, thereby making learning visible.

Learning intentions (which some people call objectives, learning goals, targets, or purpose statements) are where teacher planning begins. Learning intentions are different from standards. Standards are statements for teachers that identify what students should know and be able to do at a given point in time. Standards are tough for yet-to-be-educated students to understand, and they are too broad for students to master in a single lesson. Effective teachers start with a standard, break the learning that standard requires into lesson-sized chunks, and then phrase these chunks so that students will be able to understand them. Each one of these chunked phrases—a daily statement of what a student is expected to learn in a given lesson—is a learning intention. Learning intentions can focus on knowledge, skills, or concepts, and should be aligned to the mathematics standards and to the learning intentions of related lessons. As mathematics researchers and educators Margaret Smith and Mary Kay Stein (2011) remind us, "The key is to specify a goal that clearly identifies what students are to know and understand about

Video 2.1
Learning Intentions in the Elementary Classroom

http://resources.corwin.com/ VL-mathematics

Video 2.2
Learning Intentions in the Secondary Classroom

http://resources.corwin.com/ VL-mathematics

mathematics as a result of their engagement in a particular lesson" (p. 13). Following are some examples of learning intentions that we have seen in mathematics classrooms.

- Know that a ten is really just a group of ten ones.

- Recognize that area is a specific kind of array (built from unit squares) that measures two-dimensional space, and understand why we find area by multiplying the length times the width of a rectangle.

- Learn to add two fractions with like denominators by modeling on a number line.

- Understand how to divide a decimal number by a decimal number by considering place value.

- Examine a given data set to determine if the function that it describes is linear or exponential by assessing the way the function changes over equal intervals and relating this change to students' knowledge of a given context.

Some mathematics teachers might be concerned that statements such as these can rob students of a period of investigation and inquiry. Learning intentions don't have to be used at the outset of the lesson and may be revisited over time. Teachers can withhold their learning intentions until after an exploration has occurred. And teachers can invite students to explain what they learned from the lesson and compare that with the initial learning intention for the lesson. Interesting class discussions about the alignment (or lack of alignment) can provide a great deal of insight on student understanding.

Learning intentions are themselves evidence of a scaffolded process that unfolds over many lessons. A key to planning a lesson is in knowing where your students currently are in their learning. It would be tough to teach students that a ten is really just a group of ten ones if they don't understand the value of one, just as it would be difficult for students to determine growth patterns in functions if they don't really understand what functions are or why they're useful. However, learning intentions can (and often should) have an inherent recursive element in that they build connections between previously learned content and new knowledge. Savvy teachers embed previous content in the new content. The teacher is not only creating a need and a purpose for students to hone learned skills, but also providing opportunities for students to experience those "aha" moments that relate concepts to a previous lesson's content. In this way, students are continually connecting and deepening their mathematical knowledge.

There are a few other hallmarks of good learning intentions that Clarke, Timperley, and Hattie (2003) have identified:

- Learning intentions should be shared with students, so that students understand them and what success looks like. Recognize that not all students in the class will be working at the same rate or starting from the same place, so it's important to adapt the plan relating to the intentions to make it clear to all students.

- Learning does not happen in a neat, linear sequence; therefore, the cascade from the curriculum aim (the standard) through the achievement objective (unit goals) to the learning intention (for a specific lesson) is sometimes complex.

- Learning intentions and activities can be grouped if one activity can contribute to more than one learning intention, or one learning intention may need several activities for students to understand it fully.

- Learning intentions are what we intend students to learn, but it is important to realize students may learn other things not planned for, so teachers need to be aware of unintended consequences.

Student Ownership of Learning Intentions

Doug travels the world talking about quality instruction for all learners. He speaks to teachers and administrators, and he used to tell them that teachers should communicate their learning intentions because doing so has been shown by extensive research to boost student learning and achievement (Hattie, 2012). Furthermore, it is consistent with the first of NCTM's (2014) effective mathematics teaching practices: to establish mathematical goals to focus learning. But he found that people actually took this advice more seriously when he framed learning intentions as a students' rights issue. Students have a right to know what they're supposed to learn, and why they're supposed to learn it. After all, teachers are going to evaluate student performance and mark report cards and transcripts that last a lifetime. These records open doors to colleges and careers, or close them. It's only fair that students understand what they're expected to learn if teachers are going to evaluate that learning.

> Students have a right to know what they're supposed to learn, and why they're supposed to learn it.

Connect Learning Intentions to Prior Knowledge

While the learning intention itself is important, it needs to be based on an agreed-upon standard, phrased in a way that's easy for students to understand, and appropriately constructed around where students are in their learning. The way in which it's communicated is also key.

Activating students' prior knowledge going into a lesson is an important consideration as teachers explain the learning intentions (Bransford et al., 2000; Willingham, 2009). Many teachers begin their classes with an independent warm-up exercise. Unfortunately, some teachers just do this so that they have a chance to take attendance and make sure everyone has a pencil, thus squandering an important learning opportunity. Bell work should be an opportunity to cultivate and activate prior knowledge through written work or classroom discourse. An effective teacher uses opportunities like this to assist students in preparing for new knowledge acquisition.

Students can write or verbally share what they already know about the concept or skill they'll be learning, pose questions about it, or write about concepts they need to understand before they can tackle the day's learning. They can solve problems that are related to the day's learning (Sidney & Alibali, 2015; Sloyer, 2004). The point is to get learners ready to learn the new content by giving their brains something to which to connect their new skill or understanding.

After the opening exercise, some teachers have students turn to their groups and share what they've written or explain their reasoning in arriving at their answers. This gives students the chance to construct mathematical arguments and critique the reasoning of others, which is mathematical practice 3 (see Appendix B for a complete list of mathematical practices). An outcome of this may be to solidify their individual understanding of a mathematical concept or address any misconceptions remaining from previous experiences. This is important—connecting new learning to incorrect prior knowledge can hurt understanding (van Loon, de Bruin, van Gog, & van Merriernboer, 2013). The opportunity for students to speak also helps them firm up their understanding and learn from each other's expertise. This use of an opening routine is just one of many ways to activate students' prior knowledge, and the important thing is that it's activated. Once prior knowledge is activated, students can make connections between their knowledge and the lesson's learning intentions.

Teaching Takeaway

Tie prior learning to new learning intentions by embedding previous content in new content.

Bell work can be a good opportunity to cultivate and activate prior knowledge. The point is to get learners ready to learn the new content by giving their brains something to which to connect their new skill or understanding.

Make Learning Intentions Inviting and Engaging

The ways in which teachers talk about learning intentions make a difference. William Purkey (1992) described four patterns with which students perceived lessons: intentionally disinviting, unintentionally disinviting, unintentionally inviting, and intentionally inviting.

Teachers who were intentionally disinviting were easily recognizable because of their dismissive and harsh tone. Most of us would, thankfully, not be in that category. However, teachers who were unintentionally disinviting were negative and pessimistic about their students' capabilities, and their low expectations were apparent to the learners (and they were often successful in having low impact on student learning!). For example, consider this introduction to a lesson on adding fractions with unlike denominators. The teacher starts by saying, "Today we are going to work on adding fractions with different denominators. This is a really difficult concept, and I know that most of you are going to struggle with being able to add fractions, so you are going to have to pay close attention." Little does the teacher realize that he has just told the students that they will not be successful in this lesson. In addition to being disinviting, using this type of introduction encourages a fixed mindset in students who are thinking, "This is going to be hard and I probably won't be able to do it!"

On the other hand, there is a group of teachers Purkey categorizes as unintentionally inviting. The teachers are energetic and enthusiastic, but they lack a plan for their journey. Students like being with them, but don't benefit as fully as they could from instruction because it is inconsistent and naive. An unintentionally inviting teacher might begin the same fraction lesson by saying, "Good morning, scholars. Today we are going to learn more about fractions! I know you will find this interesting work, and I cannot wait to get started!" This is unintentionally inviting because the teacher is all about getting students excited and interested in the lesson, but notice how the statement doesn't talk about exactly what students are going to learn or why it is important. It may not take long before the students realize that despite their enthusiasm, they have no idea of what is going on.

The final category—intentionally inviting—consists of teachers who are consistently positive and are sensitive to the needs of students. They take action and promote a growth mindset. Most of all, they are purposeful and effectively transmit a sense of instructional urgency. As teachers set the learning intentions, they also set the tone for their classroom. Let's take a look at an intentionally inviting learning intention on adding fractions with unlike denominators in Mrs. Schmidt's fifth grade.

> "Good morning, scholars. You may recall that last year you worked with adding fractions with common denominators. This year we will move on to adding fractions with unlike denominators. Let's start by solving this problem.

> Joey ate $\frac{2}{5}$ of the pumpkin pie. His sister ate $\frac{1}{5}$ of the pie. How much pie did they eat? How much pie is left?

> I would like you to start by representing this problem in any way that you would like."

(After giving students the opportunity to write their ideas, the teacher gives them time to explain their work with partners or small groups while she circulates to observe and listen to discussions, noting students that may need additional support or review and those who are successful in solving the problem.)

Mrs. Schmidt now has enough information to know if students are ready for adding fractions with unlike denominators, or if some time needs to be spent reviewing and filling in the gaps from last year's work. She continues by inviting students to identify situations in which addition of fractions is important so that students understand the need for representing, understanding, and applying this concept.

Algebra teacher Jeff Turnbull has a consistent place where he posts daily learning intentions prominently on the board. In a unit on solving systems of equations, Mr. Turnbull referred back to the day's learning intention: "Use graphing to figure out x and y when you have two equations that intersect, and you don't know x or y at that point." Mr. Turnbull then said,

> "This skill is used in many different jobs. You can use this skill to figure out which cell phone plan is the best deal for you or to decide if you want to buy a monthly subway pass or pay for each ride. These are important skills, and the most important part, to me, is that it makes you a better thinker. It lets you have conversations about math at a higher level, so that you can communicate better. You see, solving for two different variables, like we're doing today, builds on the solving

Not So Inviting Learning Intentions	More Inviting Learning Intentions
We have a test on Friday, so we need to review place value.	I was thinking about our work together, and I noticed that many of us still need to think about place value. We should spend some time reviewing place value so that we know how to determine which number is greater.
By the end of the lesson, you will be able to solve inequalities with rational numbers.	Remember all of the learning we did with inequalities? We really mastered that content as a class. Now it would be interesting to examine how to solve inequalities that were more complex, maybe with several variables. And then we could graph them to visualize what is happening. I know that several of you find it helpful in understanding when we create visual representations.
Today we are going to continue our work with statistics. We will focus our learning on scatter plots for bivariate measurement data so that we can see if there are patterns of association.	Have you ever wondered if the relationship between two things was really significant? For example, I was wondering if the number of students in a class was related to their overall scores on a test. I'm sure you all can think of things you'd like to compare. Remember, we learned that correlations don't mean cause, but that there is a relationship with the numbers. Today, we get to explore scatter plots as one tool to look for associations.

Figure 2.1

equations and graphing work we've done, but the cool thing is that it opens up into more advanced algebra and even physics. It's like a gateway for you. Besides, graphs give us so much more information than substitution or elimination."

While some students know that Jeff's enthusiasm is a bit contrived, they prefer him to their previous teacher, who would tell them that they "have to learn" something, or that they will "get through" some content, as though it were a chore for which the teacher was apologizing. These unintentionally disinviting statements have a negative effect on student learning. After all, Jeff figures, how can students be expected to be engaged and excited about something if their teacher isn't engaged and excited about it?

Figure 2.1 contains a few sample learning intentions that were initially less than effective, and how teachers revised them.

EFFECT SIZE FOR
TEACHER–STUDENT
RELATIONSHIPS =
0.72

Learning intentions are more than just statements to convey to students what the learning is composed of; they are a means for building positive relationships with students. While much of this book is about instructional practices, teacher-student and student-student relationships are foundational to learning. Learning intentions that are intentionally inviting, are aligned to current student learning, are designed to advance students from surface to deeper learning, and set high expectation targets deliver positive results that accelerate learning (Hattie, 2012). Taken together, these practices make learning visible to students who understand they are under the guidance of a caring and knowledgeable teacher who is invested in their success.

Language Learning Intentions and Mathematical Practices

We have seen some of the best teachers set several learning intentions in a given lesson. These teachers communicate learning intentions in terms of content, but they also have language goals for their students and specific learning intentions related to these language goals. The language demands of mathematics are extensive, as students are expected to attend to precision, construct viable arguments, express their reasoning, and critique the reasoning of others. For students identified as English Learners, the stakes are even higher, as they do "double work" of learning mathematics while also learning the academic and disciplinary language needed (Short & Fitzsimmons, 2007). It is unfortunate that instruction of mathematical language is often overlooked, further disadvantaging those who do not possess a strong foundation of background knowledge. As well, technical mathematical terms are rarely encountered in daily life.

Language learning
intentions focus
on the academic
language and
vocabulary students
need to know to
master a lesson's
content.

Language learning intentions can be related to the vocabulary words that students will need to know in order to master the lesson's content. For example, fifth-grade teacher Katie McKenna keeps her language goals on the wall, right under her content learning intentions. For a lesson in a unit on adding and subtracting fractions, she posted the words *numerator* and *denominator*. Many students were familiar with these words, but their understanding was limited to the numerator as the "top number in a fraction" and the denominator as the "bottom number." To make matters even worse, students had been given the "hint" that *numerator* contains the letter *u* which reminds them of *up* and *denominator* begins with the letter *d* so denominator is *down*. Granted, these are challenging words for students in Grades 3 through 5, and the need to develop deeper understanding of the meanings of the numerator and denominator in a fraction is even more complex. However, intentionally introducing these words in a context and expanding the meaning of each term across the grades have a much greater impact on the development of deep understanding of what a numerator or denominator actually means in a given situation.

Language learning intentions can be constructed to highlight the use of what educational researchers call Tier 2 or general academic words (Beck, McKeown, & Kucan, 2013). Tier 2 words are words that all students should know by the time they graduate, and they extend beyond math class. These are words like *analyze, synthesize,* and *extrapolate.* Other Tier 2 words have specific meanings in mathematics, such as *set, prime, similar,* and *area,* that differ from the way these words are used outside of mathematics. These multiple-meaning words are especially vexing, as students often possess a limited set of definitions for words like these. For instance, they may understand that area refers to a space, but they do not know that finding the area of a figure requires a level of precision. Students are more likely to remember words when they are learning them for a reason, so it makes sense to set the expectation that students will use these words and phrases when they talk about their math work. Tier 1 words are everyday words like *small* and *size* and are not usually the focus of math teachers. Tier 3, or domain-specific, words are terms that are used specifically for mathematics such as *absolute value, angle bisector,* or *numerator.* Typically, general academic and domain-specific words are the focus of language learning in a mathematics classroom. Additional examples of these types of words can be found in Figure 2.2. The best teachers remind students why they're learning these words.

In addition to vocabulary, teachers can focus on the function that language serves. In mathematics, we typically *describe, explain, convince, solve, question, sequence, inform, justify, evaluate,* and the like. When students understand these terms, teachers should expect them to engage in these actions as they work collaboratively with their peers. For example, mathematics teacher Melissa Juarez's middle school students have been multiplying and dividing fractions. She had planned a lesson with their health and nutrition teacher, Chuck Branson, in which students would have to produce rewritten recipes with the correct calculations based on the number of people assigned. She explained that in order to do so,

Teaching Takeaway

Create language goals in addition to learning intentions to make the learning richer.

EXAMPLES OF TIER 2 AND TIER 3 WORDS IN MATHEMATICS

Tier 2 or General Academic Terms *Words whose meaning varies by context and discipline*	Tier 3 or Domain-Specific Terms *Terms that have a fixed meaning and are used only in the context of mathematics*
average	addend
difference	base 10
expression	cardinal number
figure	categorical variable
model	circumference
outlier	cosine
pattern	denominator
plot	linear equation
prime	number line
reciprocal	numerator
similar	quadrilateral
slope	quartile
solution	quotient
table	rhombus
unknown	trapezoid
whole	tree diagram

 This figure and a blank template are available for download at **http://resources.corwin.com/VL-mathematics**

Figure 2.2

they would need to correctly use terms such as *conversion, portions,* and *scaling* in their written explanations. "I don't just want to read your procedure. Convince me *why* your answer is correct. To do so, you'll need to identify any patterns you used to help solve the problem." She listed these terms on the whiteboard as she spoke. As she explained,

> "Some recipes are written for larger groups of people, like 14 to 20. You want to prepare it for yourself and a couple of friends. So, we'll work on the mathematical thinking here, and then you'll be able to make these recipes in Mr. Branson's class. It's not just about the calculations, but explaining how you came up with the answers. I'm interested in having you solve these problems in your expert group, inform the others in your home group, and justify your answers in writing."

During this time, Ms. Juarez accomplished several important instructional goals. The first is that she made her learning intentions clear to students, giving attention to language as well as content. In addition, the task was designed to facilitate their learning as they transitioned from surface learning of conversions to deeper learning in applying knowledge to new situations. Third, the lesson supported several of NCTM's (2014) effective mathematics teaching practices, including "implement tasks that promote reasoning and problem solving" and "use and connect mathematical representations." Finally, the task incorporates many of the standards for mathematical practice in order for students to continue to develop important mathematical habits of mind.

Social Learning Intentions and Mathematical Practices

Since high-quality math lessons involve a good deal of collaboration (as we'll discuss in the next chapter), it makes sense for teachers to set social learning intentions as well. **Social learning intentions** are those that focus on the social skills that foster effective collaboration and communication. Will has seen one frustrated teacher post the social goal "Be quiet when the teacher is talking!" This is *not* the type of social goal that we mean here, even though respect for a teacher talking is important. However, a social goal of "be quiet and listen when others are talking" is a valued skill in small and large group work. It makes sense to attend to the social skills of mathematics students. After all, Vygotsky (1962) and others have certainly shown us that all learning is a social endeavor. The ways in which peers interact and work with one another, and with their teacher, are an engine in the classroom.

Social learning intentions focus on the social skills that foster effective collaboration and communication.

EFFECT SIZE FOR
CLASSROOM
COHESION = 0.53

Social learning intentions can include things like "Ask your teammates for help," "Listen to really understand what your group members are saying," "Explain your reasoning," or "Give helpful feedback to others." These and other communication skills contribute to a sense of classroom cohesion, which Hattie (2009) describes as "the sense that all (teachers and students) are working toward positive learning gains" (p. 103). As with content and language learning intentions, social intentions should be based on what teachers learn from their students as they watch them work and review individual and group products. Listening to and observing the interactions of students in small and large group settings is essential for making such decisions.

Shortly into the school year, Mr. Milam asks his students to create a list of class norms they will agree to as they work on doing mathematics together throughout the school year. The students come up with an excellent list, and because it is their list, they work hard to follow these norms and politely remind each other of their agreed-upon ideas when they slip! Here is a list that a group of sixth graders developed.

Teaching Takeaway

Social goals can include things like "Ask your teammates for help," "Listen to really understand what your group members are saying," "Explain your reasoning," or "Give helpful feedback to others."

1. We will listen when others are speaking. That means

   - Looking at the speaker
   - Not playing with pencils or other distractions
   - Not interrupting or talking with a neighbor

2. We will work to support each other in our math groups. That means

   - Answering a teammate's question
   - Sharing our work without copying or telling others how to do it
   - Asking good questions of one another

3. We will come to class prepared to work hard to learn important mathematics. That means

   - We will be ready to start when the bell rings.
   - We will have the correct supplies (paper, pencil, notebook, textbook).
   - We will complete the practice and come with questions about parts we did not understand.

As the year progressed, students added other norms to this list. Mr. Milam did not have to spend time preaching to students about their behavior or being prepared for class. These norms had been decided and agreed upon by the entire class, and by giving students ownership, Mr. Milam thus increased the likelihood that students would take responsibility for their behavior and their work.

Sometimes social learning intentions support the mathematical practices (MPs) we alluded to in the preface. These practices are often described as habits of mind students must develop to be proficient in doing mathematics, and there is agreement that these are general practices that students must develop. The language in these practices differs based on specific states, provinces, or countries. As an example, let's consider the practices (Standards for Mathematical Practice) recommended in the Common Core State Standards (National Governors Association Center for Best Practices & Council of Chief State School Officers, 2010):

1. Make sense of problems and persevere in solving them.

2. Reason abstractly and quantitatively.

3. Construct viable arguments and critique the reasoning of others.

4. Model with mathematics.

5. Use appropriate tools strategically.

6. Attend to precision.

7. Look for and make use of structure.

8. Look for and express regularity in repeated reasoning.

In setting learning intentions, a teacher might identify a mathematical practice, such as "Construct viable arguments and critique the reasoning of others" (MP 3), and turn it into more student-friendly language, such as "Justify your thinking so that you can convince a partner you're correct." Integrated Math III teacher Brian Stone posts the mathematical practice he wants his high school mathematicians to focus on, sometimes even more prominently than the learning intention. When his students were learning about logarithms, he had "Look for and make use of structure" (MP 7) posted to remind students what to look for as they completed the tasks. Another day, when students were working on a particularly challenging task, he had posted "Make sense of problems and persevere in solving them" (MP 1). Before delving into the task, he led his students in a discussion about perseverance, and together they identified what this would sound like and look like, including items such as asking for help, asking for clarification, and tracking the speaker.

This example is from the practice standards from the Common Core, and nearly all state and national standards have a version of these higher order thinking skills. For example, in Texas, the processes are described as the following (Texas Essential Knowledge and Skills for Mathematics, 2012):

A. Apply mathematics to problems arising in everyday life, society, and the workplace.

B. Use a problem-solving model that incorporates analyzing given information, formulating a plan or strategy, determining a solution, justifying the solution, and evaluating the problem-solving process and the reasonableness of the solution.

C. Select tools, including real objects, manipulatives, paper and pencil, and technology as appropriate.

D. Communicate mathematical ideas, reasoning, and their implications using multiple representations, including symbols, diagrams, graphs, and language as appropriate.

E. Create and use representations to organize, record, and communicate mathematical ideas.

F. Analyze mathematical relationships to connect and communicate mathematical ideas.

G. Display, explain, and justify mathematical ideas and arguments using precise mathematical language in written or oral communication.

Australia's Mathematics Curriculum Key Ideas (Foundation–Year 10 Australian Curriculum, 2015) include the following:

Understanding

Fluency

Problem solving

Reasoning

You can find a nonexhaustive list of practice standards around the world in Appendix C.

Pay Close Attention	• Focus on the speaker, visually and mentally. • Ignore distracting thoughts or forming a rebuttal while you listen. • Avoid distractions.
Show That You're Listening	• Nod when appropriate. • Smile and use facial expressions. • Look at the speaker while he or she is talking. • Encourage the speaker to continue with brief verbal comments such as yes, and uh huh.
Provide Feedback	• Paraphrase what you heard ("What I'm hearing is" or "Sounds like you are saying"). • Ask clarifying questions. • Summarize the speakers' information.
Respond Appropriately	• Allow the speaker to finish (interrupting wastes time). • Be honest and kind in your response. • Treat others the way you want to be treated.

Figure 2.3

Fourth-grade teacher Andrea Villanova reminded her students to "take turns as you work to solve the problems. Remember, your group should work together to solve the problem using pictures, words, and numbers. You'll only be able to hear the reasoning of your group members if you take turns and if you listen with intention." The poster in Ms. Villanova's room outlined what it meant to listen with intention, and students had practiced each of these skills at the outset of the school year. A copy of her poster can be found in Figure 2.3.

Reference the Learning Intentions Throughout a Lesson

Excellent teachers think hard about when they will present the learning intention. They don't just set the learning intentions early in the lesson and then forget about them. They refer to these intentions throughout instruction, keeping students focused on what it is they're supposed to learn. For example, a teacher might intentionally decide to present a mathematical practice early in the lesson so students can focus on using this habit throughout their work. When a group of Mr. Stone's middle school students were experiencing productive struggle that was teetering toward the unproductive, he referred them to the word *persevere* underlined on the board in his positive discussion with them. They discussed how they could ask for help or clarification, using the ideas from the discussion earlier in the lesson, to move back toward productive struggle. Ms. McKenna referred back to her vocabulary words, *numerator* and *denominator,* referencing her language learning intention, and asked students to do the same as she worked with small groups who were constructing their knowledge, reminding them to use the terms in their explanations.

As with academic learning intentions, savvy teachers return to social learning intentions before releasing students to work collaboratively, and ask students to self-assess whether they thought they met these goals once they're finished. Even young children can rate their skill at taking turns, sharing ideas, or disagreeing respectfully during a discussion.

Success Criteria for Mathematics

Effective math teachers establish not only the learning intentions but also the success criteria. In addition to knowing what they're supposed to learn, students should know how they will know they've learned it, and how they can assess themselves along the way.

Success Criteria Are Crucial for Motivation

As mathematics teachers move away from the futile practice of relying on repetitive problem sets and toward mathematically rich tasks, the question of success criteria becomes more complicated than "You'll know you're successful if you get sixteen out of twenty of today's problems right." Besides, calculating the right answer isn't the only point of a task. Mathematics is more than getting correct answers. Mathematics is thinking about problems flexibly and working to solve them logically. As students are increasingly called upon to justify and explain their reasoning, connect multiple solutions to a problem, analyze worked examples, and address real-world problems using the tools of mathematics, teachers must offer more nuanced assessments of student learning. The great news about learning intentions and success criteria is that they have been shown to increase students' internal motivation. And a very convincing case could be made that internal motivation to succeed in mathematics is one of the most important things your students can learn.

Success criteria work because they tap into principles of human motivation (Bandura, 1997; Elliot & Harackiewicz, 1994). People tend to compare their current performance or ability with a goal that they set, or have a caring teacher help set with them. When there is a gap between where they are and where they want to be, it creates cognitive dissonance. Students are motivated to close the gap and get rid of the dissonance by working and learning. The more explicitly and precisely they can see the goal, the more motivated they will be.

It may seem obvious that teachers should know whether or not their students are learning what they're supposed to. But students need to know whether they're on the right track, too. Self-reported grades reflect the extent to which students have accurate understandings of and abilities to predict their achievement. It matters that students can describe their current performance accurately, whether that performance is high or low (Hattie, 2012). When we think about it, though, it's hard for learners to know whether they are learning something without having some criteria against which they can measure themselves. Teachers should have success criteria in mind for the lesson. As mentioned earlier, success criteria describe what success looks like when the learning goal is reached. It is specific, concrete, and measurable.

Suppose that a teacher establishes a learning intention that students should use their knowledge of area of rectangles to solve real-world problems. How would a student know whether he or she can do this? Would solving one problem involving area be enough? Some area problems are more difficult than others, involving combinations of rectangles and related shapes. Should students solve these problems independently or as part of a team? Will they need to solve three out of four correctly? Eight out of ten? Will the lengths of the sides be round numbers or numbers with decimals, or fractions of units? What if their methods are correct, but they forget a decimal place or mess up their conversions? Each of these questions guides teachers in determining what success looks like for their students. In mathematics, success criteria are measures of success demonstrated by more than simple "answer getting." Teachers

Video 2.3
Achieving Teacher Clarity
With Success Criteria

*http://resources.corwin.com/
VL-mathematics*

EFFECT SIZE FOR
SELF-REPORTED
GRADES/STUDENT
EXPECTATIONS = 1.44

who focus only on the correctness of a student's answer do so at the peril of misunderstanding the student's conceptual understanding and problem-solving process.

Without clearly defined criteria, teachers and students are not sure what type of learning has occurred, if any. As we noted earlier, some learning intentions focus on surface learning, and thus the success criteria should be aligned with that level of learning. Other times, the learning intention focuses on deep or transfer levels of learning, and the success criteria need to align with those levels.

Students are much more motivated to work toward success criteria if those criteria are specific (Locke & Latham, 1990). Criteria such as "Do your best" and "Try hard" are not very clear or actionable (they have the lowest of effect sizes and probably should never be used). "I can" statements such as "I can add fractions" may be actionable but are not very specific. Criteria such as "I will be able to clearly explain my reasoning as I factor a polynomial" or "I can solve problems that involve addition or subtraction of mixed numbers and explain my thinking" are more likely to produce results. The more specific your learning intentions and the criteria for reaching those intentions, the more likely it is that your students will achieve them. Learning intentions, which are synonymous with learning goals, should also be proximal (Bandura, 1997). In other words, they shouldn't be too distant in the future. This is important to keep in mind when assigning long projects—it really is worth establishing daily success criteria that your students can keep in mind as they work on long-term projects, especially at younger ages. Even better might be to teach students how to break larger goals down into smaller ones themselves.

At the beginning of a unit on number theory, Mrs. Martinez assigned her fifth graders a "Special Number Project" that incorporated all of the important mathematical ideas of the unit. This would be the final assessment in lieu of a written test. Students would be working on their projects throughout the unit and checking in regularly with Mrs. Martinez to show their progress. At the beginning of the unit, the project was explained, and by the third day, each student was to choose a special number between 1 and 100. Mrs. Martinez prepared a letter to parents so they were aware of what their children were doing. As the week progressed, Mrs. Martinez shared some examples of former students' projects (without giving too much information so that students would work to develop original ideas). By the end of the week, students had to turn in a brief description of their special number projects. While they were permitted to change their ideas after a conversation with the teacher, this helped them to commit to an idea rather than flounder throughout the unit. As the unit vocabulary developed, a classroom word wall was built to help students focus on the important mathematical concepts and the new vocabulary. One of the success criteria was that all of the vocabulary had to be meaningfully incorporated into the project. Students discussed what was meaningful and what was not using the project examples the teacher had shared. Mrs. Martinez met with students regularly or collected written updates on their progress throughout the unit so no one was left hanging until the last minute. The best part was that on "Project Day," students proudly carried their math projects (ranging from posters to board games to stories) into class eager to share their work with others. The project was clear, the learning intention was clear, and the success criteria were clear. Most of the students successfully demonstrated mastery of this important mathematics content and had fun doing it! (And Mrs. Martinez still has many of those projects in her files!)

Hilda Amador uses "I can" statements with her first-grade students throughout the day. She posts the statements on a language chart and leads the class in reading them aloud together. "I can find all of the two-addend combinations to make a given number," they read. Ms. Amador continues, "Here is a problem for you to solve."

> My mom went to the market and bought some apples and some pears. She bought 10 pieces of fruit altogether. How many apples and how many pears could she have bought?

Using the color tiles, you will work with your partner to model all of the different combinations of apples and pears you can find. Then you will write an equation for each combination you have found.

One caution here is to be sure that "I can" statements are specific and tied to the learning intention. General "I can" statements, while well intentioned, are not very helpful to the students or the teacher. Sample "I can" statements in mathematics can be found in Figure 2.4.

In some lessons, especially after students have explored a task to make sense of it themselves, the teacher leads a discussion to have students

SAMPLE "I CAN . . ." STATEMENTS

Grade	Statements
Kindergarten	• I can count up to ten objects to tell how many. • I can compare shapes by describing how they are the same or different.
First	• I can write numbers up to ten in words. • I can figure out the solution to a word problem by making a model and then deciding whether to add or subtract.
Second	• I can skip count by tens to 1,000. • I can draw a picture graph to represent data.
Third	• I can explain whether two fractions are equivalent. • I can solve word problems involving elapsed time.
Fourth	• I can multiply two two-digit numbers. • I can use what I know about fractions to help me compare decimals in the tenths and hundredths places.
Fifth	• I can use my understanding of division of whole numbers to explain what happens when I divide a whole number by a fraction. • I can explain why the formula for finding the volume of a rectangular solid works.
Sixth	• I can fluently divide multidigit whole numbers using the standard algorithm. • I can use what I know about fractions to find a unit rate for a given situation.
Seventh	• I can draw a triangle when given the measurements of its three angles. • I can use what I know about probability to predict about how many times a particular outcome is likely to occur.
Eighth	• I can explain why a zero exponent produces a value of one. • I can perform operations using numbers expressed in scientific notations.
Algebra	• I can create a linear equation or inequality for a given situation and use it to solve a problem. • I can factor a quadratic expression and use the information to help me understand the graph of the function.
Geometry	• I can draw a transformation of a figure if I'm given the original figure and instructions for the transformation. • I can use transformations, including dilations, to determine if two triangles are similar.

Figure 2.4

think aloud and to help clarify their thinking through posing purposeful (carefully constructed) questions. In the case of Ms. Amador's first grade, she might tell students they will need to convince her they have found all of the combinations. This reminds them of the learning intention and success criteria for the lesson before they head off to work further with their partners. "Let's review our 'I can' statement so we can keep our goal in mind." As students work together to model and write equations to represent a given sum, Ms. Amador is providing guided learning by asking purposeful questions to student groups that are struggling with the task, as well as pointing out where they are meeting success. At the end of the lesson, she returns once more to the "I can" statement. "We'll use our traffic light so you can tell me how you're doing with this." Her young learners place their magnetized name card on either the red light ("I don't know this yet"), the yellow light ("I'm almost there"), or the green light ("I can help someone else tomorrow!"). The teacher later said, "They're not always accurate in their self-assessments, but it's building a habit of noticing their own learning. I still need to formatively assess and check for understanding, but their self-assessments give me a head start on how I'll group them tomorrow."

> Internal motivation to succeed in mathematics is one of the most important things your students can learn.

Getting Buy-In for Success Criteria

Student goal setting, or having students determine their own criteria for success in mathematics, has been shown to boost achievement (Schunk, 1996; Senko & Hulleman, 2013). Interestingly, these benefits have also been evidenced when students have a teacher set goals for them, *if* students accept the goals as legitimate. Success criteria developed by the teacher allow students to understand their learning goals in measurable terms. An effective way to create this acceptance is to have students collaborate with you to determine the success criteria. Their input on what constitutes success provides the teacher with feedback about how students are viewing their progress and what they believe they will need to get there. For example, when presenting a rubric to students, it is worthwhile to discuss and collaborate on the contents of the rubric with students, to allow them to weigh in on the draft success criteria. This doesn't mean that you have to let a group of teenagers lower the bar so that they have an easier time. The teacher is still responsible for maintaining high expectations. In our experience, though, students' desire to slack off is rarely a serious problem when they have input into what determines success with a particular concept, practice, or problem.

> EFFECT SIZE FOR GOAL SETTING = 0.56

> EFFECT SIZE FOR EXPECTATIONS = 0.43

High school math teacher Brian Stone likes to present his students with a rough draft of his rubrics (some people call them scoring guides and others use checklists) when he assigns rich mathematical tasks and projects. He gives students some time to read the rubric and jot down some initial thoughts. Do they understand it? Is there anything they think needs to be changed? This opportunity can be crucial, as it gives students time to more deeply understand the assignment they're being asked to complete. It's also a sneaky way to have them start to visualize themselves completing rigorous work. For example, the rubric found in Figure 2.5 focuses on students' reflections of their success when collaborating with others.

Once his students have seen the rubric, Mr. Stone provides students time to discuss, in groups of three or four, and generate recommendations for the rubric. They can process their thoughts with each other and test their ideas on a small and relatively unthreatening audience. Remember that students, like the rest of us, are social creatures who learn and remember best when they're interacting with others. After the students chat with each other for a couple of minutes, Mr. Stone holds a quick class discussion. He calls on representatives from each group to share their feedback. Sometimes the student feedback is trivial and fun—"We should call the category on the right 'Nobel Prize' because that's the thinking of real experts." And sometimes it's substantive—"We could have a fourth column in between good and excellent, in case somebody's work is in between. That way they get a score that's more fair."

For shorter assignments with less complicated success criteria, it may not be necessary to spend this much class time making sure students know all the details of what's being asked of them. As a rule of thumb, the longer and more complex the assignment, the more class time teachers should devote to making sure that students understand the success criteria.

Mr. Stone also uses a rubric for the rich mathematical tasks he develops (see Figure 2.6). "I use a consistent rubric for the tasks because the criteria are the same, regardless of the content we're working on," he explained. "I used to make a different rubric for each task, but realized after a while that what I really wanted them to do was grasp the concepts being taught, furnish an explanation that included a rationale, and use accurate notation and terminology," he said. The justification element has been especially challenging. "Their tendency is just to explain, without furnishing the mathematical reasoning to support it,"

SELF-REFLECTION RUBRIC FOR MATHEMATICS GROUP COLLABORATIVE ASSESSMENTS

How well did I contribute as a member of my team? What were my strengths? Where will I improve for the next group competency?

Criteria	Evaluative Practitioner	Aware Practitioner	Evaluative Novice
Evaluative Thinking	There is evidence of the student's own thinking and learning processes and reflections on that learning, as well as implications for future learning.	There is evidence of the student's thinking about his/her own learning processes.	The submission focuses exclusively on a description of the student's experience rather than a reflection about that experience.
Analysis	The reflection moves beyond simple description of the experience and includes an analysis of how the experience contributed to student understanding of self, others, and course concepts.	The reflection is an analysis of the learning experience and the value of the derived learning to self or others.	The reflection contains a description of the learning experience with no clear analysis of learning, either by self or others.
Recognizes the Contributions of Others	The student recognizes and makes active use of ideas and special talents of each team member.	The student makes an attempt to include special talents of some of the team members.	The student does not recognize or use special talents of team members or ignores the ideas of others.
Ownership	The student accepts responsibility for the team's successes and struggles and states goals for future self-improvement.	The student accepts some responsibility for the team's success and struggles but does not link to future goals.	The student denies responsibility for struggles and blames other team members instead.

Source: Adapted from Buck Institute for Education and Williamson County (TN) Schools.

Figure 2.5

said Mr. Stone. "So no matter what we're studying, this is a continual teaching point. That's why I want to use a rubric that keeps this front and center." Mr. Stone also uses anonymous samples of student work with the class to demonstrate what successful and unsuccessful work looks like for each category. This gives students the opportunity to ask questions or to better understand the expectations through examples of completed work.

Whatever your success criteria, it is both fair and motivating for students to know what quality learning looks like before they begin a task. Just like making sure that students know learning intentions, ensuring that students know the success criteria has been shown by research to dramatically increase their learning (Black & Wiliam, 1998; Hattie, 2009). This makes intuitive sense, but it is lost in many classrooms.

Using exit tickets can be a means for teachers to gauge progress toward the established success criteria. Typically, exit tickets allow students to summarize or synthesize their thinking about some aspect of their learning. This task makes learning more visible to students and their teachers. As some of our students have noted, "I didn't know what I understood until I wrote it down." Middle school math teacher Andrea Martin uses exit slips each day to determine if her students have met the success criteria for that day. She changes the prompt each day. Her general prompts have included the following:

- How does your model demonstrate your thinking?
- Convince me your method and answer are correct.
- Describe any patterns you found to help you solve the problem.
- How can you solve the problem another way?

As students leave Ms. Martin's classroom, they deposit their exit slips into one of three buckets indicating their level of understanding. One of the buckets says, "I totally understand and could teach this to someone else." Another says, "I understand it, but my thinking is still a bit shaky." And the third says, "I am not sure I understand and would appreciate some support." This self-assessment helps guide Ms. Martin's work the following day. When Leo placed his paper in the bucket indicating his lack of success, he said to his teacher, "I can't figure out how to show my thinking. Maybe you could pair me up with someone so I could talk about it and then maybe I could do it." Students don't always need support from the teacher; peer support also works.

EFFECT SIZE
FOR PEER
TUTORING = 0.55

RUBRIC FOR RICH MATHEMATICAL TASK

	Conceptual Understanding	Explanation and Justification	Math Terms and Notations
4	Thorough understanding of mathematical concepts. The solution is accurate and complete, addressing all requested elements.	Explanation is clear and logical. Justification is reasoned and includes both how you arrived at the solution and why you used the method you chose.	Accurate terminology and notations are used. They are complete and can be followed in a step-by-step manner.
3	Nearly complete understanding of mathematical concepts. There may be minor errors, but they do not significantly detract from the solution.	The explanation is clear and logical. The justification is reasoned, but some gaps exist in how you arrived at the solution, or why you used the method you chose.	Terminology and notation used were accurate. There are minor errors, but the calculations can be followed in a step-by-step manner.
2	Some understanding of mathematical concepts. There are major errors that detract from the solution, although some aspects are intact.	The explanation is less clear due to gaps in reasoning or logic. Information is missing, as you did not address (1) how you arrived at the solution OR (2) why you chose the method you used.	Some errors in terminology and/or notation. The notations are incomplete, making it difficult to follow in a step-by-step manner.
1	Little understanding of mathematical concepts in evidence. Data were recopied and calculated, but the solution addresses only a few of the required elements of the task.	The explanation is faulty or vague. Only the solution is furnished, but you did not provide a justification of how you arrived at the solution and why you chose the method you used.	Inaccurate and incomplete use of terminology and notation. A solution is furnished, but no other calculations are apparent.
0	*Did not complete*	*Did not complete*	*Did not complete*

Figure 2.6

Video 2.4
Continual Assessment
for Daily Planning

*http://resources.corwin.com/
VL-mathematics*

Preassessments

Another factor that influences teacher clarity involves the precision of the lessons to meet the needs of students and not just to cover content. Teachers need to determine the gap between students' current level of performance or understanding and the expected level of mastery (as indicated in standards documents, for example). It's not hard to imagine that there are students who have already mastered the content that's about to be taught to them. What a waste of precious instructional time! It's also not hard to imagine that there are students who need instructional time focused on a specific aspect of a concept. The only way that a teacher can know this, and increase his or her precision in determining learning outcomes and thus clarity, is through the use of preassessments. Preassessments, or diagnostic testing as it is sometimes called, allow teachers to establish a baseline level of student knowledge before they begin teaching. It will also give teachers information to plan differentiated instruction that fills gaps and scaffolds instruction into smaller pieces for struggling students, plan tasks that move students prepared to learn the concept, and extend tasks for students who are ready to move on. Preassessments also enable teachers to determine what learning has occurred over the time of lesson(s) or units. When teachers use only postassessments, such as end-of-unit tests or projects, they will know who has demonstrated the expected level of achievement (and who has not), but they won't know who has learned what because learning is a measure of change over time.

Will remembers a colleague being delighted when her students showed mastery after her unit on the collection, display, and interpretation of data. Her students could calculate mean and median. They could use that information to visually represent data. They understood a variety of plots and graphs. She had great hopes for them for the coming year. After all, they had mastered this first unit so quickly! However, the teacher soon grew frustrated when her students didn't learn much quite so easily in the next unit. It turned out that her students had previously learned to analyze simple data the year before arriving in her classroom. In other words, what she thought had been new material in that first unit was really a review. When confronted with new concepts in subsequent units, their learning stalled, in part because she was pacing her instruction based on their early, and somewhat deceptive, success. Will's colleague would have known this in advance if she had given a preassessment before beginning the unit, thus allowing her to make adjustments to her pacing based on their existing knowledge and gaps. The ideal preassessment mirrors the postassessment in rigor and in the content it assesses, even though the questions may be different.

Another value in giving preassessments is for the teacher to establish appropriate success criteria. Will's colleague could have asked her students to design their own data collection tools, analyze more challenging data sets, or learn in some other way—or she could have moved more quickly to the next unit instead of wasting valuable instructional time. Many researchers argue that the bigger value in giving preassessments is in knowing your individual students' understandings going into a lesson (Stiggins, 2001). Armed with data from preassessments, teachers can effectively differentiate instruction and meet more students' instructional needs (Ainsworth & Viegut, 2006). You will read more about differentiating instruction later in this book. Preassessment data will also be a tremendous help as you connect your lessons to students' prior knowledge. You will know what you can connect your lesson to and what you can't. We will discuss assessment more in Chapter 7.

Conclusion

We have taken the position that students deserve to know what they are expected to learn. To our thinking, this is more than writing the standard on the dry-erase board. It's more than complying with a teacher evaluation tool that requires objectives to be written. Part of the joy of teaching and learning mathematics comes when learners know what they are expected to learn and why. In sum, teachers should establish learning intentions that

- connect to prior knowledge,
- are engaging and inviting,
- contain both content and mathematical practices, and
- address language and social goals.

In addition, teachers should make the learning intentions explicit at some point in the lesson and reference them to mark progress toward them. When the learning intentions are well developed, the teacher is able to increase his or her clarity mindfully, and mathematics can be enjoyed for its own sake.

Just as important are the success criteria that are used to motivate students and allow them to develop the habit of self-assessing. But keep in mind that your students will not become motivated and reflective learners overnight. Expert teachers know that student motivation levels can increase over time, but that it happens gradually. Those moments in which previously underperforming students "see the light" and suddenly understand the importance of mathematics may initially be short-lived. But over time, these instances become more frequent and sustained, and shift a student's personal view of mathematics. After all, nothing is more motivating than a sense of competence. Daily success criteria give students a chance to experience competence more frequently, not just when they receive a grade on the unit test. The key is to remain encouraging, but also to remain patient with the process. Remember to encourage students' growth, effort, and perseverance, rather than praising their intelligence or innate math ability, or their grades. The way you encourage students will help to shape their mathematical mindsets toward becoming more growth-centered and motivated (Dweck, 2006). Show students that you believe in them, but do it thoughtfully, persistently, and warmly.

Reflection and Discussion Questions

1. Learning intentions can help students make connections between current learning and previously learned content. Identify the learning intention for a lesson you have recently taught. What previously learned content is connected to this learning intention? Did your students see the connection? If so, how did this impact their engagement in the learning? If not, how might you modify the learning intention and experience to bring more attention to this connection?

2. Learning intentions should be intentionally inviting to students. Look back over your learning intentions from recent lessons and rewrite them to be more inviting to students. Use the examples in Figure 2.1 for guidance.

3. A lesson can have mathematical content and/or practice learning intentions, language learning intentions, and/or social learning intentions. Consider again your recent lessons and learning intentions, keeping in mind that not every lesson will incorporate every type of learning intention. Which relevant types of learning intentions did you make known to students? What other types of learning intentions might you consider? How can you determine where you want to focus your lessons?

4. Review the list of Tier 2 words in Figure 2.2. Download the blank template and make a list of the specific general academic (Tier 2) words that are important in your mathematics course(s) along with any Tier 3 (domain-specific) words your students must master. What are your strategies for helping students find success with this vocabulary?

5. Look at Mr. Stone's general math rubric in Figure 2.6 and consider one of your learning intentions with its success criteria. Make notes about the specific things you would expect to see from your students in each of the three areas of the rubric, Conceptual Understanding, Explanation and Justification, and Math Terms and Notations.

MATHEMATICAL TASKS AND TALK THAT GUIDE LEARNING

3

M s. Clark was planning a lesson on counting the value of coins for her first graders. Her learning intention for the lesson was for students to determine the value of up to four coins including pennies, nickels, and dimes. Her success criterion was for students to successfully apply their understanding to a new situation. She considered the work in the first-grade text that included drawings of several coins of which students were to determine the total value. Since they had been spending a lot of time on this skill, she was certain this would not be very challenging for her students. Instead, she decided to give them the following task.

> You are going to the store and you want to buy a banana that costs 25¢. You have lots of pennies, nickels, and dimes. What coins can you use to pay for the banana?

Ms. Clark brought a variety of coins to class so that each group had a selection of coins to help them with the problem. She was surprised at the reluctance of the students to get started on what she thought would be an enjoyable task. It turned out some students didn't recognize the real coins (even though they recognized the drawings in the textbook). Other students recognized the coins but had no idea of how to put them together to make 25¢. Ms. Clark did not jump right in to tell the students what to do. Instead, she encouraged them to work in groups to support each other in solving the problem. She was intrigued to watch the groups form based on what students could do (recognize or count the coins). Soon, one group of students raised their hands to show their answer of two dimes and a nickel. When Ms. Clark asked if there was another way to make 25¢, the students were dumbfounded. They had never solved a problem with more than one correct answer! Interestingly, the students set to work to find other solutions, challenging themselves to find all of the possible combinations!

Making Learning Visible Through Appropriate Mathematical Tasks

The banana problem is an example of students having surface learning (recognizing coins and/or knowing the value of individual coins) and taking that learning to a more complex level through deep learning (combining the value of various coins) to transfer learning. Not only did they have to recognize and add the value of the coins, but unlike the textbook exercises, they also had to determine which coins to use. Giving students appropriate tasks at the right time in their learning cycle is crucial to move students from surface to deep and transfer learning.

Exercises Versus Problems

It is important to have a common understanding of the types of tasks we assign to students. **Exercises**, which typically make up most of traditional textbook practice, are provided for students to practice a particular skill, usually devoid of any context. Although these are casually referred to as problems, in reality they are simply practice exercises.

Problems have contexts—they are usually written in words that can be situations that apply or provide a context for a mathematical concept. One category of problems is an application that focuses on the use of particular concepts or procedures. Another category of problems is nonroutine or open-ended problems that involve much more than applying a concept or procedure. We will explore each of these types of problems in more detail in the next section.

There are a few items that we need to address before we more fully explore the types of tasks that are useful in various phases of learning in mathematics.

- Spaced practice—also known as distributed practice—is much more effective than mass practice. We will discuss this more in Chapter 4. In practical terms, this means that students should do a few exercises or problems on a given concept each day over several days rather than a lot of problems for only one or two days.

- Math is not a speed race. Teachers should be very careful with timed tests. Neither fluency nor stamina requires that students work as quickly as humanly possible. Giving students a test that requires them to speed through problems reinforces an idea that they should prioritize by doing the "easy" problems first and not spend valuable time on problems that require deeper thinking. Too often, timed tests or speed games are used to check for fluency with basic mathematics facts. The problem is, speed is not part of fluency. Fluency requires flexible, accurate, and efficient

Exercises are meant to practice a particular skill, but are noncontextual.

Problems are usually written in words that can be situations or provide a context for a mathematical concept.

EFFECT SIZE FOR SPACED VERSUS MASS PRACTICE = 0.71

thinking. Fluency also requires a level of conceptual understanding. One would not be considered fluent in a foreign language if he or she could speak it by mimicking without any comprehension! Students would be better served with practice developing fluency rather than racing through written tasks or activities. In addition, speed races also make some students believe that they are not good at math. The attitude students have toward mathematics is important and can impact their willingness to try.

- Tasks should not focus exclusively on procedures. Sara excelled in math at a young age. She seemed to understand numbers, and she was very good at learning a procedure and executing it repeatedly on her own. But she was never asked to explain why these procedures worked. Bring down the last number under the house when doing long division? Sure, why not. Why does that lead to a correct answer? How do I apply that skill to real-world situations if I don't understand what it means? Sara had no idea, and it didn't seem to matter to her teacher. This was a case of focusing on procedural skills and sacrificing conceptual understanding.

We are not arguing that students shouldn't learn long division. But we don't think that students gain much from doing long division mindlessly, either. The goal should be for students to develop a transferable and flexible understanding of processes like division, and they should have the opportunity to construct this understanding in a meaningful context. Doing extensive, repeated, context-free long division exercises is just not aligned to this goal.

Instead, students should be expected to engage in reasoning, exploration, flexible thinking, and making connections. They know that learning isn't easy, and they should enjoy the success of meeting the challenges that learning demands of them (Hattie, 2012). Students need deliberate practice, guided by the teacher, not repetitive skill-and-drill tasks. Some tasks should provide students an opportunity to engage in mathematical modeling—taking a problem or situation, representing it mathematically, and doing the mathematics to arrive at a sensible solution or to glean new information that wouldn't have been possible without the mathematics.

Still other tasks require that students practice applying a concept in different situations. To facilitate strategic thinking, some tasks should be open-ended and have multiple paths to get to the solution or, in some cases, solutions. Math tasks don't always have to be fun, but they can be interesting and useful.

Should students work on exercise sets, in which they develop skill in long division? Sure, but these types of tasks won't be discussed here for several reasons. First, we have seen that teachers are already quite good at assigning exercises from a textbook, and reading about this would be a waste of your time. More importantly, though, the research evidence suggests that application of a concept, in varying contexts or in ways that offer sense-making opportunities, is more effective in building true fluency than doing repeated, nearly identical manipulations of numbers (NCTM, 2014).

It is useful for students to be able to perform math operations flexibly and efficiently, as it frees up cognitive space to apply these operations to novel situations and relate these operations to other mathematics concepts. But in most mathematics classes, this type of automaticity tends to be emphasized way too early in the learning cycle. It also tends to take up a disproportionate amount of class time. Procedural fluency cannot be developed without true and meaningful comprehension, and "drill-and-kill" exercises without understanding can harm students' mathematical understandings, their motivation level, and the way they view mathematics. Students who learn procedures at the expense of mathematical thinking often fail to develop an understanding of what they're doing conceptually, and teachers find that it's more difficult to motivate students to really understand a concept if they can already execute a shortcut. What's needed is a restoration of the balance: A strong conceptual foundation makes fluency building more efficient, meaningful, and useful for students. So it really is worth devoting a lot more learning time to the conceptual understanding that undergirds procedural knowledge. Children need to learn the relationship between procedures and concepts in order to become increasingly fluent thinkers.

Problems fall into two categories: applications and nonroutine problems. **Applications**—often called word problems or story problems—are problems, usually related to real-life experiences, in which students use or apply a mathematical concept or skill they have learned. Interestingly, these problems usually follow the exercises in a traditional textbook lesson. However, they should also be used to introduce an idea in order to allow students to model a situation and develop conceptual understanding, connect that understanding to procedural skills, and then practice that skill through more applications and exercises. For those familiar

> Procedural fluency cannot be developed without true and meaningful comprehension, and 'drill-and-kill' exercises without understanding can harm students' mathematical understandings, their motivation level, and the way they view mathematics.

> **Applications** are problems, usually related to real-life experiences, in which students use or apply a mathematical concept or skill they have learned.

with Cognitively Guided Instruction (Carpenter et al., 2014), this is the pathway used in that philosophy. Application problems can range from straightforward (solution reached by applying well-practiced operations) to difficult (involving application of new ideas, several steps, and/or multiple representations).

Non-routine or complex problems are problems that involve more than applying a mathematical procedure for solution. These types of problems are usually met with student reactions of "I don't know what to do!" because a simple procedure is not the pathway to a solution. Rather, students need to use a variety of strategies and some "out-of-the-box" thinking to solve these types of problems.

When we think about the kinds of mathematical tasks we want to use with our students, and when we should use each kind of task (and there is a place in mathematics instruction for each type of task), we need to think about what we want to achieve with the task. What are our learning intentions? What role does the task play in helping students meet the success criteria for the lesson?

In the next sections, we will examine two frameworks for classifying problems. One focuses on the level of difficulty/complexity of the task, and the other focuses on the kind of thinking required by the student. One is not better than the other, but given your own realm of experience, one may be more helpful than the other as you work to connect exercises/problems with surface, deep, and transfer learning. We will go into more detail with examples in future chapters. Our intention here is to get you familiar with the descriptions and the need for hard thinking about the kinds of tasks you assign to your students to make your teaching positively impact student learning.

Difficulty Versus Complexity

In order to help students master all dimensions of rigor (conceptual understanding, procedural fluency, and applications) and to help students' progress toward owning their own learning and then transferring that learning to new situations, it is important for teachers to think carefully about the level and type of challenge a given task provides. Unfortunately, some people confuse difficulty with complexity. We think of **difficulty** as the amount of effort or work a student is expected to put forth, whereas **complexity** is the level of thinking,

Non-routine or complex problems are problems that involve more than applying a mathematical procedure for solution.

Difficulty is the amount of effort or work one must put in.

Complexity is the level of thinking, the number of steps, or the abstractness of the task.

DIFFICULTY AND COMPLEXITY

Figure 3.1

the number of steps, or the abstractness of the task. We don't believe that teachers can radically impact student learning by simply increasing the volume of work. We know that students learn more when they are engaged in deeper thinking. Figure 3.1 shows how we think of this in four quadrants.

The fluency quadrant that includes tasks of low difficulty and low complexity is not unimportant; it's where automaticity resides. For example, once students have mastered conceptual understanding of addition and subtraction (what do they mean and what do they look like?) and learned thinking strategies and procedures for computing sums and differences, they need to build fluency so that they are flexible, accurate, and efficient with these operations. Students should be able to do basic mathematical calculations quickly and effortlessly in order to free up the cognitive space to connect the operations to more complex examples or to larger concepts. There are times when you will want students to build automaticity on certain types of procedures. Instant retrieval of basic number facts is foundational for being able to think conceptually about more complex mathematical tasks. Hattie and Yates (2014) assert that these retrievals are the product of

> a combination of exposure to others, working it out for yourself, playing with concrete materials, experimenting with different forms of representation, and then rehearsing the acquired knowledge unit within your immediate memory, transferring it into long-term memory, and having it validated thousands of times. (p. 57)

Video 3.1
What We Mean
by Tasks With Rigor

*http://resources.corwin.com/
VL-mathematics*

If students' mathematical experiences are limited to this quadrant, learning isn't going to be robust. The stamina quadrant—high difficulty but low complexity—is where tasks that build perseverance reside. Stamina refers to the idea of sticking with a problem or task even when the work is difficult and requires patience and tenacity. This type of task would be a problem or exercise (yes, they both have a place here) in which students are taking their current knowledge and extending it to a more difficult situation. The first-grade banana task that opened this chapter is a good example of a task that promotes stamina. Students were able to complete earlier work with counting coins in the textbook examples, but they needed to apply this knowledge differently and think strategically about the different ways to find *all* of the possible solutions, and then justify how they knew they had them all.

The daily practice of having students work independently to resolve a problem before consulting peers is one example of helping to build stamina, as it draws on the learner's capacity to stick with a problem. Add to that the additional step of consulting one another and then returning to the problem individually a second time to make any corrections, and now you're extending their stamina even further.

The strategic thinking quadrant addresses tasks that have a lower level of difficulty, but a higher degree of complexity. Some rich mathematical tasks fall into this category, as they draw on students' ability to think strategically. An example of strategic thinking is having students connect their understanding of division of whole numbers to division of decimals before any specific procedure is explored. In this task, students must think about what they know about division and what they know about decimals to make conjectures about place value in the quotient.

Mr. Beams has a very strange calculator. It works just fine until he presses the = button. The decimal point doesn't appear in the answer. Use what you know about decimals and division to help him determine where the decimal point belongs in each quotient. Be ready to justify your thinking!

1. $68.64 \div 4.4 = 156$

2. $400.14 \div 85.5 = 468$

3. $0.735 \div 0.7 = 105$

4. $51.1875 \div 1.05 = 4875$

This task requires students to extend their understanding from previous learning to situations that are much more complex. Complexity is often supported by having students work in groups and justify their thinking. Students will likely be stretched to consider how to resolve problems collaboratively, attend to group communication and planning, and monitor their own thinking and understanding.

The final quadrant, which describes expertise, includes those tasks that are both complex and difficult. These tasks, in one form or another, push students to stretch and extend their learning. A favorite task for fifth or sixth graders is the Handshake Problem, which includes both complexity and difficulty.

Twenty-five people attended a party. If each person shakes hands with every other person at the party, how many handshakes will there be?

This problem can be pretty overwhelming as there is not a particular process or operation that will lead to a solution. Rather, students might work together to use a combination of problem-solving strategies to get started, including acting it out, looking for a pattern, making a table, or starting with a simpler problem. What makes this problem even more interesting (and complex) is the opportunity for students to make a generalization (find a rule) so they can determine the number of handshakes for any number of guests—even 1,000!

This is certainly not an exhaustive list; rather, it is meant to be illustrative. As part of each lesson, teachers should know the level of difficulty and complexity they are expecting of students. They can then make decisions about differentiation and instructional support, as well as feedback that will move learning forward.

Students need regular contact with tasks that allow them to explore, resolve problems, and notice their own thinking. They need tasks that present the right amount of challenge relative to their current performance and understanding, and to the success criteria deriving from the learning intention. Teachers should select tasks that help students push their thinking, but are not so difficult that the learner sees the goal as unattainable. Teachers *and* students must be able to see a pathway to attaining the goal. This supports the second effective teaching practice in NCTM's *Principles to Actions*: Implement tasks that promote reasoning and problem solving. The tasks that teachers assign must

1. Align with the learning intention.
2. Provide students an opportunity to engage in exploration and make sense of important mathematics.
3. Encourage students to use procedures in ways that are connected to understanding.
4. Provide students opportunities to implement the standards for mathematical practice.
5. Allow teachers and students to determine if the success criteria have been met.

This is why relating a task to prior learning is so important (Hattie, 2012).

A Taxonomy of Tasks Based on Cognitive Demand

A second framework for thinking about how to strategically select mathematical tasks aligned to learning intentions and success criteria is one that presents a taxonomy of mathematical tasks based on the level of cognitive demand each requires (Smith & Stein, 1998). **Cognitive demand** is the kind and level of thinking required of students in order to successfully engage with and solve the task (Stein, Smith, Henningsen, & Silver, 2000).

This taxonomy has been embraced by the National Council of Teachers of Mathematics (NCTM, 2014) for good reason, as it provides a powerful

Cognitive demand is the kind and level of thinking required of students in order to successfully engage with and solve a task.

CHARACTERISTICS OF MATHEMATICAL TASKS AT FOUR LEVELS OF COGNITIVE DEMAND

Levels of Demands

Lower-Level Demands (Memorization)

- Involve either reproducing previously learned facts, rules, formulas, or definitions or committing facts, rules, formulas, or definitions to memory

- Cannot be solved using procedures because a procedure does not exist or because the time frame in which the task is being completed is too short to use a procedure

- Are not ambiguous; such tasks involve the exact reproduction of previously seen material, and what is to be reproduced is clearly and directly stated

- Have no connection to the concepts or meaning that underlie the facts, rules, formulas, or definitions being learned or reproduced

Lower-Level Demands (Procedures Without Connections)

- Are algorithmic; use of the procedure either is specifically called for or is evident from prior instruction, experience, or placement of the task

- Require limited cognitive demand for successful completion; little ambiguity exists about what needs to be done and how to do it

- Have no connection to the concepts or meaning that underlie the procedure being used

- Are focused on producing correct answers instead of on developing mathematical understanding

- Require no explanations or explanations that focus solely on describing the procedure that was used

Higher-Level Demands (Procedures With Connections)

- Focus students' attention on the use of procedures for the purpose of developing deeper levels of understanding of mathematical concepts and ideas

- Suggest explicitly or implicitly pathways to follow that are broad general procedures that have close connections to underlying conceptual ideas as opposed to narrow algorithms that are opaque with respect to underlying concepts

- Usually are represented in multiple ways, such as visual diagrams, manipulatives, symbols, and problem situations; making connections among multiple representations helps develop meaning

- Require some degree of cognitive effort; although general procedures may be followed, they cannot be followed mindlessly—students need to engage with conceptual ideas that underlie the procedures to complete the task successfully and that develop understanding

(Continued)

(Continued)

Higher-Level Demands (Doing Mathematics)

- Require complex and non-algorithmic thinking—a predictable, well-rehearsed approach or pathway is not explicitly suggested by the task, task instructions, or a worked-out example

- Require students to explore and understand the nature of mathematical concepts, processes, or relationships

- Demand self-monitoring or self-regulation of one's own cognitive processes

- Require students to access relevant knowledge and experiences and make appropriate use of them in working through the task

- Require students to analyze the task and actively examine task constraints that may limit possible solution strategies and solutions

- Require considerable cognitive effort and may involve some level of anxiety for the student because of the unpredictable nature of the solution process required

Source: Smith and Stein (1998). Used with permission.

Note: These characteristics are derived from the work of Doyle on academic tasks (1988) and Resnick on high-level-thinking skills (1987), the *Professional Standards for Teaching Mathematics* (NCTM, 1991), and the examination and categorization of hundreds of tasks used in QUASAR classrooms (Stein, Grover, and Henningsen, 1996; Stein, Lane, and Silver, 1996).

Figure 3.2

---

structure to types and characteristics of mathematical tasks, providing teachers with criteria that enable them to align the type of task they choose with the learning intention and success criteria for a given outcome (see Figure 3.2).

Traditionally, the majority of classroom instructional time is spent on tasks with lower level cognitive demands that require memorization and/or procedures without connections. These are not bad tasks, and there is a time and place for them, but they do not provide students the range of learning experiences they need to develop mathematical habits of mind, such as looking for patterns and using alternate representations (Levasseur & Cuoco, 2003). Memorization tasks that follow the development of conceptual understanding facilitate learning at the surface level. And surface learning is important and should not be minimized. There has been much misdirected criticism of surface learning because it is often confused with shallow learning. That said, too much emphasis on surface learning at the expense of learning that deepens over time and transfers to new and novel situations does not provide students with true mathematical experiences. Balance is warranted.

Tasks with higher levels of cognitive demand on Smith and Stein's taxonomy—those that connect procedures to understanding—require students to understand relationships between concepts and processes as they analyze and explore the task and its parameters. But the process doesn't stop there. Tasks that call for higher level cognitive demand extend even further to those requiring more complex thinking. There is no predictable or well-rehearsed pathway (algorithm) that is suggested by the task, or by a similar and already-worked example. Tasks such as these provide students an opportunity to engage transfer learning.

However, effective teachers don't leave these things to chance. Instead, they provide problem-solving experiences in which students engage with rich tasks that require them to mobilize their knowledge and skills in new ways. A close association between a previously learned task and a novel situation is necessary for promoting transfer of learning. In time, these become tasks that stretch students' problem-solving abilities as they self-monitor and self-regulate their learning. This is transfer learning in action.

EFFECT SIZE FOR PROBLEM-SOLVING TEACHING = 0.61

Whether you are looking at a task in terms of difficulty versus complexity or the level of cognitive demand students must employ, appropriately challenging tasks may produce some level of student anxiety when they are first introduced. As we have noted before, that's okay, because students should expect learning to require an effort as they grow to appreciate cognitively demanding tasks. An often-needed requirement for learning to occur is some form of tension, some realization of "not knowing," a commitment to want to know and understand—or, as Piaget called it, some "state of disequilibrium" (Hattie, 2012). When students are assigned rich tasks, they use a variety of skills and ask themselves questions, make meaning of mathematics, and ultimately build a healthy and realistic relationship to mathematics as something that is engaging, interesting, and useful—and something that makes sense.

Figure 3.3 includes examples of mathematical tasks for each level of cognitive demand.

We will refer back to these tasks and present additional tasks for your consideration in the coming chapters. In the meantime, we encourage you to sharpen your pencils and experience the levels of cognitive demand along with some metacognition by completing these tasks. Note that answers are not provided in the back of this book!

EXAMPLES OF TASKS AT EACH OF THE FOUR LEVELS OF COGNITIVE DEMAND

Lower-Level Demands *Memorization*	Higher-Level Demands *Procedures With Connections*
What is the rule for multiplying fractions? Expected student response:	Using pattern blocks, if two hexagons are considered to be one whole, find $\frac{1}{6}$ of $\frac{1}{2}$. Draw your answer and explain your solution. Expected student response:
You multiply the numerator times the numerator and the denominator times the denominator. or You multiply the two top numbers and then the two bottom numbers.	 First you take half of the whole, which would be one hexagon. Then you take one-sixth of that half. So I divided the hexagon into six pieces, which would be six triangles. I only needed one-sixth, so that would be one triangle. Then I needed to figure out what part of the two hexagons one triangle was, and it was 1 out of 12. So $\frac{1}{6}$ of $\frac{1}{2}$ is $\frac{1}{12}$.
Procedures Without Connections Multiply: $$\frac{2}{3} \times \frac{3}{4}$$ $$\frac{5}{6} \times \frac{7}{8}$$ $$\frac{4}{9} \times \frac{3}{5}$$ Expected student response:	*Doing Mathematics* Create a real-world situation for the following problem: $$\frac{2}{3} \times \frac{3}{4}$$ Solve the problem you have created without using the rule, and explain your solution. One possible student response:
$$\frac{2}{3} \times \frac{3}{4} = \frac{2 \times 3}{3 \times 4} = \frac{6}{12}$$ $$\frac{5}{6} \times \frac{7}{8} = \frac{5 \times 7}{6 \times 8} = \frac{35}{48}$$ $$\frac{4}{9} \times \frac{3}{5} = \frac{4 \times 3}{9 \times 5} = \frac{12}{45}$$	For lunch Mom gave me three-fourths of the pizza that we ordered. I could only finish two-thirds of what she gave me. How much of the whole pizza did I eat? I drew a rectangle to show the whole pizza. Then I cut it into fourths and shaded three of them to show the part Mom gave me. Since I only ate two-thirds of what she gave me, that would be only two of the shaded sections. 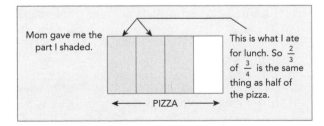

Source: Smith and Stein (1998). Used with permission.

Figure 3.3

Making Learning Visible Through Mathematical Talk

We're mindful that these tasks don't exist in a vacuum. These meaningful tasks are fueled by the discourse that occurs in productive class conversations. The language, thinking, and reasoning that occur when discourse happens further contribute to surface, deep, and transfer learning. Discourse is facilitated through purposeful questioning and thoughtful prompts and cues that usually begin with the teacher. Just as there is a need to select tasks that align with learning intentions and success criteria, there are a variety of "math talk" routines and techniques teachers can use to build student understanding and assess how that understanding is developing, and to guide students in self-questioning and self-verbalization to extend metacognition. As teachers consider routines and techniques that facilitate rich classroom discourse, they should also be thinking about the role of discourse in supporting surface, deep, and transfer learning.

> EFFECT SIZE FOR SELF-VERBALIZATION AND SELF-QUESTIONING = 0.64

Characteristics of Rich Classroom Discourse

Let's begin by examining the characteristics of classroom discourse that builds student understanding and confidence.

1. Teacher questioning and prompts support students in building understanding based on previous knowledge and making connections rather than the teacher being the authority.

2. Mistakes are valued and seen as opportunities for students to clarify their ideas through discussing and justifying their thinking and listening to the ideas of their peers.

3. Students consider different approaches to the mathematics and how those approaches are similar or different.

4. There is an element of productive struggle among students that is accompanied by perseverance, so that the focus is on how students are going to use mathematics to make sense of the task and how to approach a solution path.

5. Students are encouraged to use a variety of representations to build understanding and justify their thinking.

So, how do we facilitate this kind of rich discourse in our classroom? Read on!

Posing Purposeful Questions

Let's begin by delving into questioning techniques that have different purposes and goals throughout a lesson. In subsequent chapters, we will refer back to these general categories of questions and offer concrete examples of when in the learning cycle these techniques are most appropriate. Purposeful questions serve a variety of outcomes (NCTM, 2014), including the following:

Video 3.2
Questioning That
Guides Learning

*http://resources.corwin.com/
VL-mathematics*

- Encouraging students to explain, elaborate, and clarify thinking to build understanding
- Revealing students' current understanding of a concept
- Making the learning of mathematics more visible and accessible for students

By the way, these are not discrete outcomes. It is likely that questions that are intended to support students in building understanding and applying current knowledge to new situations are also providing the teachers information about students' current understanding of a concept. And of course, making the learning of mathematics more visible and accessible for students is the overarching goal for all of our work in recognizing and applying impactful instruction.

Questions That Check, Build, and Deepen Student Understanding

Have you ever started a lesson that builds on previous understandings only to find the students seem to be in the Twilight Zone? Mrs. Norton recalls a situation just like that. After teaching fifth-grade mathematics for many years, she was "promoted" with her students to teach sixth-grade mathematics the following year. When they were ready to extend their understanding of fractional numbers, she thought that there wouldn't be much need for review. After all, fifth grade was the "year of the fraction," and she knew her students had developed understanding through the use of concrete explorations and a variety of applications. So she began the first lesson asking students to solve this example and be ready to explain their thinking:

$$\frac{2}{3} + \frac{1}{2}$$

Imagine her surprise when every student had the answer $\frac{3}{5}$. After she calmed down a bit, she asked her students, "How would you convince me your answer is correct?" Interesting discourse about the sum and whether it was reasonable began to take place. Students began to think about the value of each addend in reference to $\frac{1}{2}$ and one whole rather than a procedure that made no sense. They came to the conclusion that the answer had to be greater than one and that $\frac{3}{5}$ was only a little more than $\frac{1}{2}$; therefore it wasn't reasonable. Several things happened in this lesson. First, and foremost, Mrs. Norton realized that even though she had progressed through the "steps" of concrete, pictorial, and abstract representations in teaching how to add fractions, her students had developed no number sense about fractions. She also realized how powerful the question she asked was for the students so they could begin by taking time to think about what these fractions meant and determine why their answer was not sensible. Subsequent review and lessons built on fraction benchmarks helped to develop deeper understanding of this important concept. In this lesson, Mrs. Norton valued students thinking through the questions she posed. Subsequent discourse provided her with information about her students' misconceptions and, at the same time, pushed student thinking forward.

Purposeful questions promote understanding that can be surface, deep, or transfer depending on where students are in the spiral. Rather than telling students what to do, good questions will move student thinking forward, possibly causing some disequilibrium along the way, so students can work to build on what they know and how to make sense of a given example or problem context. These questions are used not only to prompt student thinking but also to help students explain and justify their thinking. Let's revisit the decimal examples from earlier in the chapter. Good questions will help to promote student understanding even when a concept is new. As students discuss their thinking about where the decimal point belongs in the quotient of $0.735 \div 0.7 = 105$, Mr. Beams's questions require them to think more deeply about what is actually happening with the numbers.

Marcus: I think the decimal point belongs before the 1.

Mr. Beams: How many of you agree with Marcus? *(Pause.)* Marcus, can you explain why you think the decimal point belongs there?

Marcus: Well, both of the numbers I am dividing have the decimal point before the first number, so the decimal point should also be before the first number in the answer.

Mr. Beams: What do the rest of you think about Marcus's reasoning? *(Some nods and other hands are waving to get Mr. Beams's attention.)* What are some other ideas that you have?

Lisa: I think the decimal point belongs between the one and the zero because this problem means how many groups of seven tenths can I make from 735 thousandths.

Bill: But I don't get what you just said. How do you find how many tenths are in thousandths? You didn't convince me that 1.05 is the correct answer.

(A long pause takes place and quiet conversations are happening around the room. Mr. Beams lets this go on for a while and then reconvenes the class by asking the following question.)

Mr. Beams: Can anyone answer Bill's question? How can you explain how many tenths are in 0.735?

Martina: If you look at the place value of 0.735, you see that there is a seven in the tenths place. That means I have seven tenths and some more in that decimal number. If I want to know how many groups of 0.7 I can make, I can determine there is one group of 0.7 and I have a little left to make part of another group. So the decimal belongs after the 1.

Mr. Beams: Can anyone repeat what Martina just said?

Mr. Beams: What does 1.05 mean?

Patricio: It means there is one group of seven tenths in 1.05 and part of another group.

> ### Teaching Takeaway
>
> Use questions, prompts, and cues to both help children deepen understanding and also better understand student misconceptions or partial understanding.

A lot is going on here. Notice that Mr. Beams never tells the students what to do. Marcus's response to the task tells Mr. Beams that some students are looking for a procedure that is neither accurate nor based on mathematical understanding. Mr. Beams allows students some time to talk to each other to make sense of the situation. His questioning carefully draws students back in and allows them to make sense of the example and think of it in terms of previous understandings of division.

While questions that check for understanding are a crucial way to guide learning, the best teachers probe further for more specific information. They don't just want to know whether or not a student understands something; they want to see if the child can explain his or her thinking and apply what is understood, or in this case, misunderstood. If a student doesn't understand, good questions enable teachers to probe deeper in order to find the point at which a misconception, overgeneralization, or partial understanding led students astray. In the back of the teacher's mind is the question "What does this child's answer tell me about what he or she knows and doesn't know?" This is followed by "What question should I ask next?" This is what helps the student begin to move from surface to deep learning.

Funneling and Focusing Questions

You might agree that formal evaluation tools like rubrics are great for longer term, mathematically rich tasks and projects, but it's important to have methods of checking for understanding that you can do anytime you like, regardless of the task. Teachers need to know how much students have actually learned, and how successful a lesson is, in real time so that they can make midcourse adjustments and differentiations. The tools teachers rely on most are the questions we ask of our students. But too often, the questions we pose are interrogative rather than invitational. By this we mean that questions that constrain student responses to short replies are not going to yield much information to the teacher. In addition, these narrow questions don't do much to provoke thinking in students, or to help them notice their own learning. Herbel-Eisenmann and Breyfogle (2005) distinguished between two patterns of teacher-student interactions: funneling questions and focusing questions. **Funneling questions** (Wood, 1998) occur when a teacher guides a student down the teacher's path to find the answer. In these situations, the teacher is doing the cognitive work. **Focusing questions** support students doing the cognitive work of learning by helping to push their thinking forward.

In the book *Principles to Actions,* the National Council of Teachers of Mathematics (NCTM) makes clear the difference between funneling questions and focusing questions. Funneling questions limit student thinking by hinting at an answer, and take the thinking away from the students. Focusing questions encourage students to figure things out for themselves. "What are the measures of central tendency we can use with these data? What are mean, median, and mode?" would be funneling questions, while "What can you tell from the data?" would be a focusing question.

Funneling questions guide students down the teacher's path to find the answer.

Focusing questions allow students to do the cognitive work of learning by helping to push their thinking forward.

EFFECT SIZE FOR QUESTIONING = 0.48

Funneling Questions. Consider how little information is revealed in the following exchange, reported by Herbel-Eisenmann and Breyfogle (2005) as an example of a funneling questioning pattern:

Teacher: (0,0) and (4,1) [are two points on the line in graph B]. Great. What's the slope? *(Long pause—no response from students.)*

Teacher: What's the rise? You're going from 0 on the *y* [axis] up to 1? What's the rise?

Students: 1

Teacher: 1. What's the run? You're going from 0 to 4 on the *x* [axis].

Students: 4.

Teacher: So the slope is _____?

Students: 0.25 *(in unison with the teacher).*

Teacher: And the *y*-intercept is?

Students: 0.

Teacher: So $y = \frac{1}{4}x$? Or $y = 0.25x$ would be your equation. (p. 485)

Funneling questions can create the illusion of deep student learning, but really, they only require the student to know how to respond to the teacher's questioning pattern without understanding the mathematics. These types of questions limit student thinking and leave little opportunity for metacognition. This routine could also be interpreted as scaffolding. But it isn't really, since the questions direct students to what to do rather than giving them opportunities to think about and make connections in ways that effective scaffolding provides. Although the teacher is checking for understanding, the information she gets from her students is limited to whether they are correct or incorrect and doesn't consider anything about understanding or transfer of that understanding.

There can be a role for carefully thought out funneling questions as a new topic is introduced, which has greater impact than a teacher just giving procedural steps to follow. We will talk more about this as we consider surface learning strategies in Chapter 4.

Focusing Questions. The second type of questioning pattern the researchers discuss is called a focusing questioning pattern. These questions are designed to advance student learning, not simply assess it. These are the types of questions you want to ask. Here is the beginning of the same sequence, but this time the teacher goes into a *focusing question sequence* instead of a funneling (Herbel-Eisenmann & Breyfogle, 2005):

Teacher:　(0,0) and (4,1) [are two points on the line in graph B]. Great. What's the slope? *(Long pause—no response from students.)*

Teacher:　What do you think of when I say slope?

Student 1:　The angle of the line.

Teacher:　What do you mean by the angle of the line?

Student 1:　What angle it sits at compared to the *x*- and *y*-axis.

Teacher:　*(Pause for students to think.)* What do you think [student 1] means?

Student 2:　I see what [student 1] is saying, sort of like when we measured the steps in the cafeteria and the steps that go up to the music room—each set of steps went up at a different angle. (p. 487)

As the conversation progressed, the students engaged in figuring out how to find the slope. Students who do this are much more likely to understand slope and remember what they figured out a week later, and are much better able to transfer their knowledge—in this case, how to find the slope—to new situations, like projecting sales for a company, constructing a skateboard ramp, or learning how to find derivatives in calculus class.

You've heard the adage that "great teachers don't tell you what to see, but they show you where to look." Focusing questions open up kids' thinking and show them where to look, while funneling questions narrow their thinking in a direction that the teacher has already decided; they tell them what to see. Funneling questions don't allow for multiple paths to solving a problem, for new approaches, or for students to think about their own thinking. With focusing questions, children get to figure it out, so they learn more. They remember the content better, and they can transfer and apply it to new situations. Figure 3.4 contains examples of how funneling questions in mathematics can be transformed into focusing questions.

FUNNELING AND FOCUSING QUESTIONS IN MATHEMATICS

Funneling Questions	Focusing Questions
How do you find the mean of the data? What about the median and the mode? What about the interquartile range?	What do you notice about the data? How would you describe them to someone? What makes you say that? What other ways might you be able to describe them?
How can I get rid of the 2? What do I have to do to the other side? What about the 4?	What do you think about when you see this equation? How do you want to solve it?
How do I find the area of this trapezoid? Do you see the rectangle and the triangles? I can just add them up. How can I find the area of the rectangle?	I want to know the area of this trapezoid, but I'm not sure how to find it. Any ideas? Where should we start?
Let's add these fractions by finding the least common denominator. What's the first step in finding the least common denominator?	What should we do with these fractions? [*Student: "Add them."*] Why add them? [*Student refers to word problem.*] Okay, so how would you add them?

Figure 3.4

Some other useful focusing questions to have in your back pocket are the following:

- What are you trying to find?
- How did you get that?
- Why does that work?
- Is there another way you can represent that idea?
- How is this connected to (other idea, concept, finding, or learning intention)?

Questions that check for understanding are a crucial aspect of visible learning. The best teachers probe deeper for more specific information. They don't just want to know whether or not a student understands something. If the student does, they want to see if the child can explain his or her thinking and apply what is understood. If the student doesn't understand, these teachers probe deeper to find the point at which a misconception, overgeneralization, or partial understanding led them astray. In the back of the teacher's mind is this question: "What does this child's answer tell me about what he or she knows and doesn't know?" This allows the teacher to determine the type of learning that the student needs next.

A key to effective checking for understanding is to avoid false positives. In other words, you don't want to fool yourself into believing that your students know something when they really don't. Novice teachers often ask a question, wait for a volunteer to respond, and then think the class gets it because the volunteer has the correct answer. This pattern doesn't work very well to get all students learning. The teachers who rely primarily on volunteers are almost always disappointed when more accurate data prove that the majority of their students haven't learned as much as their handful of volunteers. This is one advantage of having students work in groups. As you walk around and listen to group conversations, pausing to ask probing questions can provide information about where students are in their understanding rather than where one student is.

Here's one last important hint about asking good questions: The types of questions we are calling for are likely not the questions that we experienced from teachers when we were students. It takes thoughtful planning to prepare the kinds of questions that will best support your students' learning while making them more independent learners. Asking good questions models for students the kinds of questions they can ask themselves when they are stuck. Good questions are seldom spontaneous. As you are putting the practice of posing purposeful questions (NCTM, 2014) into action, give yourself time to stop and think about what question you want to ask that serves student learning and fuels constructive communication.

Prompts and Cues

Questions are the starting place that helps teachers check for understanding. Prompts encourage students to do cognitive or metacognitive work. They can take the form of a statement or a question. When Daniel Castillo said to a student who was stuck, "Based on what you know about functions, can that be true?" he wasn't just checking for understanding. He was asking the student to return to her background knowledge. Prompts should challenge students rather than do the thinking for them. **Prompts** are often used to activate background knowledge and interrupt the temporary forgetting of prior knowledge in the face of new learning. Saying "Think about what you already know about

> **Teaching Takeaway**
>
> Use questions to better understand student misconceptions or partial understanding.

> **Prompts** are questions or statements used to remind students to leverage what they already know in order to think further.

finding a common denominator as you read that question again" can remind them to use what they do know. Prompts are a bit narrower than questions, as they come after you've had a chance to engage with the child using those focusing questions. When questions don't spur action, prompts can move students forward.

Another prompt is revoicing what the student has said to give all students a chance to think about it, clarify whether you have understood the explanation accurately, and give the student talking an opportunity to think about his or her thinking. For example, "So you're saying that we'll have three-eighths left over?" This can be especially powerful if a student's thinking seems unclear, or if he or she spoke in a way that makes it tough for other students to hear (Chapin, O'Connor, & Anderson, 2009). Another move is to ask another student, "Can you say what [student name] just said, in your own words?" This is especially helpful for English learners, and it helps the rest of the group to process what the first student said. Figure 3.5 includes sample prompts with examples.

Cues are more direct and overt than prompts, as they shift the student's attention to the relevant information or study action needed to move forward. Examples of effective cues are when a teacher points to a vocabulary word posted on the wall, to the lesson's learning intentions, to another student who is using her notes, to a figure in the textbook, or to sentence starters on a table tent. If a student is looking at a page that's different from what you assigned, then a verbal cue might be in order, such as a whispered "The class is on the other side of this paper," or even better, "Look around at everyone else's paper." This doesn't take away children's thinking if they've already shown that they're proficient in turning to the right page, since it was probably an error of whoever passed out the papers. Just like questioning patterns, you could imagine funneling cues—"Look at the left side of data table #3 when you're deciding which numbers to use"—and focusing cues—"Think about how you could know which numbers to use" or "Remember that you have resources here to help you." Figure 3.6 includes definitions of several types of cues.

In using prompts and cues, teachers must be careful that they ask all students to think about why their work is correct or incorrect. Teachers can inadvertently create a situation where students know their answer is incorrect because the teacher uses certain prompts or cues that he or she does not use when seeing a correct answer. The prompt "Does that

Cues are more overt attempts to draw attention to relevant information or a certain action needed to move forward.

Teaching Takeaway

Use prompts and cues to help students zero in on new learning, remember critical points, and connect to previous learning.

TYPES OF PROMPTS FOR MATHEMATICS

Type of Prompt	Definition	Example
Background knowledge	Reference to content that the student already knows, has been taught, or has experienced but has temporarily forgotten or is not applying correctly.	• When trying to solve a right-triangle problem, the teacher says, "What do you recall about the degrees inside a triangle?" • As part of their study of solid figures, the teacher says, "Think about what you remember about vertices, edges, and faces."
Process or procedure	Reference to established or generally agreed-upon representation, rules, or guidelines that the student is not following due to error or misconception.	• When a student incorrectly orders fractions thinking the greater the denominator, the greater the fraction, the teacher might say, "Draw a picture of each fraction. What do you notice about the size of the fraction and the number in the denominator?" • When a student is unsure about how to start solving a problem, the teacher says, "Think about which of the problem-solving strategies we have used might help you to get started."
Reflective	Promotion of metacognition—getting the student to think about his or her thinking—so that the student can use the resulting insight to determine next steps or the solution to a problem.	• The student has just produced a solution incorrectly, and the teacher says, "Does that make sense? Think about the numbers you are working with and the meaning of the operation." • A teacher says, "I see you're thinking strategically. What would be the next logical step?"
Heuristic	Engagement in an informal, self-directed, problem-solving procedure; the approach the student comes up with does not have to be like anyone else's approach, but it does need to work.	• When the student does not get the correct answer to a math problem, the teacher says, "Maybe drawing a visual representation would help you see the problem." • A teacher says, "Do you think you might find it easier to begin with a simpler but similar problem? What might that problem look like?"

Source: Adapted from Fisher and Frey (2014).

Figure 3.5

TYPES OF CUES FOR MATHEMATICS

Type of Cue	Definition	Example
Visual	A range of graphic hints to guide students' thinking or understanding	• Highlighting areas within text where students have made errors • Creating a graphic organizer to arrange content visually • Asking students to take a second look at a graphic or visual from a textbook
Verbal	Variations in speech to draw attention to something specific *or* verbal "attention getters" that focus students' thinking	• "This is important . . ." • "This is the tricky part. Be careful and be sure to . . ." • Repeating a student's statement using a questioning intonation • Changing voice volume or speed for emphasis
Gestural	Body movements or motions to draw attention to something that has been missed	• Making a predetermined hand motion such as equal or increasing • Placing thumbs around a key idea in a problem that the student is missing
Environmental	Use of the classroom surroundings or physical objects in the environment to influence students' understanding	• Using algebra tiles or other manipulatives • Moving an object or person so that the orientation changes or the perspective is altered

Source: Adapted from Fisher and Frey (2014).

Figure 3.6

Video 3.3
Student Discourse That Builds Understanding

http://resources.corwin.com/ VL-mathematics

answer make sense? Really think about it." can be used even following a correct answer to help that learner think about how to justify his or her thinking.

Too often, we ask questions or give students prompts or cues only when they are incorrect. Try asking students a question or providing a prompt when they are correct. Notice if they automatically assume they are incorrect because you stopped to ask a question. Productive questions, prompts, or cues should be a regular part of our instruction moves repertoire!

Conclusion

The tasks and assignments teachers provide for students are an important consideration. The wrong task may not only be a waste of time; it may fail to develop the type of thinking students need to be successful in mathematics. Quality tasks can be used to guide students' learning at the surface, deep, and transfer levels. These tasks can be considered across a number of dimensions, including difficulty and complexity. Assigning students ten more math problems may or may not ensure that they are engaged on complex thinking. In addition to the difficulty and complexity consideration, teachers have to consider the level of cognitive demand expected in the tasks and assignments they use to facilitate (and assess) learning.

We focused intentionally on the tasks and talk students must do before discussing types of learning. As we will see in the chapters that follow, understanding surface, deep, and transfer is really important, and identifying the right approach at the right time is a critical consideration for mathematics teachers and a key message from this book. Having said that, the type of learning students will do is based in large part on the types of tasks that teachers use during lessons. Again, a misalignment between the tasks and the types of learning puts students at risk. With the information about tasks in hand, we'll now turn our attention to the types of learning expected of students.

Reflection and Discussion Questions

1. Make notes of the questions you typically ask in your math lessons. Think about them in terms of the focusing and funneling questions framework discussed in this chapter. Which way does your questioning sequence lean? How can you make focusing questions a stronger presence in your mathematics classroom?

2. Identify two or three mathematics tasks you've asked your students to work on recently. Think about each task in light of its difficulty and complexity (see Figure 3.1). In which quadrant does each task fit? Is each the right kind of task given your learning intentions?

3. Think about these same tasks in terms of the cognitive demand they make on students (see Figure 3.2). How could you revise or reframe the tasks to require a higher level of cognitive demand?

SURFACE
MATHEMATICS
LEARNING MADE
VISIBLE

K ate Franklin is planning a unit introducing multiplication for her third-grade class. Other than some earlier work with skip counting and simple arrays, this will be the students' first real experience with multiplication. As Kate plans, she considers the types of learning that students will undergo as they make sense of these concepts by experiencing different situations. For example, students will model multiplication situations to develop conceptual understanding, learn appropriate vocabulary and notation for multiplication, develop strategies to build fluency with basic facts, apply understanding to worded problems (applications) as well as open-ended problems, and make connections to understand the relationship between multiplication and division. Wow! That is a lot to think about. While the textbook will help to guide her through some of this progression, Mrs. Franklin knows how important it is to carefully plan the learning intentions for each lesson while keeping the bigger picture in mind. She knows she also needs to identify the success criteria for her students to show and know they are progressing with understanding through each lesson. Mrs. Franklin plans so that by the end of this unit, her students will be confident that they understand the content, can apply concepts, and are ready to connect these concepts to future topics.

On the first day, Mrs. Franklin has made a conscientious decision to hold off on sharing the learning intention for the lesson until after students have completed an activity that introduces the meaning of multiplication as equal groups. She introduces the lesson with a game called *In the Doghouse*. She models the game with her students. It looks something like this. Students work with a partner. One rolls a die and lays out the corresponding number of rectangles made of construction paper (the doghouses). The second person rolls the die and puts the corresponding number of counters (dogs) in each doghouse. The students describe the number of doghouses and the number of dogs in each doghouse and then they determine the total number of dogs in all of the doghouses. They record their work on the table in Figure 4.1.

After students have a chance to ask questions, they play the game. When the students have played five rounds, Mrs. Franklin asks them to find the total number of dogs for all five rounds.

In the next part of the lesson, Mrs. Franklin leads a discussion in which students talk about what the numbers mean for each round and how they might write an equation for what they have modeled. Since most of the students recall earlier work with repeated addition, someone quickly

IN THE DOGHOUSE

Round	Number of Doghouses	Number of Dogs in Each Doghouse	Total Number of Dogs	Equation
1	5	3	15	
2				
3				
4				
5				
		Total Dogs for 5 Rounds		

Figure 4.1

comes up with $3 + 3 + 3 + 3 + 3 = 15$. This continues for a few more examples, and then Mrs. Franklin models her thinking. "This is sure a lot of writing. I am going to show you a simpler way that mathematicians write this same idea because we know that there are usually many ways to accomplish things in mathematics." She then introduces the multiplication sign and writes the equation $5 \times 3 = 15$. She also introduces vocabulary in the context of this example (multiplication, multiply, times, groups of) and adds these words to the mathematics word wall. The class follows with a discussion about what each of the numbers means in that equation. Mrs. Franklin then directs them to work together to record similar equations in the last column of their chart as she circulates to check on students' understanding of the task.

Now Mrs. Franklin is ready to introduce the learning intention for the lesson. "We are using equal-group activities to write and understand multiplication equations." She then asks the students how *In the Doghouse* helped them with this learning intention. After a short discussion, Mrs. Franklin presents the success criteria, saying, "I will know and you will know if you have successfully learned this by completing an exit ticket at the end of our mathematics time that lets you show how you can use equal groups and equations to represent multiplication." Students continue with additional work and discussion, moving to

EXIT TICKET FROM *IN THE DOGHOUSE* ACTIVITY

Name: _____ Date: _____

Jose and Robin played a game of *In the Doghouse*. Jose was player 1 and rolled a 4. Robin was player 2 and rolled a 5. Draw a picture of their game board.

How many dogs were in the doghouses?

For round 2, Martin wrote the following on his table. Find the total number of dogs that were in the doghouse.

Round	Number of Doghouses	Number of Dogs in Each Doghouse	Total Number of Dogs	Equation
1				
2	3	4		
3				
4				
5				
		Total Dogs for 5 Rounds		

Write an equation to represent Martin's work.

Figure 4.2

pictures of groups and items and writing multiplication equations for each. Mrs. Franklin is also ready with some supporting activities for students who appear to be struggling to make the connection between the pictures and the equation. Toward the end of the lesson, Mrs. Franklin gives each of the students the exit ticket in Figure 4.2.

This lesson is an example of developing surface learning for the initial acquisition of conceptual understanding of multiplication. Subsequent lessons will continue to focus on helping students to make connections to other multiplication situations as well as using various representations to develop fluency with multiplication facts. In this lesson, Mrs. Franklin also intentionally gives students the language and structure they need to speak clearly about the mathematical ideas they are learning, so students can talk about and explore these new ideas with each other. The activity connects to the language and notation that pave the way for the rich discourse and focus on structure and relationships that are at the heart of mathematics learning. Let's leave Mrs. Franklin and her third graders as we take a closer look at surface learning.

The Nature of Surface Learning

As we noted in the first chapter, almost everything in published research works at least some of the time with some students. Our challenge as a profession is to become more precise in what we do and when we do it. Timing is everything, and the wrong practice at the wrong time undermines efforts. Knowing when and how to help a student move from (sufficient levels of) surface to deep is one of the marks of expert teachers. Instructional practices that foster deep learning are not necessarily the most effective ones to employ when students are still at the surface level of developing mathematical understanding on any given topic. Deep learning is about noticing relationships, extending ideas to new situations, and making connections, but children first need to learn the ideas that they can then make connections among and between. That is what surface learning is about!

As we also mentioned in Chapter 1, the phrase *surface learning* may hold a negative connotation for many people. It's easy to assume that by "surface" we mean "superficial" or "shallow," or that by surface-level learning, we mean rote memorization of procedures and vocabulary that have typically been taught at the beginning of a lesson and are disconnected from conceptual understanding. This is not what we mean by

Teaching Takeaway

Surface learning happens best when employing specific high-impact approaches that foster initial acquisition of conceptual understanding followed by associated procedural skills.

Video 4.1
Surface Mathematics
Learning: Connecting
Conceptual Exploration
to Procedures and Skills

*http://resources.corwin.com/
VL-mathematics*

surface learning. Rather, the phrase *surface learning* represents an essential part of learning made up of both conceptual exploration and learning vocabulary and procedural skills that give structure to ideas.

In this chapter, we will examine the importance of surface learning and consider the use of high-impact approaches that foster initial acquisition of conceptual understanding and procedural skills. We will first guide you in the selection of mathematical tasks that promote surface learning, building on our example with Mrs. Franklin. Next, we'll discuss the types of mathematical talk that can guide students who are in the surface phase of a topic. These include the following:

- Number talks
- Guided questions
- Worked examples
- Direct instruction

Finally, we will profile some other teaching methods that have high effect sizes when fostering students' surface learning of mathematical concepts and procedures. Featured practices include strategic use of the following:

- Vocabulary instruction
- Manipulatives for surface learning
- Spaced practice with feedback
- Mnemonics

Keep in mind that the goal during the surface phase of learning is to create sufficient time and space for students to acquire and consolidate knowledge, with an eye toward deepening their knowledge. Don't stay in this phase longer than you need to, but don't rush through it and leave learners behind. Our mantra is "As fast as we can, as slow as we must."

Two important reminders are key to visible learning for mathematics:

1. **The teacher clearly signals the learning intentions and success criteria** to ensure that students know what they are learning, why they are learning it, and how they will know they have learned it. This clarity should guide all instructional decisions.

2. **The teacher does not hold any instructional strategy in higher esteem than his or her students' learning.** Visible learning is a continual evaluation of one's impact on students. When the evidence suggests that learning has not occurred, the instruction needs to change (not the child!).

Selecting Mathematical Tasks That Promote Surface Learning

As we discussed in Chapter 3, one of the most important responsibilities of a teacher is to select the right task for the learning intention at hand. In selecting tasks that build surface knowledge, teachers want to find tasks that raise questions for students—What is this called? How can I write this? What does this symbol represent? Surface learning does not have to be the result of lectures and flash cards. Teachers can use tasks (such as *In the Doghouse*) to create situations that help students make meaning of the mathematics at hand accurately and efficiently. Tasks that are efficient are often also more engaging, which raises student motivation.

Many tasks that foster surface learning will be of low difficulty and low to moderate complexity (see Figure 3.1). We can make many tasks lower in difficulty by using smaller numbers and/or simpler situations, especially when a new idea is introduced. For example, primary students learn about the notation of addition and subtraction by using it first to record what they have done in solving problems using manipulatives or other models. K–5 teachers ask students to solve problems using manipulatives and other strategies so that they are reasoning about the solution and thinking about the context. The problems are straightforward and the numbers may be small. Notation is introduced as efficient ways to record thinking and build on previous experiences. In the opening example, $5 \times 3 = 15$ was connected to $3 + 3 + 3 + 3 + 3$ as a way to record 5 groups of 3. Discussion and opportunities to connect notation to actual tasks support students' learning and understanding. This is true throughout all of a student's mathematics education, from learning numerals in kindergarten to the symbolic notations of algebra, geometry, statistics, and calculus.

We can look at similar tasks in middle school as students learn to operate with integers. By keeping the range of numbers small and the situations simple (for example, temperature increasing/decreasing or spending/borrowing money), students are free to consider how the problems are similar to those in elementary school as well as learn how notation changes

SURFACE LEARNING OF MULTIPLICATION IN THE SOLO FRAMEWORK

Learning Intentions		Success Criteria
SOLO 1: Represent and solve problems involving multiplication of whole numbers		
Uni-/Multi-Structural	Represent equal-group situations for multiplication using models and drawings.	Students can represent equal-group situations using groups and counters, pictures, or words.
Uni-/Multi-Structural	Represent equal-group situations for multiplication using symbols in equations. Know the appropriate vocabulary/description for each term in the equation (factor, product, groups of, items in a group, total number of items).	Given a multiplication situation with equal groups using concrete materials, pictures, or words, students can write an equation to represent the situation. Students can identify the meaning of each term in a multiplication equation and represent it using pictures or words.

Source: Adapted from Biggs and Collis (1982).

Figure 4.3

when recording operations with integers. The complexity of these tasks is low to moderate for students with adequate background knowledge.

Let's put Mrs. Franklin's learning intentions for the lesson she used to introduce multiplication into the first level of the SOLO framework discussed in Chapter 1. The unistructural and multi-structural levels are about having students develop surface learning about multiplication that will support future opportunities to make connections and see relationships (see Figure 4.3).

Mathematical Talk That Guides Surface Learning

Neuroscientists in the 1990s noticed something surprising when they measured brain cell activity of monkeys that were watching the movements of other monkeys. They found that brain cells called motor neurons in the observing monkeys were active, even though these observing monkeys were sitting still. Interestingly, these were some of the same neurons that became active when the observing monkeys were the ones doing the motion. So, when a monkey watches another monkey pick up a banana, a lot of the same brain cells in the observing monkey are just as electrically active as they would be if that monkey were the one picking up the banana (Rizzolatti & Craighero, 2004). Neuroscientists called these specialized brain cells mirror neurons. Later, they showed that mirror neuron systems in the human brain work similarly to understand intentions of others (Iacoboni et al., 2005). To these brain cells, observing someone do something uses many of the same neural pathways as when you perform the action yourself. These mirror neuron systems may help explain the power of number talks, guiding questions, worked examples, and direct instruction. Doing math is not eating bananas. But it turns out that when students explain their thinking verbally, in a way that other students can understand, all students are better able to consider the ways that other people think and adopt some of these practices themselves. By listening to others think, the student is guided through the same thought processes that someone else used, as if an apprentice. By using guiding questions, teachers can indirectly model a path for students' thinking without telling them what to do (which often becomes the right way or only way in a student's mind). This modeling helps to provide structure to advance student thinking.

What Are Number Talks, and When Are They Appropriate?

Number talks are a powerful protocol for students to share their thinking processes aloud (Humphreys & Parker, 2015). Mrs. Manno includes a number talk in her fourth-grade morning meeting every day. A **number talk** is a short, ongoing, daily routine that provides students with meaningful, ongoing practice with computation. A number talk helps students develop computational fluency because the expectation is that they will use number relationships and the structures of numbers to add, subtract, multiply, and divide. These brief (around five minutes) opportunities for students to share their thinking can be used as review or practice on a current topic. Mrs. Manno knows her students need some additional work with subtraction of whole numbers, so she is using today's number talk for work on this topic. She starts with the following example:

$$3{,}000 - 1{,}345 =$$

A **number talk** is a brief, ongoing, daily routine that helps students develop computational fluency through the opportunity to share their thinking processes aloud.

Video 4.2
Number Talks
for Surface Learning

*http://resources.corwin.com/
VL-mathematics*

She gives students some time to think about this—as number talks are usually done with mental calculations—and students signal when they think they have the answer by putting their thumb up against their chest. This is intentional so that waving hands of eager students do not distract those students who need time to think. Mrs. Manno reminds students who have an answer to think about how to find it using a different strategy. When most of the students have indicated they have an answer, Mrs. Manno begins to collect student solutions and writes them on the board without signaling if they are correct or incorrect. Once the answers have been collected, the focus shifts to student thinking. A student is called upon to share his thinking while Mrs. Manno records on the board. A conversation might begin as follows:

Juan: I used a counting on strategy, so I started with 1,345. I added 5 more to get to 1,350.

Mrs. Manno: *(Writes as she revoices)*

1,345 + 5 = 1,350

Juan: Then I added 50.

Mrs. Manno: Why did you add 50?

Juan: So I would get to 1,400. That will make it much easier to get to 3,000.

(Mrs. Manno records the next step beneath the first step.)

1,345 + 5 = 1,350

1,350 + 50 = 1,400

Juan: Now I added on 600 to get to 2,000 and then I added 1,000 to get to 3,000.

Mrs. Manno: *(Continues to record, asking)* Am I following your thinking correctly?

1,345 + 5 = 1,350

1,350 + 50 = 1,400

1,400 + 600 = 2,000

2,000 + 1,000 = 3,000

Mrs. Manno: So how did you get your final answer?

Student: I kept track of the numbers I was adding on as I went along. $5 + 50 + 600 + 1,000$ is $1,655$.

Mrs. Manno: Did anyone else do it this way? *(Several students indicate they also used the same method.)* Did anyone use a different strategy?

Students begin to share their thinking, including those students who may have made a mistake in their initial computation, but self-correct after "seeing" classmates' thinking. Although number talks are brief, they should be done daily to be effective. Students love the opportunity to share their thinking and convince others they are correct or to question the work of others (MP 3). Mrs. Manno reports that if they do not have time for a number talk on a particular day, students will remind her as they head home that they missed their number talk, which means they have to do two the next day! By the way, it was likely not a coincidence that Mrs. Manno's students had the highest district scores on the state tests for their grade level.

> EFFECT SIZE FOR SELF-VERBALIZATION AND SELF-QUESTIONING = 0.64

What Is Guided Questioning, and When Is It Appropriate?

In Chapter 3, we discussed two types of questions—focusing questions and funneling questions. The lines between some of these ideas are not always clear and straight. There is some overlap between when students move from surface learning to deep learning. There is not a clear delineation between good focusing and good funneling questions. There is a time for both. The key is understanding what comprises good funneling and good focusing questions and when to use each.

Too often, a lesson begins with the teacher giving explicit instruction in how to do some mathematics, whether it's second graders working on understanding regrouping or sixth graders' introduction to proportional reasoning. This flies in the face of helping students to use new information as an opportunity to make sense of mathematics by understanding a situation, building on previous knowledge, and extending this knowledge to new ideas. It's like reading a mystery novel and someone tells you "who dunnit" before you have had the opportunity to make sense out of what is happening and make your own conjectures. Instead of giving away the ending, carefully constructed **guided questions** are designed to help students make sense out of what is going on and guide them to draw conclusions on their own.

> **Guided questions** are questions designed to help students make sense out of what is going on and guide them to draw conclusions on their own.

SHAPES WITH FOUR SIDES

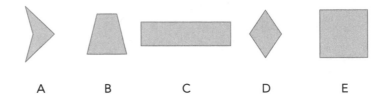

| A | B | C | D | E |

Figure 4.4

Mrs. Rodriguez is working on the following learning intention with her second-grade students: "Discover and define attributes of two-dimensional shapes." The first activity focuses on working with different kinds of quadrilaterals. She wants this work to be engaging and clear and not just a list of vocabulary words to memorize. She decides to do this by giving students several riddles to solve, and she begins by working together with the class to solve the first riddle:

> What shape am I?
>
> I have four sides.
>
> I have four right angles.
>
> My sides are all the same length.

She asks, "What clue would be a good place to start?" This gives students the opportunity to explore and see the advantage or disadvantage of starting with each clue. There is a great deal of discussion happening in each group of students, and Mrs. Rodriguez notices they are having a hard time coming to a consensus. So, she pulls the students back together and asks, "What if we began with the first clue, 'I have four sides.' Draw some shapes with four sides." She selects a few students to draw their shapes on the board, and she draws some shapes that the students haven't thought of (see Figure 4.4). Then she continues, "Look at these shapes. What is the same? What is different?"

COMPARING ATTRIBUTES OF FOUR-SIDED SHAPES

Same	Different
All of the shapes have four sides.	Shapes D and E look like the sides are all the same length. The other shapes have sides that are different lengths.
All of the shapes have four corners (angles).	A and D have pointy corners, and the others have fat corners.
	C is long and skinny.
	B and E are kind of fat.

Figure 4.5

Students then discuss what is similar and what is different using their own words. Mrs. Rodriguez keeps track of the ideas students raise, saying, "You all have some excellent ideas, and it would be helpful to keep track of them so we can look back as we look at the other clues. I am going to make a table on the board to record your ideas. Let's also label the shapes so if there is something special about a shape, you can identify which one it is." (See Figure 4.5.)

After the students complete their list, Mrs. Rodriguez can identify some vocabulary that will help her students. She reminds them that another name for corner in these shapes is angle. She points to the angles in shapes C and E and asks, "How would you describe these angles?" Students use their own words, comparing the angles to the corner of a window or the corner of a room. Mrs. Rodriguez writes the words *right angle* on the board and explains that the corners they have described that look like the corners of the window or the room are called right angles. She continues, "Can you find some other corners or angles in the room that are right angles?"

"Let's take a look at the second clue. Do any of our shapes have four right angles?" Students talk in small groups, and the class agrees that shapes C and E have four right angles. Some of the students are also debating whether shape D has four right angles. Rather than tell the students, Mrs. Rodriguez suggests they cut out a shape that looks like shape D and asks how they might compare it with C and E. After a brief discussion, the students agree that if they turn D so the bottom is straight, they can see it doesn't have four right angles.

"Which shapes now fit the first two clues?" asks Mrs. Rodriguez. As the students respond, she circles C and E on the board. "How can we use the final clue to solve the riddle?" The students explain their thinking and agree that the sides of shape E are the same length, so that shape must be the answer. Mrs. Rodriguez agrees and follows up by reminding students that this shape is a square. She concludes the lesson by asking, "What are the characteristics of shape E that the clues tell us?" She leaves the students to ponder this question: "Do all squares have all of these characteristics?"

Students continue working in small groups to solve a few other riddles that deal with two-dimensional shapes. At the conclusion of each riddle, the class meets to discuss their representations and their solutions. Mrs. Rodriguez then introduces the appropriate vocabulary and adds these words and pictures to the mathematics word wall.

Think about how, rather than telling students what to do, her questions and prompts led students to think about what was needed to solve the riddles and how they could justify their solutions. Mrs. Rodriguez used guiding questions to help students get started on the task and was ready for follow-up examples to which students could apply what they just learned. Making a table was an important strategy to organize their ideas and also linked to understanding new vocabulary.

Asking good questions when a new concept is being introduced—meaning questions that do not give too much information but rather guide students' thinking—requires practice. We have to make a conscientious decision about the questions we want to ask as we are *planning* lessons and more so when we are actually in the midst of teaching. That means your questions depend on the responses and questions of your students and what you see evidenced in their work. In order for surface learning to take place, questions should engage students as well as guide them to the understandings and connections that are determined by your learning intentions. One word of advice: too often we respond by giving students too much information rather than asking a question that will push their thinking forward just enough to allow them to think differently about a situation. Give yourself permission to stop and think about the "right" question to ask at any given point in the lesson. Good questioning takes lots of practice.

Video 4.3
Guided Questioning
for Surface Learning

*http://resources.corwin.com/
VL-mathematics*

Video or audio recording a lesson and taking the opportunity to watch or listen to the recording, to focus on the questions you have asked, can be very helpful in developing expertise. Some call this practice micro-teaching, which is when a lesson or "mini-lesson" is video recorded and then reviewed and analyzed by the teacher in order to improve the teaching and learning experience. Jim Knight and his colleagues (Knight & van Nieuwerburgh, 2012) analyzed the work of teachers and instructional coaches over a three-year period as they interacted with video and audio recordings of lessons, and they found that these tools propelled improvements in instructional quality more effectively than lesson debriefing alone. Similar effects were also seen with individual teachers who coached themselves by watching videos of their own teaching.

> EFFECT SIZE FOR MICRO-TEACHING = 0.88

In the shape lesson, Mrs. Rodriguez explicitly modeled making a table to help her students organize their thinking to help solve the problem. You might be thinking to yourself that you would never do that, because you believe effective math teachers are the ones who give their students the space to figure things out for themselves. After all, students can gain a longer-lasting and more meaningful understanding when they make sense of problems, persevere in solving them, and own their learning. But also note that Mrs. Rodriguez didn't rush in immediately. She let her students work through the riddle on their own first, and stepped in when she saw them struggling to reach a consensus. The principle of productive struggle or productive failure (Kapur, 2008) suggests that students who confront and fail a challenging problem and are then provided further clarifying instruction outperform traditionally taught students. There can be value in presenting a task before kids have all of the prerequisite skills, letting them struggle a little, and then looping back and teaching them the skill within the meaningful context of the task. However, productive struggle should not be confused with impossible tasks.

What Are Worked Examples, and When Are They Appropriate?

A **worked example** is a math problem that has been fully completed to show each step of a mathematician's arrival at a solution. These have been shown to be useful for students in completing problems more efficiently and accurately (Atkinson, Derry, Renkl, & Wortham, 2000; Sweller, 2006). It is important, of course, to identify from the beginning whether a worked example is correct or erroneous. Worked examples

> A **worked example** is a mathematical problem that has been fully completed to show each step of a mathematician's arrival at a solution.

> EFFECT SIZE FOR WORKED EXAMPLES = 0.57

SAMPLE PROMPTS TO USE WHEN SELF-QUESTIONING

Although it is acceptable to ask procedural questions, be sure to ask students to explain and/or justify their reasoning.

1. Why is _____ not included in the answer?

2. What did [student name] _____ do as his [or her] first step?

3. What should [student name] have done to _____?

4. Would it have been OK to write _____? Why or why not?

5. Why did [student name] combine _____ and _____?

6. Why did [student name] first _____ then _____?

7. Is _____ the same expression as _____? Explain.

8. Would [student name] have gotten the same answer if he [or she] _____ first?

9. Why did [student name] change _____ to _____?

10. Explain why _____ would have been an unreasonable answer.

11. How could [student name] have figured out that his [or her] answer did not make sense?

12. How did [student name] know that _____ was not equal to _____?

13. What did the _____ represent in this word problem?

14. How did the _____ in the equation affect the graph?

15. Why did [student name] _____ from both sides of the equation?

Source: McGinn, Lange, and Booth (2015). Used with permission.

Figure 4.6

that are erroneous as well as those that are correct can spark students' thinking as they hypothesize why the mathematician made the decisions he or she did to arrive at a solution. These examples can range in topic, but generally provide students with examples of mathematical reasoning, especially in demonstrating for students how to speculate, problem solve, and formulate reasons. McGinn, Lange, and Booth (2015) advise that worked examples should be developed in such a way that they provide the opportunity to highlight an anticipated misconception and that they are followed by a similar problem that students can solve collaboratively or independently. **Caution:** especially with younger students, be sure your students have a good conceptual understanding before they respond to incorrect worked examples so that they do not replicate error patterns in future work. The questions one should verbalize should focus less on procedural knowledge and more on querying the reasoning used—in other words, more "why" questions and fewer "what" questions. Figure 4.6 contains suggested self-questioning prompts that can be utilized by the teacher while thinking aloud using a worked example.

Fifth-grade math teacher Susana Knowles sometimes uses a process called My Favorite Mistake to share her thinking. Ms. Knowles has students complete a problem or exercise on an index card at the beginning of class, and then quickly sorts through them to locate one that has a common error or an interesting strategy to get to the correct solution. She rewrites it so that the child's handwriting is not recognizable, and always assigns a pseudonym. "I always call him 'Amazing Aloysius,' because he dazzles us with what he knows and doesn't know, and always makes us think. Amazing Aloysius might make an error or has an interesting path to a solution so that the rest of us can learn," she explained.

During a unit on subtracting decimals, Ms. Knowles gave her students the following to solve.

$$3 - 1.473$$

She chose this particular example, because it is one that students often struggle with as they work to regroup. Several students made the same error, so Ms. Knowles copied the following on the board.

$$
\begin{array}{r}
\scriptstyle 2\ 9\ 9\ 9 \\
3.\cancel{000} \\
-\ 1.473 \\
\hline
1.526
\end{array}
$$

For several minutes, the teacher speculated about ways that the student arrived at the solution, asking herself aloud, "I wonder why Amazing Aloysius decided to rewrite this problem vertically?" "I wonder why he chose to put a decimal point followed by three zeroes?" and "I wonder why he crossed off the zeroes and made them all nines?" She paused after each question and let students reply. "It gives them the chance to see how I can ask myself questions to justify what the student did and why he may have done it. It also clears up misconceptions that students may have based on earlier misconceptions."

What Is Direct Instruction, and When Is It Appropriate?

Video 4.4
Direct Instruction: The Right Dose at the Right Time

http://resources.corwin.com/ VL-mathematics

There are times in a lesson or sometimes with particular students—particularly when students are struggling to understand an idea and other student-centered approaches are not yielding the results a teacher wants—when assistance or explanation from a teacher helps to focus the mathematics so that students can get a different perspective (in this case, the teacher's perspective). Before delving into this, we need to recall from Chapter 1 what we mean by direct instruction. As we hope you will see, direct instruction does not mean lecturing. Instead, as Lobato, Clarke, and Ellis (2005) note, there should be "teaching actions that serve the function of stimulating students' mathematical thoughts via the intro-duction of new ideas into the classroom conversation" (p. 136).

Often in mathematics, "direct instruction" is interpreted to mean "show-and-tell" math where the teacher launches a lesson by showing students how to do a procedure, gives them all the vocabulary terms they could ever want, and then sends them off to work on problems independently. This often happens in traditional lecture pedagogy. But we are *not* talking about a scripted transmission model or didactic teaching. By contrast, recall that in Chapter 1 we defined direct instruction more as a carefully scaffolded and guided instructional process that is done with great intention. It is when the teacher decides the learning intentions, makes them clear and visible to students, may do some demonstration, checks for understanding, and recaps what they have done by tying it all together with closure.

It is important to recognize that there is a big difference between teaching and telling. Direct instruction should focus on teaching and improve the ways in which teachers provide students with information. As Munter et al. (2015a) noted, "Those more aligned with direct instruction do not argue that teachers should simply provide facts and procedures to students and ask students to memorize and practice them over and over until proficient. Likewise, those more aligned with dialogic instruction do not advocate 'pure discovery learning,' in which students somehow manage to re-invent the mathematics curriculum" (p. 24). There are three important things to keep in mind about direct instruction:

1. It should not be used as the sole means for teaching mathematics (Munter et al., 2015b). It should be used strategically to build students' surface knowledge when they need it.

2. It does not have to—nor should it—consume a significant portion of the instructional minutes available for learning. The majority of instructional time should actually be devoted to students doing mathematics and talking about their work and understandings to build deeper level learning.

3. It does not have to be used solely at the outset of a new unit of study or the beginning of a lesson. There is evidence that effective direct instruction can follow students' exploration of an idea or concept (Loehr, Fyfe, & Rittle-Johnson, 2014). There is also evidence that students can solve problems targeting concepts that are new to them (Kapur, 2012).

Irrespective of where and when within a lesson or unit it occurs, there are times when students need some direct instruction, as it is especially useful in developing students' surface-level learning.

Direct Instruction of the Mathematical Practices

We do not want to limit the discussion about direct instruction to skills. Yes, there is evidence that computational and procedural skills can be increased through direct instruction (e.g., Flores & Kaylor, 2007). Direct instruction can also be used to develop students' thinking. Think back on the list of mathematical practices we introduced in the preface (National Governors Association Center for Best Practices & Council of Chief State School Officers, 2010):

1. Make sense of problems and persevere in solving them.

2. Reason abstractly and quantitatively.

3. Construct viable arguments and critique the reasoning of others.

4. Model with mathematics.

5. Use appropriate tools strategically.

6. Attend to precision.

7. Look for and make use of structure.

8. Look for and express regularity in repeated reasoning.

The mathematical practices are worth explicitly applying again and again, in many different contexts, across a wide range of math content.

Like the practice or process standards in non-Common-Core states and nations around mathematical problem solving, reasoning, communication, and modeling (see Appendix C), these are habits of mind and ways of thinking that students may, or may not, figure out on their own. We really hope that teachers don't wait for students to figure out ways of attending to precision through precise mathematical language any more than we hope that they will wait for students to learn how to use certain features of graphing calculator software. Designing lessons and activities that naturally involve students using these practices is the most ideal. These practices are something that students must experience and do as they develop as budding mathematicians. Direct instruction can allow students to see these mathematical practices in action. None of us developed our ability to use appropriate tools strategically in isolation or in one sitting. Rather, we developed that practice over time as we were provided examples and non-examples, listened to others, and tried our hand at it. For novices, the mathematical practices often need to be taught directly, explicitly, intentionally, and frequently through teacher modeling. Over time, and with practice, students will begin to incorporate these habits into their daily work. In other words, direct instruction about the mathematical practices can provide students with surface levels of comprehension about them, setting them up to move to deep learning and transfer their learning, which occurs when they begin to practice the mathematical practices and consolidate their understanding in collaboration with others.

Ms. Senger has a bulletin board dedicated to the mathematical practices. There is a poster for each practice that describes the practice in language that is accessible to her seventh- and eighth-grade students. Early in the year, she begins class by discussing one of the practices, what it means and what it looks like. She purposefully designs lessons so that a practice is transparent, and she often stops and points out when students are using the practice during the lesson. She does this for each practice over the first few weeks of school. These mathematical practices are worth explicitly applying again and again, in many different contexts, across a wide range of math content. By mid-October, the students are well versed in each of the practices. Ms. Senger then plans her mathematics tasks and lessons so her students are using several of the practices at any given time. Ms. Senger leaves the bulletin board up all year because these habits of mind are constantly under development, and students should be thinking about how to use them throughout a lesson. In fact, at the end of some lessons, Ms. Senger's exit ticket asks students to reflect and describe which practices they used that day and what they learned about doing mathematics from their use.

The practices are not just for older students. Some of the most effective mathematics lessons in earlier grades include students using these practices to make sense of the mathematics they are doing. Let's revisit Mrs. Franklin's class as they are beginning to work with ideas of multiplication. The game they are playing has them modeling equal-group situations as they begin to make sense of the structure of multiplication. As students learn how to write a multiplication equation and use the appropriate vocabulary to describe what the numbers in the equation mean, they are using precision. What is so powerful about these practices is that instruction should not stop in order for students to apply these practices; rather, the practices are an integral part of doing mathematics. And these practice-related experiences have positive effect sizes.

> EFFECT SIZE FOR VOCABULARY PROGRAMS = 0.67

> EFFECT SIZE FOR CLASSROOM DISCUSSION = 0.82

Mathematical Talk and Metacognition

When using the above mathematical talk activities (number talks, guided questioning, worked examples, and direct instruction), teachers are able to demonstrate the kinds of questioning and listening strategies that exemplify excellent mathematical practice, as well as give their students opportunities to begin building these habits of mind.

Perhaps more importantly, this is when students can begin to practice the self-verbalizing and self-questioning skills that will help them think critically about the conceptual and procedural processes they are using. Teachers can model these talk patterns for students and encourage them to practice them in a number of ways. For example, teachers can get students in the habit of using "I" and "Because."

> EFFECT SIZE FOR SELF-VERBALIZATION AND SELF-QUESTIONING = 0.64

A lot of teachers say "we" or "you" during their lessons, but "I" statements do something different and more powerful for the brains of students. They activate the ability—some call it an instinct—of humans to learn by imitation. The use of "I" statements also encourages empathic listening, which is why this approach is used in conflict resolution and marriage counseling. When students are encouraged to use "I" statements, they recognize that they are the force acting upon and understanding the mathematical ideas and employing the mathematical practices. This is particularly useful when constructing viable arguments and critiquing the reasoning of others (MP 3). When students hear their teachers and peers using "I" statements regularly, they will begin to build the habit too.

Another important habit to build is using the word "because." In mathematics, it's important to explain *why* you're thinking what you're thinking. If a teacher or peer is explaining his or her own thinking, using *because* reduces the chance that students will be left wondering how someone knew to do something or why that person was thinking a certain way. Similarly, reduce the *what* and increase the *why* and *how* questions. Thinking about one's thinking is a metacognitive act, and students will start to think more metacognitively when they hear others, including their peers, do so. Metacognition is thinking about one's own thinking, and there is plenty of research showing that students who use metacognitive strategies tend to achieve more (Schoenfeld, 1992; Veenman, Van Hout-Wolters, & Afflerbach, 2006).

Some of the metacognitive strategies useful in mathematics include having a plan for approaching the task, using appropriate skills and strategies to solve a problem, monitoring and noticing when a problem doesn't make sense, self-assessing and self-correcting, evaluating progress toward the completion of a task, and becoming aware of distractions (Rosenzweig, Krawec, & Montague, 2011; Throndsen, 2011).

A handful of your students might do this instinctively, but if you're serious about all of your students reaping the benefits of thinking about thinking, you'll need to teach metacognitive strategies explicitly, and mathematical talk can be a great vehicle for doing so. Remember that students need to be taught to assess their learning in relation to the success criteria. This is key to moving them forward from surface learning to deep learning. Figure 4.7 contains sample sentence frames that teachers can use to facilitate student metacognitive thinking, organized into the three phases of planning, monitoring, and evaluating.

Strategic Use of Vocabulary Instruction

Vocabulary knowledge is a strong predictor of understanding across content areas (Graves, 2006), and at the 0.67 effect size, strong vocabulary programs fall well into the zone of desired effects. With quality instruction, students move from everyday language to more formal mathematical language, eventually developing a mindset for thinking mathematically. This also speaks to mathematical practice 6, which, in referring to attending to precision, includes precision with mathematical language. Furthermore, Simpson and Cole (2015) note that vocabulary instruction has to extend beyond word learning and believe that "for students to be successful in mathematics classrooms, educators must

SENTENCE FRAMES THAT CAN
BUILD METACOGNITIVE THINKING

Planning

I wonder why . . .

I already know something about this topic. It is . . .

I know the word _____, but I don't know what _____ and _____ mean.

I see lots of graphics and charts. I'll need to use those to help me understand what I'm reading.

I think/believe/assert that . .

Monitoring

This wasn't what I expected. I expected _____ because _____.

What can I write or draw that might help me remember and understand?

Based on . . . I infer . . .

My idea/answer is similar to . . . because . . .

My idea/answer is different from . . . because . . .

I discovered from . . . that . . .

I found out from . . . that . . .

A question I have is . . . because . . .

Evaluating

How well did I understand the task or problem?

What strategies worked well for me?

What strategies did not work for me?

What should I do next time?

Do I need some help for next time?

Figure 4.7

Video 4.5
Vocabulary Instruction to
Solidify Surface Learning

*http://resources.corwin.com/
VL-mathematics*

become cognizant of the role of language in establishing classroom norms, negotiating identities, and challenging inequitable distributions of power" (p. 369).

Vocabulary instruction, like other aspects of the mathematics curriculum, must be taught for depth and transfer (Bay-Williams & Livers, 2009), but it often begins during the surface phase of learning so that students can begin to build the academic language they'll need to discuss and debate their thinking with precision going forward. Unfortunately, too many children and adolescents experience vocabulary instruction as making passing acquaintance with a wide range of words that are disconnected from conceptual understanding. Students assume that many of the words won't be used again, and that next week there will be a new list.

So what does it mean to know a word? Vocabulary knowledge should be viewed across five dimensions (Cronbach, 1942, cited in Graves, 1986):

- *Generalization* through definitional knowledge
- *Application* through correct usage
- *Breadth* through recall of words
- *Precision* through understanding examples and non-examples
- *Availability* through use of vocabulary in discussion

Furthermore, there are different types of words that serve different functions. As we discussed in Chapter 2, researchers (e.g., Beck et al., 2013) suggest that vocabulary can be divided into three main categories:

- Tier 1—everyday words
- Tier 2—general academic words that change their meaning in different content areas and contexts
- Tier 3—domain-specific words that are consistently used in a given content area

In addition to identifying words that students need to know, the timing for providing instruction on those words is important. In too many cases, students are exposed to new words before they need to use them. Livers and Bay-Williams (2014) suggest that mathematics teachers have three options for introducing vocabulary:

- *Preteaching*—providing instruction at the beginning of a lesson
- *Just-in-time*—during the course of the lesson as students need to use the word
- *Formalizing*—or at the end of the lesson once students have explored a concept

These researchers note, "Vocabulary support must assist in giving students the appropriate terminology they need to engage in the lesson but not give away the mathematical challenge of the lesson" (p. 154). How many of us have heard (or even taught) students to *reduce* fractions? But we are not reducing anything at all! When we change $\frac{12}{24}$ to its equivalent $\frac{1}{2}$, we are simplifying or renaming the fraction, not reducing it! Livers and Bay-Williams (2014) created a decision flowchart that teachers can use to decide when to teach vocabulary as part of a lesson (see Figure 4.8). They begin with a decision about the difference between teaching a concept and context. A concept, the mathematical idea of the lesson, is different from the context in which words are used. One implication from their work is that teaching vocabulary at the beginning of a lesson should happen when building upon a familiar context and previously learned content or concept. Similarly, when teaching a new concept or content, the vocabulary should be introduced during or after the lesson. In other words, as with questions, there are appropriate moments for the introduction of vocabulary words during the surface phase of learning, but only once students have had time to cognitively grapple with a new idea.

There are several teaching strategies one can use to foster good use of academic language. We'll focus on two: word walls and graphic organizers.

Word Walls

A **word wall** is an ongoing, organized display of key words that provides visual reference for students throughout a unit of study or a term. To keep students focused on the academic vocabulary expected of them, teachers post the targeted vocabulary on the wall, bulletin board, or white board. Teachers may elect to include a brief definition, picture, or example with the word. Words can be placed on the word wall at the beginning of a unit or as new vocabulary is introduced throughout the unit. Students are reminded to use the words as they talk with one another. Cunningham (2000) warned that having a word wall is unproductive unless we are also

A **word wall** is an ongoing, organized display of key words that provides visual reference for students throughout a unit of study or a term.

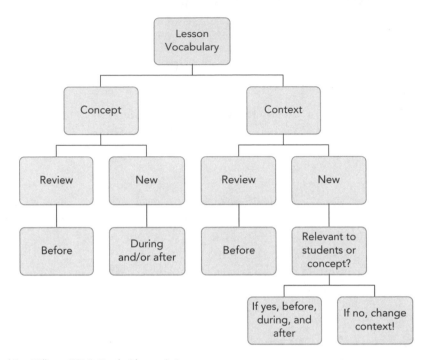

Source: Livers and Bay-Williams (2014). Used with permission.

Figure 4.8

"doing" the word wall—meaning actively referencing it throughout the lessons. Biddle (2007) notes that her students use the math word wall in their discussions and in their journal writing.

Word walls can be used especially in vocabulary-heavy units such as geometry. However, they can also be effective as new concepts are introduced or as words take on new contexts. Mr. Gray began his fifth-grade year with a study of number theory. Some of the vocabulary (factor, multiple, product) was review and other terms (divisible, prime, composite, prime factorization) were new to the students. Mr. Gray prepared the words for the word wall by writing them on colorful cardstock with a contextual example for each word. At the beginning of the class, he asked students to add the new words for that day to the wall. Students became "detectives" as they watched and listened for the words to be used in the lesson. Students were responsible for recording the words and the examples in the vocabulary section of their mathematics journals for future reference. Interestingly with the words and examples, students did not mix often-interchanged words such as factor or multiple and prime or composite. Mr. Gray took down the words at the end of the unit so that students were not overwhelmed with the number of new and review vocabulary as the year progressed, although they regularly reviewed previously learned vocabulary.

Graphic Organizers

Students can also master vocabulary by creating graphic organizers such as a Frayer model, Word Splashes, or Anchor Charts. A **graphic organizer** is a visual display that demonstrates relationships between words, facts, concepts, or ideas.

Grecia Cordova uses the Frayer model to help her students develop a deeper understanding of new vocabulary (Frayer, Frederick, & Klausmeier, 1969). Her sixth-grade students divide a 4 × 6 index card into four quadrants and write the targeted word in the upper left-hand quadrant. The definition, written in the students' own words after the teacher explains the meaning, is included in the upper right-hand corner. Next, they write a non-example or opposite of the word in the bottom right-hand corner. In the bottom left-hand corner, students illustrate the meaning of the word. The image they choose is vital and is thought to embed newly learned information into a visual memory students can retrieve. Ms. Cordova explains, "I ask students to create these word cards as I introduce new terms for them, and then they use these for rehearsal and memorization." An example of Horacio's word card for *polygon* appears in Figure 4.9.

Strategic Use of Manipulatives for Surface Learning

Manipulatives, such as Cuisenaire rods, linking cubes, algebra tiles, and tangrams, have long been used in mathematics classrooms, and with good reason—because they work (Domino, 2010; Gersten et al., 2009). Manipulatives can also be virtual (check out the National Library for Virtual Manipulatives at Utah State University, http://nlvm.usu.edu/en/nav/vlibrary.html). Whether physical or virtual, these tools are used by students, either individually or in small groups, to explore math concepts

> A **graphic organizer** is a visual display that demonstrates relationships between words, facts, concepts, and/or ideas.

> **Manipulatives** are concrete models students can use to show and work with representations of mathematical concepts.

> EFFECT SIZE FOR MANIPULATIVES = 0.50

HORACIO'S WORD CARD

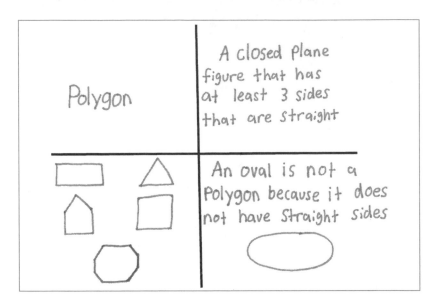

Figure 4.9

in order "to help them build links between the object, the symbol, and the mathematical idea they represent" (National Research Council, 2001, p. 354). This is an example of using a surface learning technique with an eye toward deep learning, in that the use of manipulatives bridges students' learning as they move from surface to deep.

Understanding place value in our number system is one of the most foundational ideas for elementary children to understand. A full comprehension of place value includes understanding the relationship between the place each digit holds in a multidigit number and the value of that place. For example, in the number 3456, the digit 3 actually represents three thousands, whereas in the number 2453, the digit 3 represents three ones. Without this understanding, students cannot compare or order numbers, and they have great difficulty developing strategies for whole-number operations.

There are many place value tools, such as arrow cards, expanded notation, and base ten blocks, but Mr. Martin's favorite are coffee stirrers and

MANIPULATIVES ON A PLACE VALUE MAT

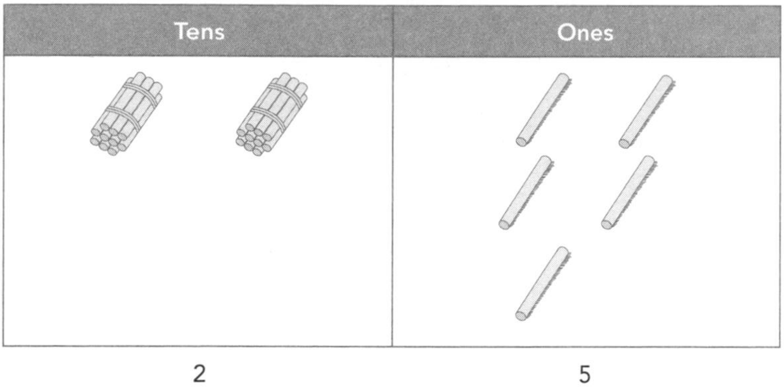

Tens	Ones
2	5

Source: Clipart courtesy FCIT, http://etc.usf.edu/clipart.

Figure 4.10

small rubber bands or twist-ties. He begins by having each first grader make his or her own place value mat (Figure 4.10), and students begin to count with the straws. However, as soon as they get ten ones, they put a rubber band around the straws and the ten becomes a new unit with its own place on the place value chart. Students build numbers up to ninety-nine. They compare the models on their place value chart with numbers on the hundreds chart that hangs in the classroom. They write the numerals under their models and compare their number with the numbers that others in their group have modeled. As students begin to add (put together) two-digit and one-digit numbers, they physically put ten ones together and move that bundle to the tens place before they ever write an equation. In Grade 2, Mrs. Sofal continues to build on previous experiences as students extend their place value chart to the hundreds place and continue to regroup in addition and subtraction. This provides students with the opportunity to make sense of place value in a very physical way, thus building the surface learning that will become deep learning as they apply this knowledge to develop algorithmic procedures.

In middle school, Sara uses algebra tiles to teach addition of integers. It is important that students see this as another example of addition that they have studied since kindergarten. The students understand addition as an operation that joins sets of objects or numbers together, so she uses algebra tiles to extend this understanding to adding positive and negative numbers. Sara wants to emphasize that we are still adding two sets (in this case, sets of tiles representing negative 4 and positive 2), so she writes the example using the signs with each number: $^-4 + {}^+2 = x$. She asks the class what the example represents, and Ian responds, "We're putting together a set of four negative tiles with a set of two positive tiles." The class uses the tiles to create a model of the situation. They talk about what happens when one negative joins one positive and after discussing several real-life examples, they agree that this would result in zero. As they return to their models, they can see that they have two pairs that combine to make zero. They note that there are two negative tiles left, so the sum is $^-2$.

By using algebra tiles to work these problems and recording their work in sketches and equations, students build their surface learning knowledge of adding integers and connect it to their previously learned knowledge of adding whole numbers. As their surface learning of adding integers becomes stronger, they will transition to the convention of not writing the sign for positive addends. From these patterns, as they take their learning into the deep phase, they will begin to make generalizations and develop the rules we use to add integers efficiently.

Strategic Use of Spaced Practice With Feedback

We have situated the dual approaches of spaced practice (often known as distributed practice) and feedback within our discussion of surface learning, because like the previous strategies (especially metacognition in number talks, guided questions, and worked examples), they teach children as much about thinking as they do about tasks. In building the learner's awareness of the processes they use, we bridge surface-level acquisition and consolidation by fostering the skills they will need to plan, investigate, and elaborate as they deepen their learning. In this context, spaced practice is about maintenance of recently acquired knowledge, not rehearsal. **Spaced practice** has to do with the frequency of different learning opportunities—having multiple exposures to an idea over several days to attain learning, and spacing the practice of skills over a long period of time.

By way of example, most textbooks focus student practice on the current skill being taught. A student might be expected to do up to 25 exercises that focus on a particular skill such as adding mixed numbers. Some teachers will adjust the assignment to doing a specific set, perhaps odd-numbered examples. But the point is that once the assignment is complete, there is no ongoing practice. Assignments or class practice is more effective when done in regularly spaced intervals, rather than clustered together for a short, intensive period of time (massed practice). Although explanations for why this phenomenon exists vary, recall of information is better after spaced practice when compared with massed practice sessions. However, spaced practice shouldn't be limited to practicing computational skills. Effective teachers build problems that require previously learned concepts and skills into warm-ups, homework, and collaborative group work in order to maintain knowledge that might otherwise atrophy.

Mathematics educator, author, and consultant Steve Leinwand (2016) describes a 2–4–2 strategy for mathematics homework that is designed to build distributed practice into the homework process. Daily homework includes 2 problems on the new skill, 4 cumulative review problems, and 2 problems that support reasoning and justification by requiring students to show and explain their work. The four cumulative review problems come from content taught the day before, the week before, and the month before the current assignment (one item each); the fourth problem in this group could be a diagnostic readiness check for a lesson in the near future or an additional cumulative review problem. By incorporating this idea of distributed practice into a homework routine, teachers can more easily ensure they are using this research base effectively.

Distributed practice events can further provide students and the teacher with essential **feedback** about the progression of learning. Brookhart (2008) defines feedback as "just-in-time, just-for-me information delivered when and where it can do the most good" (p. 1). At their best, these spaced practice events can and should be used formatively by the student such that his or her learning becomes visible. Feedback to the

Spaced practice is having multiple exposures to an idea over several days to attain learning, and spacing the practice of skills over a long period of time.

EFFECT SIZE FOR SPACED VERSUS MASS PRACTICE = 0.71

Feedback is "just-in-time, just-for-me information delivered when and where it can do the most good" (Brookhart, 2008, p. 1).

EFFECT SIZE FOR FEEDBACK = 0.75

student is important at this stage, and we encourage teachers to extend beyond feedback about the task (e.g., noting the number of correct and incorrect responses).

Rather, feedback about the process, not just the task, moves students to deeper learning. We want students to note their errors and have chances to address them. But simply supplying the correct answer for the incorrect one doesn't do much for their thinking. Feedback that prompts a student to seek more information or reconsider her approach and reasoning, or points out a path to pursue, gives the student agency and puts her in the driver's seat of her own learning. In turn, it reduces reliance on outside judgments of her progress (you) as she begins to see it for herself, and better still, realizes she can act upon it. That, by the way, contributes to a positive math mindset (Boaler, 2016). For example, saying to a student, "You identified that you answered the third one incorrectly. Could a mathematics model help you sort out the problem?" mediates her thinking, without doing all the thinking for her. We'll discuss feedback in much greater depth in Chapter 7, especially as it applies to the ability to self-regulate.

Strategic Use of Mnemonics

EFFECT SIZE FOR
MNEMONICS = 0.45

Mnemonics are
memory devices
that assist learners
to recall substantial
amounts of
information.

Mnemonics are memory devices that assist learners to recall substantial amounts of information, such as mathematical concepts like orders of operation and the quadratic formula. "It is a memory enhancing instructional strategy which involves teaching students to link new information that is taught to information they already know" (DeLashmutt, 2007, p. 1). As is often the case, mnemonics could be a short song, an acronym, or a visual image that is easily remembered to help students who have difficulty recalling information.

How often have you used this strategy (even if you couldn't name it) to recall a string of words? "Roy G. Biv" to remember the colors of the light spectrum (red, orange, yellow, green, blue, indigo, and violet) or "HOMES" to recall the names of the U.S. Great Lakes (Huron, Ontario, Michigan, Erie, and Superior). In addition to name and musical mnemonics, other techniques include using an image or an expression ("Every Good Boy Does Fine" to recall that the lines on the musical treble staff are E, G, B, D, and F). A mnemonic device is a memory aid used to link a string of words together.

Mnemonics can be useful if used appropriately. Too often, they are used to replace an understanding or to present students with a trick that overrides an important understanding, and often lead to misconceptions (Karp, Bush, & Dougherty, 2014). Thus, it is important to ensure that students understand the reasoning behind the mnemonics and not just the procedures for using them. Mnemonics work to get students to surface-level understanding, but we cannot leave them there. As Jeon (2012) notes, simply memorizing the order of operations through a mnemonic such as PEMDAS, or Please Excuse My Dear Aunt Sally, does not mean that students know how to use the information.

Mnemonics are especially helpful with the vocabulary of mathematics. For example, the fact that both **d**enominator and **d**own start with the letter **d** is helpful to remember that the denominator is the bottom number in a fraction. Some teachers extend this to connect the **u** in numerator with the word **u**p. This mnemonic does not replace an understanding of what the numerator and denominator mean; it simply helps students place the labels correctly as they work with the terms.

A challenging set of vocabulary in measurement is the metric system prefixes. One common device for helping learners sequence them correctly is **K**ing **H**enry **D**oesn't **U**sually **D**rink **C**old **M**ilk. The first initials of this sentence correspond to the prefixes *kilo-, heca-, deca-,* unit, *deci-, centi-,* and *milli-.* Students must still know the prefixes and how they correspond to the scale of the unit. In addition, they have to distinguish between the two d prefixes (*deca-,* or ten times, and *deci-,* or one tenth). Using understanding (**deci**mals involve units smaller than 1) rather than depending on memorization makes sense and therefore makes it more likely for students to remember the distinction.

Conclusion

A strong start sets the stage for meaningful learning and powerful impacts. Teachers need to be mindful of where their students are in the learning cycle. Surface learning sets the necessary foundation for the deepening knowledge and transfer that will come later. But there's a caveat: teaching for transfer must occur. Too often, learning ends at the surface level. But the challenge is this: we can't over-correct in the other direction, bypassing foundational knowledge in favor of critical and analytic thinking. Students need and deserve to be introduced to new knowledge and skills thoughtfully and with a great deal of expertise on the part of the teacher. And teachers need to recognize the signs that it is time to move forward from surface learning to deep learning.

Reflection and Discussion Questions

1. Consider the mathematical discourse in your classroom. What opportunities do students have to explain and justify their thinking? What questioning strategies could you use to provide additional opportunities for students to show their deep learning through explanation and justification?

2. Consider the important mathematical topics for your grade level. What is the surface learning phase of each topic? What would that look like in the uni-/multi-structural levels of a SOLO chart? What specific strategies might you use to help students develop surface learning for each of these topics?

3. How do you use manipulatives in your mathematics instruction? Are students encouraged to use multiple representations as they work on mathematics collaboratively? What strategies can you use to make these tools more available to your students?

DEEP MATHEMATICS LEARNING MADE VISIBLE

5

Fifth-grade teacher Mrs. Wolf is about to begin a unit on volume. Students enter the classroom to find a container of one-inch cubes and some graph paper at each set of desks. On the board is the following task.

> The Build-a-Block Company sells children's cube-shaped building blocks. Each block is 1 inch long. They want to sell the blocks in boxes of 36. Use the tools at your table groups and what you know about measurement to design a box that would hold 36 cubes.

Students set off to work with little explanation from Mrs. Wolf. When the first group comes up with a solution, she stretches their thinking by asking how they would describe their box to someone on the phone. This starts a discussion among the group members while others continue to work. Groups that finish early are challenged to find other possible boxes that will hold the thirty-six cubes. When all of the groups have found at least one solution to the problem, Mrs. Wolf has each group post its solution about the length, width, and height of their boxes in the table in Figure 5.1, which is on the front board. They are told to leave the volume columns blank for now.

As students complete the chart, Mrs. Wolf challenges them with the following prompt. "Use any patterns you see to convince me that we found all of the possible boxes that can hold thirty-six cubes."

The discussion that continues brings up a variety of important mathematical questions. Students debate whether a $3 \times 4 \times 3$ box is the same as or different from a $3 \times 3 \times 4$ box. They start to organize the table at their seats to show that they have indeed found all of the possible combinations. They notice that if they multiply the dimensions, the product is thirty-six, which is the number of blocks in the box.

The next day, Mrs. Wolf introduces the learning intention, which is for students to find patterns that will help them generalize finding the volume of a rectangular solid. Students will know they have achieved understanding when they are able to find the volume of any rectangular solid based on their understanding of patterns. That is the success criterion, and students know it. Mrs. Wolf then facilitates a discussion in which students tie together the mathematical ideas from the "Box Problem." Through their discussion, they begin to recognize that the size and shape of their boxes have something to do with how

A TABLE FOR STUDENT RECORDING ON THE BOX PROBLEM

Length	Width	Height	Volume

Figure 5.1

many cubes would fit inside, which creates an initial understanding of volume—a new term that Mrs. Wolf introduces and defines. Mrs. Wolf then explicitly guides students to see how the discoveries they have made can be generalized for finding the volume of any rectangular solid. Through purposeful questions and prompts, she helps the students make the connection between their patterns (multiply the three dimensions) and the formula for volume ($L \times W \times H$) as a way of demonstrating how volume can be found more efficiently than always stacking cubes in imaginary boxes. At this point, they work in groups to complete the volume column of their table. To continue deepening this learning about volume, and move students toward transfer, Mrs. Wolf will go on to other tasks that week that give students the opportunity to apply the same thinking to different rectangular solids, and more complex shapes composed of several rectangular solids.

Mrs. Wolf intentionally began this class unit using a high cognitive demand task that required students to use their previously mastered skills about measuring three-dimensional objects in a way that resulted in deeper learning and, ultimately, extension into a new idea. Notice, there was no formal introduction to this particular exploration task other than answering questions individual groups might have. Both deep and surface learning happened over these two days in Mrs. Wolf's class. Students built on previous experiences to see patterns and make generalizations, which enabled them to enter into a new conceptual understanding that they will continue to explore throughout the deep phase of their learning. And of course, if students began to struggle as they moved deeper, Mrs. Wolf knew she could always pull back and inject a dose of surface learning to support the students who needed it.

The Nature of Deep Learning

Deep learning focuses on recognizing relationships among ideas. During deep learning, students engage more actively and deliberately with information in order to discover and understand the underlying mathematical structure. This is particularly linked to mathematical practices 3, 7, and 8 in the Common Core and the mathematical process standards or higher order thinking standards in other states and countries that speak to displaying, explaining, and justifying mathematical ideas and arguments; communicating; interpreting; reasoning; and analyzing mathematical relationships and connections (see a nonexhaustive list of state and national practice standards in Appendix C).

By way of example, we'll look at Common Core Math Practices (MPs) and the Texas Essential Knowledge and Skill (TEKS) process standards, as those are specifically described.

> Common Core MP 3: Construct viable arguments and critique the reasoning of others.
>
> TEKS G: Display, explain, and justify mathematical ideas and arguments using precise mathematical language in written or oral communication.

This practice requires students to engage in active mathematical discourse. **Discourse** reaches beyond discussion because it includes ways of representing, thinking, talking, agreeing, and disagreeing. It is the way ideas are exchanged and what the ideas entail. It is shaped by the tasks in which students engage as well as by the nature of the learning environment (NCTM, 1991). This might involve having students explain and discuss their thinking processes aloud, share and explain their representations, or indicate agreement/disagreement with a hand signal. Students who are using this practice are able to explain their thinking and articulate the relationships they see in mathematics. They

Discourse is about the exchange of ideas, including ways of representing, thinking, talking, agreeing, and disagreeing.

are able to ask questions to help clarify an argument another student makes and to reason about what makes one case stronger than another.

In the case of Mrs. Wolf's lessons on volume, students used this practice to justify their thinking by proving that their individual solutions were accurate, debating whether packages with the same dimensions in a different order were the same or different, and proving that they had determined all of the possible box shapes and sizes.

Video 5.1
Deep Learning: Applying Understanding to Mathematical Situations

http://resources.corwin.com/ VL-mathematics

> Common Core MP 7: Look for and make use of structure.
>
> TEKS B: Use a problem-solving model that incorporates analyzing given information, formulating a plan or strategy, determining a solution, justifying the solution, and evaluating the problem-solving process and the reasonableness of the solution.
>
> TEKS F: Analyze mathematical relationships to connect and communicate mathematical ideas.

Students who engage in such practices focus on identifying and evaluating efficient strategies to reach a solution. For example, primary students can use a hundreds chart to count by tens starting with any one-digit number. They might recognize that the tens digit increases by one each time they count down in a vertical column on the chart. Middle school students might find patterns in a table to guess a rule and complete the table.

> Common Core MP 8: Look for and express regularity in repeated reasoning.
>
> TEKS D: Communicate mathematical ideas, reasoning, and their implications using multiple representations including symbols, diagrams, graphs, and language as appropriate.

These practices are about students noticing when a calculation or pattern happens over and over. This requires teachers to plan lessons that invite students to recognize the repetition. It calls for teachers to recognize any "a-ha" moments students have and to facilitate discourse so that students can make connections, describe patterns, and generalize. The goal of this practice is for students to look for efficient ways to describe and use repetition to develop fluency.

REPRESENTING 4 × 30

Hundreds	Tens	Ones
	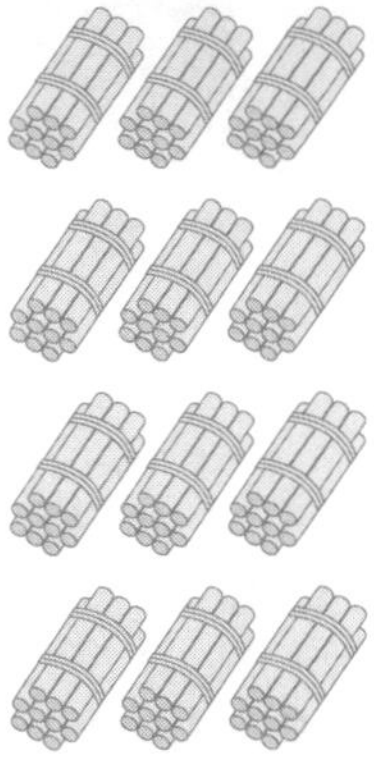	

Source: Clipart courtesy FCIT, http://etc.usf.edu/clipart.

Figure 5.2

The fourth graders in Mr. Hunt's class are working on multiplication of two-digit times one-digit numbers. They use objects on a place value chart (Figure 5.2) to physically show what happens when you multiply a one-digit number times multiples of ten. After several concrete examples, Mr. Hunt demonstrates how to record the equations using numerals. Students continue with several additional examples, when Helen is suddenly very excited and announces, "All of the answers end in zero!"

A few things are happening here. Helen notices repetition, and Mr. Hunt needs to seize the moment to help students make connections to place value and to generalize why that pattern works. It is also a good time to remind students of precision with vocabulary. He replies, "What do you notice about the place value of the one-digit factor when you are multiplying by a multiple of ten?" Students look over the examples they have completed. Students are a bit reluctant to respond, so Mr. Hunt continues with another question to guide their thinking. "What do all of the examples we have been solving this morning have in common?" His question nudges students to focus on finding similarities and connecting them to make a generalization. Billy says, "One of the factors is a multiple of ten and the other is a one-digit number." Mr. Hunt

MOBILE DATA PLANS

Plan	Monthly Cost for Voice and Text	Monthly Cost for Data
A	$0	$10/10 MB
B	$15	$5/5 MB
C	$10	$5/5 MB
D	$20	$1/1 MB

Figure 5.3

then asks them to consider what is happening to the place value of the one-digit factor. Helen responds, "Since it is ten times greater, the place value of the factor moves to the tens place because I have ten times as many." Students need time to explore the pattern they have found and connect it to mathematical understanding (the place value of the digit moves one place to the left), which lays the foundation for multiplying by multiples of 100 and by decimals in later grades.

Let's take a look at a middle school example. In Mr. Bintz's eighth-grade mathematics class, the students are graphing a set of data about various mobile phone plans. Mr. Bintz gives the class a data chart (see Figure 5.3) and asks the students to work in small groups to create graphs that represent the pricing for at least two plans for various amounts of data used each month.

As the students figure out how to use their data to create graphs to compare plans, their talk focuses on the wide range of both voice and text charges and data charges. As they graph (shown in Figure 5.4), students start to notice that the lines they are drawing are parallel and wonder how that could be given the data they have. Mr. Bintz encourages students to use what they know about lines and functions to figure out why this appears to be true. "Remember, you have to convince your parents and yourself that you're choosing the most cost-effective plan. What do the parallel lines tell you about the pricing of the various plans?"

Many arithmetic algorithms take advantage of repeated reasoning. If these algorithms are explored at only a surface level, students may know about "just count up the zeroes in the factors and put that many zeroes in the product," but they won't know the mathematics behind that pattern or

GRAPHIC REPRESENTATION
OF CELL PHONE PLANS

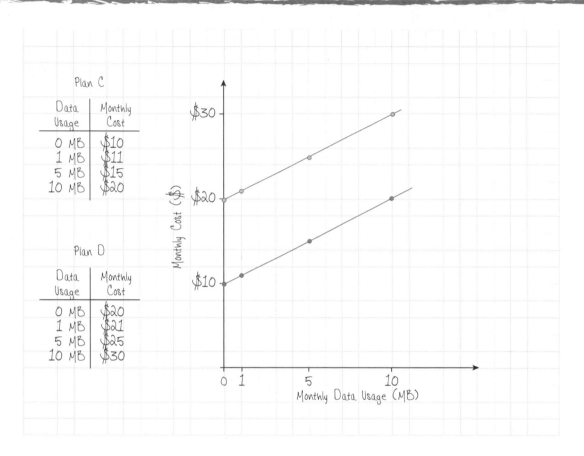

Plan C

Data Usage	Monthly Cost
0 MB	$10
1 MB	$11
5 MB	$15
10 MB	$20

Plan D

Data Usage	Monthly Cost
0 MB	$20
1 MB	$21
5 MB	$25
10 MB	$30

Figure 5.4

shortcut, about how multiplication relates to place value. So they will miss the beauty of this relationship, and when it's time to apply this principle in a different context, they will get stuck. In Mr. Bintz's class, the pricing for data was always at the same rate, just $1/1MB, although that rate was presented in different forms. Students could see that pricing can be presented in various ways to make plans appear more or less appealing depending on the area of concern. A deeper understanding of the mathematics helps students use their learning to understand the world around them.

All of these examples are instances of deep learning. Deep learners are able to make connections and think metacognitively—to think about their thinking, discuss ideas, take action, and see errors as a necessary part of learning. Surface learning is an essential part of the learning process by giving students tasks in which they are building a knowledge base of conceptual understanding that connects to flexible and efficient procedures. This prepares students to engage with more cognitively challenging tasks, and to use more rigorous discourse to identify patterns and make generalizations. Remember that this is a cyclical process, and students are constantly moving between surface learning and deep learning.

In the rest of this chapter, we will highlight the nature of mathematical tasks, questioning techniques, and discussion structures that teachers can use both in collaborative groups and in whole-class discussion to help students to make conceptual connections, and begin to apply their thinking to new contexts and situations in order to deepen their learning and move themselves in the direction of the transfer phase of learning.

Selecting Mathematical Tasks That Promote Deep Learning

As we saw in the case of Mrs. Wolf's class, mathematical tasks that promote deep learning necessitate students to use their surface learning to make connections and find relationships among ideas. These tasks require greater cognitive demand, are usually more open-ended, and have multiple routes to a solution or multiple solutions. By working through these challenges, learners build their deep thinking capacity.

It is important to know how much surface learning is necessary in order to prepare for a related task that leads to deep learning. In the case of Mrs. Wolf's class and their Build-a-Block containers, the teacher decided to provide students with an opportunity to begin to explore the study of volume. However, if she had not explicitly connected the mathematical experiences inherent in this task with important surface learning (leveraging prior knowledge of measurement and multiplication as well as developing vocabulary), it is likely this would have been an engaging activity that had no real learning outcome. Similarly, students needed to connect the patterns they discovered to the formula for finding the volume of a rectangular solid to determine how the dimensions of different solids were related to volume. The deep learning activity, connected to important surface learning, provided students with opportunities to see how and why generalizations or mathematical rules work!

In Chapter 3, we talked about exercises versus problem solving. Figure 5.5 gives examples of each using the same mathematics concepts. Think about good problems or rich tasks that can help promote deep learning that connects to surface learning.

It is not enough to provide students with rich tasks that support deep learning. Instructional protocols should include implementing whole class activities and small group activities, facilitating discourse, and knowing when to interject an idea or ask a question versus when to let productive struggle happen. A teacher's finesse in using a combination of these protocols differentiates routine instruction from effective instruction.

Mathematical Talk That Guides Deep Learning

In a recent study in England, John found that 89 percent of class time was teacher talking (Hattie, 2012). We have seen similar patterns in other countries. It seems that students come to class to watch the teacher work. It is too often the teacher who is posing questions. It is the teacher who is playing traffic cop—calling on students (hands raised, of course) and deciding who will speak next and when. Only about 5 to 10 percent of teacher talk triggers more conversation or dialogue engaging the student. But listening needs dialogue, which involves students and teachers joining together in addressing questions or issues of common concern, considering and evaluating different ways of addressing and learning about these issues.

Too much teacher talk reduces opportunities for students to use their own prior achievement, understanding, sequencing, and questioning. This means less thinking and less learning for kids. Limiting teacher talk is so important for teachers, coaches, and administrators to recognize as crucial in successful student learning! There are several considerations that can help to move the talk away from the teacher and into the mouths of students.

> Too often, it is the teacher who is doing most of the talking. It is the teacher who is posing questions. It is the teacher who is calling on students, deciding who will speak next and when.

EFFECT SIZE FOR CLASSROOM DISCUSSION = 0.82

EXERCISES VERSUS RICH TASKS

Exercises	Rich Tasks
Find the circumference of a circle with a 1. diameter of 8 inches 2. diameter of 30 feet 3. radius of 10 mm 4. radius of 40 cm	Design a tape measure that, when wrapped around a cylinder, could be used to directly read the diameter of the cylinder.
Complete the following addition and subtraction exercises: $\begin{array}{r} 543 \\ +345 \\ \hline \end{array}$ $\begin{array}{r} 716 \\ +617 \\ \hline \end{array}$ $\begin{array}{r} 449 \\ +944 \\ \hline \end{array}$ $\begin{array}{r} 613 \\ +316 \\ \hline \end{array}$ $\begin{array}{r} 543 \\ -345 \\ \hline \end{array}$ $\begin{array}{r} 716 \\ -617 \\ \hline \end{array}$ $\begin{array}{r} 944 \\ -449 \\ \hline \end{array}$ $\begin{array}{r} 613 \\ -316 \\ \hline \end{array}$	Choose a three-digit number where the hundreds digit is at least two more than the units digit. For example, 572. Reverse the digits and subtract: $$\begin{array}{r} 572 \\ -275 \\ \hline 297 \end{array}$$ Reverse the digits of the answer and then add these two numbers: $$\begin{array}{r} 297 \\ +792 \\ \hline 1089 \end{array}$$ Repeat the process with a different starting number. What do you notice? Why do you think this happens?
Complete the following: $1 + 5 =$ $2 + 4 =$ $3 + 3 =$ $4 + 2 =$ $5 + 1 =$	Choose any number between 2 and 9. First add it to itself and record your answer. Then increase your chosen number by 1, and decrease your chosen number by 1. Then add the two resulting numbers. What do you notice?
Order the following fractions by first converting them all to a common denominator of 60. $\dfrac{19}{15} \quad \dfrac{7}{12} \quad \dfrac{5}{6} \quad \dfrac{11}{15} \quad \dfrac{41}{30}$	Draw an X on the following number line where you think the fraction $\dfrac{11}{8}$ should be. Explain why you put your X where you did. Draw and label a few other points to help you explain your reasoning. $0 \rule{6cm}{0.4pt} 2$

Figure 5.5

Accountable Talk

Think of high-stakes discussions you have witnessed in your life. Perhaps you visited a state legislature in session and watched the members debate the merits of a bill. You may have listened to testimony in court when you were on jury duty. Perhaps you attended a school board meeting because the board members were considering an initiative in which you were interested. In all of these cases, the level of accountability was high. Everyone who spoke was accountable to ensure that the discussion remained on topic, that accurate information was presented, and that they thought deeply about what was being said by others. If any of these principles are violated, it seriously compromises the integrity of the collective work of the institution.

These same three tenets form the heart of accountable talk in the classroom, an approach to framing discourse practices of students (Resnick, Michaels, & O'Connor, 2010). They also describe the quality indicators of high levels of engagement and critical thinking among learners. Accountable talk is frequently framed as a set of expectations for students that is supported through the use of language frames that scaffold the use of language to explore a topic. These language expectations are distributed across five conversational moves shown in Figure 5.6.

However, in the rush to get students to engage in accountable talk, the responsibility of the teacher may be overlooked. Accountable talk begins with the teacher. Unless the teacher is consistently modeling how these conversational moves are used, and using appropriate prompts and questions to facilitate these moves, students will not integrate them into their own discussion. And we don't mean simply modeling them once or twice and then moving on. Students need to be drenched in accountable talk; it should flood the classroom. The daily enactment of these principles by the adult in the room communicates volumes about the expectations for classroom discourse. Examples of these teacher prompts (Resnick et al., 2010) include the following:

- *Marking the conversation*—"That's an important point."

- *Challenging students*—"What do you think about that question Vanessa asked?"

- *Keeping everyone together*—"Who can repeat what Pedro just said, using your own words?"

ACCOUNTABLE TALK MOVES

Move	Examples
Press for clarification and explanation	• Could you describe what you mean? • Can you provide an example that supports your claim? • Can you tell me more about your thinking about . . . ?
Require justification of proposals and challenges	• Where did you find that information? • How did you know that? • How does that support your claim?
Recognize and challenge misconception	• I don't agree because . . . • Have you considered an alternative such as . . . ? • I think that there is a misconception here, specifically . . .
Require evidence for claims and arguments	• Can you give me an example? • Where did you find that information? • How does this evidence support your claim?
Interpret and use each other's statements	• David suggested . . . • What I heard Marla say was . . . • I was thinking about Jackson's idea and I think . . .

Figure 5.6

- *Keeping the channels open*—"Did everyone hear that? Devon, can you say that again?"
- *Linking contributions*—"Allie, can you put your idea together with the one Oliver just suggested?"
- *Pressing for accuracy*—"Where can we find that?"
- *Pressing for reasoning*—"Why do you think so?"

- *Building on prior knowledge*—"How does your idea connect, Tonya, with what we've been studying?"

- *Verifying and clarifying*—"I want to make sure I understand. Are you saying . . . ?"

Imagine how your conversational moves can elevate the discourse in the math classroom. Students who are routinely exposed to a teacher who engages as an active participant will absorb some of these same practices. Having said that, students need much more in terms of the norms and structures of classroom discussion.

Supports for Accountable Talk

There are a couple of habits we suggest teachers and students adopt to work accountable talk into their daily routines.

Language Frames

Language frames are scaffolds that prompt the type of talk we want from our students. These language frames might be the tap on the shoulder your students need to engage in productive conversation around a math task. Figure 5.7 contains several language frames that we have found useful for students to use to jumpstart their conversation. These should be provided as an optional support and not a mandate for students.

Language frames are scaffolds that prompt the type of talk we want from our students.

Revoicing and Restating

Talking about mathematical ideas with clarity is not always easy, even for adults. **Revoicing** and restating are two of five math talk moves, along with wait time, prompting, and reasoning (Chapin et al., 2009). The teacher revoices a student comment or embeds the thinking in a question to help the student clarify thinking for herself and for others in the class. Revoicing opens a conversation in which a student can shed more light on her thinking. This should value the thinking of every student, not solely those who understand. Students are more willing to take a chance to share ideas when they know they will have the support of the teacher in making those ideas clear. Even when students are thinking deeply, it is not always easy to voice their ideas.

Revoicing is when a teacher restates a student comment or embeds the thinking in a question to help the student clarify thinking.

SAMPLE LANGUAGE FRAMES
FOR MATHEMATICS

- In order to solve this problem, I need to know _____.

- This is a _____ problem because I see _____.

- I started with an estimate by _____.

- We used the problem-solving strategy _____ and our answer is _____ because _____.

- In order to _____, we follow these steps _____.

- I use the _____ operation because the question asked me to _____.

- Describe the process: First, I _____. (step/process) Then, I _____. (step/process) Next, I _____. Finally, I _____.

- My/our answer is _____. I/we think this answer is reasonable because _____.

- Another way to solve this would be _____.

- Can you explain how/why _____?

- If I change _____, my answer would be different because _____.

- I respectfully agree/disagree with _____ because _____.

- I can check my answer by _____.

Available for download at **http://resources.corwin.com/VL-mathematics**

Figure 5.7

Restating, which is similar to revoicing, is a move that is extended to other students by asking them to rephrase or repeat what a peer has said. This empowers students to know that their thinking is valued by the teacher and by their peers, and it allows them to listen to classmates and verify that the interpretation of their thinking is accurate. Teaching students how to restate comments made by others in their groups grants permission for students to challenge each other and request clarification. Without this explicit expectation, students are often reluctant to correct their peers, and the collaborative conversations falter. However,

Restating is a way for students to rephrase or repeat what a peer has said.

be aware that modeling, practice, respect, and trust are important components to successful mathematical arguments and critiquing the reasoning of others.

Note that student thinking does not necessarily need to be accurate in order to be revoiced or restated. In fact, incorrect thinking can often lead to powerful small group or whole class conversations. Revoicing and restating are valuable protocols for helping students to self-verbalize (explain ideas to themselves and others) and self-question (ask themselves and others questions about their thinking).

Teach Your Students the Norms of Class Discussions

You will want to make sure your whole class and small group discussions are worthy of precious instructional minutes, and high-quality discussions hinge on effective classroom management. This means that norms and rules of class discussions should be explicit at the beginning of the school year, and these norms need to be consistently maintained, revisited, and discussed when necessary. The social norms of discussion will not on their own guarantee that the discourse promotes thinking. However, they form the essential foundation that accountable talk is built upon.

Norms and rules are not the same. Norms are the agreements of a group about how the members will work together, and they usually describe four dimensions: trust, belonging, sharing, and respect (Center on Disability & Community Inclusion, 2014). The rules and procedures that follow are meant to align with these agreements. But before you can bring your norms for class discussion to students, you will need to be clear on what you believe is important in order to have students succeed. For instance, how important is a growth mindset in your classroom? How should the community respond to mistakes? Is it safe and trustworthy for students to admit they do not know? How should people be treated and supported? The rules and procedures created should align with the norms you have identified. Yet too often, they contradict expressed norms.

Fourth-grade teacher Darren Hardy realized this when he filmed his own class as they discussed a problem he had posted on the board. "I set up the video camera because I wanted to see what was going on during discussions. I knew that I kept hearing from the same handful of kids, but couldn't figure out what was getting in the way of the others being able to participate," he said.

What Mr. Hardy saw surprised him. "It's my classroom. You think I'd have been aware of it. But because I had the camera at the back of the room, I got a completely different view." He saw students sitting in the back of his classroom who didn't participate and didn't attend to the conversation. "I realized that I had clustered a number of students who are English learners in a place in the classroom that didn't offer them a decent sight line. It was harder to hear back there." Mr. Hardy made a number of changes, including rearranging the desks in a U-shape to afford a better view for everyone, reassigning seats to pair quiet students with more participatory ones, and especially in altering his practices. "I saw that I needed to move around the room more, and give students a chance to talk to one another first before opening it up to the class. This has caused the ones who want to answer everything to spend their time talking first with their partner. It also gives those quiet ones a chance to check in with someone else before talking to the large group. There's some rehearsal taking place, which has been a big help for the English learners."

Mr. Hardy altered his procedures to better reflect one of his classroom norms: "Everyone belongs to this classroom community." The rules you develop should be developmentally appropriate and allow for you to manage discussion without thwarting it. Will students in your class need to raise their hands and wait to be called on? Many teachers of intermediate students begin to fade this rule so that students learn how to yield and gain the floor. Will you expect your students to speak in complete sentences? Teachers of younger students teach their students how to stretch their statements so that others can better understand their thinking. Do you want them to ask questions if they don't understand something another student said? Make sure that there are expectations that students talk directly to one another during discussion, rather than addressing only you.

Teachers at an elementary school adopted some simple signals during discussion that are used in every classroom to increase participation and provide support:

- A hand cupped around the ear means "Please speak more loudly because I am having trouble hearing you."

- A thumbs-up means "I agree with what you're saying, and I have a reason I can explain."

> Norms are the agreements of a group about how the members will work together, and they usually describe four dimensions: trust, belonging, sharing, and respect.

Teaching Takeaway

Clarify norms first for yourself, then for your classroom, making sure that rules and procedures reinforce the norms and are developmentally appropriate.

- Hands crossed over one another means "I disagree, and I have a reason I can explain."

- Hands rolling end over end are meant to encourage the speaker to "Keep going with your idea. Tell us more."

In addition, the primary students stand next to their seat or place on the carpet and face the class to talk. The principal explained that this makes it easier for small people to track the discussion because they can see who is talking. As well, the gestures provide the classroom teacher with a way to monitor the thinking that is occurring within the group, and not just with the speaker. When they see signs of disagreement or agreement, they know who to engage in further discussion. They report that the hand signals are especially valuable for supporting mathematical discourse, as it interrupts the conventional expectations that while one person answers, the rest are simply passive observers rather than active thinkers. This makes the difference between a few students being engaged in a discussion, and having an entire class of active learners.

Mathematical Thinking in Whole Class and Small Group Discourse

Let's apply some of the ideas of the previous section to facilitating worthwhile mathematical discourse. Recall that discourse encompasses both the way ideas are exchanged and what the ideas entail.

Video 5.2
Student Collaboration and Discourse for Deep Learning

http://resources.corwin.com/ VL-mathematics

Without intending to, discourse can devolve into the same kind of Initiate-Respond-Evaluate (I-R-E) questioning cycle used with individual students. Instead of mathematical thinking, students are primarily engaged in simple recall of information and reproduction of processes, such that accuracy is valued over the thinking that went into it. Unlike I-R-E, classroom discourse that values mathematical thinking allows students to speculate, hesitate, change their viewpoints, and take risks. This means that space must be created for students to engage with quandaries that may initially confound them. Yackel and Cobb (1996) described norms that promote true mathematical discourse, and they called these sociomathematical norms:

- *Explanations* are mathematical arguments, not procedural summaries of the steps that were used to arrive at an answer. Explanations include justifications.

- *Errors* are opportunities to reconsider a problem from a different point of departure. Even when the answer is correct, there is further discussion about more efficient and more sophisticated pathways.

- *Mathematical thinking* requires that teachers cultivate a sense of intellectual autonomy that prizes participation in the discussion about possible solutions.

What are the talk moves of a skilled mathematics teacher that promote conceptual thinking? When looking for explanations, skilled teachers follow up with questions and prompts that ask for elaborations and justifications. They draw other students into the discussion to probe their thinking, especially in seeking to locate areas of disagreement or contradiction. They use errors as opportunities to reboot the discussion by requiring students to wrestle with a discrepancy rather than furnishing them with an easy answer. We're not romanticizing mistakes; we all like to be right, and feeling like you're wrong all the time is discouraging. But skilled teachers hunt for the partial understandings that lead students down an incorrect path. Keep in mind that an erroneous answer has its own logic. When these errors occur, take the time to find out how that occurred by unearthing the logic behind it. Figure 5.8 includes the conversational moves of a skilled math teacher.

Small Group Collaboration and Discussion Strategies

Discourse can bloom out of observed small group collaborative learning. When students use tools in different ways to approach a task, small group discussion is the perfect time for students to notice and relate one another's techniques. As they compare various approaches to the same problem, they may notice an underlying structure that is useful.

Remember Brian Stone, the high school math teacher from Chapter 2 who so effectively collaborates with students on his success criteria? He is always on the lookout for connections to the practice standards, and he regularly has students construct viable arguments and critique one another's reasoning. The small groups in Mr. Stone's math class were considering which of three representations they thought would

CONVERSATIONAL MOVES OF A SKILLED MATHEMATICS TEACHER

Purpose	Conversational Move
Require explanations by following up with questions and prompts that ask for elaboration and justification.	Convince me why you believe your thinking is correct.
Probe student thinking for disagreement or contradiction to draw students into the discussion.	Do you agree with _____? Why or why not? Can you find an example when _____ doesn't work?
See errors as opportunities.	You made a really interesting mistake here. Can you tell us what you were thinking as you did this?
Hunt for partial understandings that lead students down an incorrect path.	Let's go back and see what you did so far. Show me each of your steps to this point.
Unearth the logic behind erroneous answers to help correct the logic.	Talk to me more about the reason you did _____. Will this always work? What about if you were to _____ (providing an example of when it doesn't work)?

Figure 5.8

be most useful in a lab report on radioactive dating: parts per million, percentage, or fraction.

> "These are all representations you could use in a lab report if you're a scientist—it's up to you to decide which is best for this situation. Most importantly, be sure to justify your reasoning and say why your choice is the best. You have ninety seconds to decide with your group."

As he circulated around the room to eavesdrop on group discussion, Mr. Stone heard one group having a particularly thoughtful and passionate debate, so he brought the class back together to listen in.

> "All right, I need everyone's attention. I need everyone except for Mohamed and Musab to quiet down, and I would like Mohamed and Musab to continue with their debate, but just turn up the volume. Let's all listen to their arguments."

Mohamed continued arguing that parts per million made more sense because the numbers wouldn't take up so much room on the page, and would be easier to write, while Musab made the case that everyone was used to working with percentages. After about a minute, Mr. Stone interjected, "Now I want to pause this discussion so we can hear from Addison. Addison, you were saying you wanted to use fractions for a representation. Why did you say you wanted to use fractions?" The two-way debate turned into a three-way debate, until a fourth student stepped in and made the case for scientific notation. Notice how the classroom discourse started in small groups, and how Mr. Stone attended to the talk that was happening in those small groups and then used that talk to ignite a whole class discussion.

Learning can be a social endeavor. Humans learn better when they interact with other humans. In addition, students learn a lot more language when they are required to produce language. Mathematics is a language, foreign to some and familiar to others. One of the best ways to apprentice students into the language of mathematics, which then facilitates their mathematical thinking and reasoning, is to have them collaborate with their peers in solving complex, rich tasks.

EFFECT SIZE FOR COOPERATIVE VERSUS INDIVIDUALISTIC LEARNING = 0.59

When Is Collaboration Appropriate?

Our recommendation, based on personal experiences and reviews of evidence, is that 50% of classroom time (averaged over a week) be devoted to student discourse and student interactions with their peers. To our thinking, effective collaborative and cooperative learning tasks must do the following:

EFFECT SIZE FOR CLASSROOM DISCUSSION = 0.82

- Be complex enough so that the students need to work together. Less complex tasks entice learners to divide and conquer the task. Also, the task should be complex enough for the number of students in the group. If there are too many students, someone might not participate.

- Allow for argumentation in which students agree and disagree with one another, negotiate understanding, make claims supported by reasons and evidence, and reach consensus or agree where they disagree.

- Include sufficient language support so that students know how to say what they want to say. That may mean teaching vocabulary, providing sentence frames, using teacher modeling, or mobilizing peer language brokers.

- Provide both individual and group accountability so that learning is visible for students and teachers. In addition, these types of accountability prevent one student from completing the task for the other members of the group.

When these conditions are met, students spur each other's thinking. In order for them to do so, they need to be taught how to collaborate and how they will be held accountable for their own learning as well as that of the group.

Grouping Students Strategically

We all made the mistake early in our teaching careers of letting students choose their own groups, and then got upset when students didn't focus on, or complete, the task. We came to realize that socializing when in the company of friends was inevitable and developmentally appropriate, and that most of our students did not have the self-regulation skills to focus on academic work while face-to-face with their afterschool buddies. Importantly, in time, each of us came to the further realization that we needed to actually teach those self-regulation skills as carefully as we taught the subject content.

EFFECT SIZE FOR CONCENTRATION/ PERSISTENCE/ ENGAGEMENT = 0.48

EFFECT SIZE FOR ABILITY GROUPING = 0.12

Another error we made in our grouping practices was in grouping by math ability. Researchers are in conflict about whether or not grouping students by their perceived ability is appropriate in a math class. Some researchers have found a small but positive effect on student math outcomes in the short term, probably due to teachers having an easier time differentiating instruction (Gentry & Owen, 1999; Kulik & Kulik, 1992). But a larger number of researchers have found that grouping students by their abilities within a class hurts student motivation and makes them dislike math (Boaler, 1997; Zevenbergen, 2005). Whether or not your students like math is important, because long-term learning of mathematics is dramatically related to how many math courses people take in their lives, and only slightly related to how well they do in the courses they take (Bahrick & Hall, 1991; Ellis, Semb, & Cole, 1998). It might seem a bit counterintuitive, but fixed ability grouping does not help students to understand the math they're learning. John's analysis of 129 studies on in-class ability grouping found a small effect size of 0.12, leading him to describe this practice as "a disaster."

As you would expect, this is a controversial and touchy topic. We recommend that when taking ability into account, you make sure that these groupings are flexible and balanced, and allow for a moderate but not extreme range of skill levels. Sitting the students who need more time and repetition together, or the ones who are already ahead of the curriculum, should not be fixed, rigid, or permanent. Meeting with a small group of students for some needs-based, teacher-guided instruction is valuable and allows for more robust and responsive differentiation of instruction. But permanently tracking students contributes to a destructive and fixed mindset, enough to counteract any growth mindset activities such as number talks you may have planned. The minor convenience of having similarly achieving students seated at the same table is vastly outweighed by the destructive effects on students' mindsets. Most importantly, the students placed most at risk by the practice of permanently assigned ability groups within the classroom are those that can least afford it: students who struggle with math concepts, are learning English as a subsequent language, or have disabilities.

We have seen some of the most effective teachers make good use of flexible groupings that shift partnerships throughout the week to foster collaborative and cooperative learning. In Natalia Smith's fourth-grade class, students sometimes enter the room to find that the tables have been rearranged, and their name placard is somewhere different from where they usually sit. Ms. Smith tailors her table arrangements and groupings to her preassessments, learning intentions, and tasks of the day. She always plans these seating arrangements ahead of time using an alternate ranking system. Using an appropriate metric, such as the results of a diagnostic screening assessment, the last administered assessment, or her evaluation of each student's communication skills, the members of the class are rank ordered from most to least skilled. The list is then split in half, and the two students from the first half of the list are paired with the corresponding two students on the second half of the list. Therefore, in a class of twenty-four, students ranked first and second are paired with those ranked thirteenth and fourteenth.

THE ALTERNATE RANKING METHOD FOR GROUPING

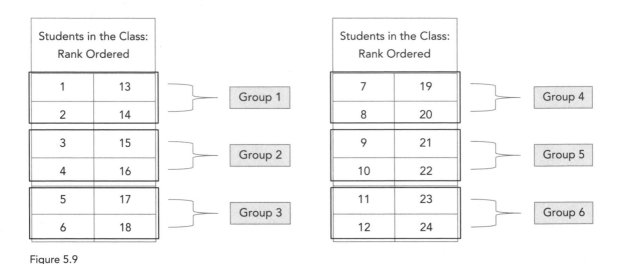

Figure 5.9

We call this method alternate ranking, and it ensures that there is a range of skills within each group, but not such a broad gap that they will just furnish the answers rather than truly work together. In other words, highly skilled students are paired with those possessing an average level of skills (see Figure 5.9). In turn, those with an average skill level are paired with those who are the least skilled. It doesn't work to pair the top two students in the class with the two at the bottom. Bennett and Cass (1989) studied the work accomplished in small groups, noting that when the balance of high-achieving students within a group outweighed the number of low-achieving students, those in the majority took control and performed the task without input from those who needed more time, explanation, or repetition. This phenomenon disappeared when the groups were balanced, and the skills the group possessed were moderately, but not extremely, different.

The most frequent group size is four students, but we have seen groups of three or five work well, too. Groups of six tend to be too big for all group members to contribute, and groups of two tend to lack the cognitive diversity necessary for interesting academic discourse. However, groups of two work for brief conversations, even if they are less effective for rich tasks that require deeper discussion and dialogue. Teachers sometimes have one or two students who will make the case that they should be allowed to just work alone. Often, this is because they have been in groups gone bad and ended up doing all of the work for the other members of the group. Fortunately, they have a caring adult in their lives (that's you) who understands that students not only learn math better in groups but also learn key collaborative and interpersonal skills that will be required of them in college and the workplace. And they have a teacher who knows how to include individual and group accountability into the tasks.

If you dig a little deeper into the experiences and skills of students who request to be excused from collaborative learning, you'll often find it's their interpersonal skills, not their mathematical ones, that are lacking. The prospect of having to manage all of those social relationships while performing cognitive tasks may be overwhelming for them. But these soft skills are vital for their success. So consider reducing the size of the group just a bit for that child. Perhaps he'll work in a group of three, while the other groups have four or five students. Over time, as social skills strengthen, you can increase the number of partners the student will be working with.

Above all, don't fall into the trap of considering the least common denominator when making decisions about collaborative work. Just because one or two students will be more challenged by collaboration doesn't mean that it should be eliminated from your classroom. You wouldn't do this with the curriculum: "There are two students who really struggle with fractions, so that means I won't teach fractions to anyone this year." Why would you do so with collaborative learning?

Video 5.3
Grouping Strategies
for Deep Learning

*http://resources.corwin.com/
VL-mathematics*

What Does Accountable Talk
Look and Sound Like in Small Groups?

Consider the following scenario. Seventh-grade students were working with ratios and proportions. Their teacher, Bianca Rayos, had selected a task from Illustrative Mathematics (www.illustrativemathematics.org/content-standards/7/RP/A/1/tasks/470).

The task begins . . .

> Travis was attempting to make muffins to take to a neighbor that had just moved in down the street. The recipe that he was working with required $\frac{3}{4}$ cup of sugar and $\frac{1}{8}$ cup of butter.
>
> Travis accidentally put a whole cup of butter in the mix.
>
> 1. What is the ratio of sugar to butter in the original recipe? What amount of sugar does Travis need to put into the mix to have the same ratio of sugar to butter that the original recipe calls for?
>
> 2. If Travis wants to keep the ratios the same as they are in the original recipe, how will the amounts of all the other ingredients for this new mixture compare with the amounts for a single batch of muffins?
>
> 3. The original recipe called for $\frac{3}{8}$ cups of blueberries. What is the ratio of blueberries to butter in the recipe? How many cups of blueberries are needed in the new, enlarged mixture?

Sakina starts with her group, saying, "I think we need to set up the ratio first. I think it's $\frac{3}{4}$ to $\frac{1}{8}$. Do you all agree?" Mrs. Rayos is observing the conversation and asks Angelina to restate what Sakina just said. "The original recipe was $\frac{3}{4}$ cup of sugar and $\frac{1}{8}$ cup of butter, so I wrote it as $\frac{3}{4} : \frac{1}{8}$."

Francisco speaks next, adding, "I think we have to get the denominators the same. If we write the fraction equivalent $\frac{3}{4}$ as $\frac{6}{8}$, then they're the same. I think that's the next step." Cassandra doesn't agree, so she restates Francisco's comment, adding her own: "I think you're saying that we need to make the denominators the same so we can add or subtract, but the problem is really about a ratio, so I think we need to get them to whole numbers."

Francisco responds, "I'm not sure how to get them to whole numbers. How do we do that?" Everyone in the group goes back to work thinking about Francisco's question. Cassandra says, "I think I know how to do it, but I'm not sure. Let me explain my thinking and let me know what you think. I think we have to multiply the sugar times eight. Eight times $\frac{3}{4}$ equals six. And we multiply the butter times eight, which is eight times $\frac{1}{8}$ or one. But I'm not sure that's right." Sakina adds, "I think you have it. You multiplied both of them by eight so we could work with whole numbers to get a ratio. Just like you wrote, the ratio of sugar to butter is 6:1."

Notice how students pressed each other for clarification and explanations, and asked each other for support. See how together they worked out any misconceptions and made sure that their final answer was understood by everyone in the group. In other words, through the conversation, they were holding themselves and each other accountable for deep learning. But these types of student conversations do not just happen on their own. Great teachers do a lot of behind-the-scenes work to make them happen.

Supports for Collaborative Learning

It would be unfair to hold students accountable for academic conversations without providing them the supports they need to be successful. One crucial support is to teach students how to work collaboratively during the first month of school. But savvy teachers know that they need to revisit teaching collaborative skills and routines throughout the year. It's certainly worth reviewing expectations for collaborative work, but sometimes a teacher will need to completely reteach these expectations as well. A return from a weeklong break from school can be the perfect time to refresh everyone on how things are done in your classroom.

Contribution Checklists

One support you can offer is a readily available checklist of ways that students can contribute. These lists can include student behaviors like asking questions, checking others' work, keeping the team on task, encouraging others respectfully, making sure the answer makes sense, making sure everyone can explain the reasoning, and drawing connections to things they've already learned. These lists can also include more task-specific roles, like "checking the units." The behaviors can be listed on a poster, projected onto a screen, taped to their tables, or inserted into table tents, which are inexpensive pieces of plastic that hold paper in a vertical position on a table so that it is in students' lines of sight. A sample checklist is included in Figure 5.10.

CONTRIBUTION CHECKLIST

Have you considered . . .

- ❑ asking questions of others to support their thinking?
- ❑ checking your own and others' work for accuracy?
- ❑ keeping the team on task?
- ❑ encouraging others respectfully by providing positive comments?
- ❑ making sure the answer makes sense and, if not, figuring out why?
- ❑ making sure everyone can explain the reasoning for the answer?
- ❑ drawing connections between this problem and other types of problems or tasks?
- ❑ sketching a visual representation of the task you're trying to solve?
- ❑ looking for another way to solve the task?
- ❑ suggesting tools that might help your teammates approach the task?
- ❑ drawing connections between the task and your real-world experience?

Available for download at **http://resources.corwin.com/VL-mathematics**

Figure 5.10

Allow Students to Move

Study after study encourages regular physical movement in the classroom (Jensen, 2005; Parks, Solmon, & Lee, 2007). Orlowski and her colleagues (Orlowski, Lorson, Lyon, & Minoughan, 2013) summed up the research well:

> Classroom-based physical activity is an instructional tool teachers can use to boost mood, energy level, and student learning. . . . Evaluations of active environments have demonstrated positive changes in student classroom behavior, word recognition and reading fluency, math scores, time on task, and concentration levels. (p. 48)

Depending on your school culture, the grade level you teach, and your relationship with students, you will likely be able to just explain the benefits of movement and then have students join you for stretches or jumping jacks every twenty minutes or so as a break from sitting in their chairs. The benefits to their learning would be well worth the time invested in these routines. An added bonus is that group exercise can have a positive impact on your classroom culture.

EFFECT SIZE
FOR CLASSROOM
COHESION = 0.53

Peer Support

You can get students to move around the room to interact with different peers or ideas. If you have already numbered the students in their groups, you can have all the number ones stand in one corner of the room, twos in another, threes in a third, and fours in a fourth corner. Once your students are in their corners, they can engage in dialogue with their peers from other groups, comparing and contrasting their teams' different approaches to the math task at hand, asking each other for help, or engaging in some other type of meaningful dialogue.

EFFECT SIZE
FOR PEER
TUTORING = 0.55

Some teachers have students make appointment calendars before beginning a lesson. In this format—also known as clock partners—teachers take time before the lesson gets started for students to find three or four different partners around the room. At spaced intervals, students go and find, for example, their "one o'clock appointment," "two o'clock appointment," and so on. Students like the freedom to choose their partners (and it is easier to allow them to choose partners for short conversations than for longer tasks or projects), but we have also seen teachers just assign appointment calendars to students. You can also instruct your students to go and meet with a student at another table whom they haven't talked to yet that day, appointment or not.

Movement isn't just for students, and you probably wouldn't like sitting in a school chair for forty or eighty minutes at a time either. As we are researching and writing this book, all of us authors are periodically getting up out of our seats and stretching, going for brief walks around the house, or doing some other form of light exercise. We encourage you to do the same if you will be writing, grading, or constructing lesson plans for long periods of time. Our experience lines up perfectly with the research: we feel more energized, sharper, and happier when we treat our minds to these movement breaks. Ultimately, we get more work done.

EFFECT SIZE
FOR TACTILE
STIMULATION
PROGRAMS = 0.58

Supports for Individual Accountability

Some teachers are resistant to assigning a lot of collaborative work because they were scarred by their own experience with poorly designed group work when they were in school. They remember doing all the work, while their classmates coasted by without doing much at all. (We call them worker bees and hitchhikers.) That wasn't fair, and teachers don't want their students to have the same experience. What was missing from so many of these group tasks was individual accountability. It's important to find ways to ensure that students are individually accountable for deep learning and doing their best to contribute to a group's math work.

Importantly, not all tasks require individual accountability. Sometimes, a quick collaborative conversation is all that is required. When this is the case, teachers can use a think-pair-square to encourage conversations. Rather than having some students share out to the whole class after their partner conversation, we prefer to have partnerships join forces (squaring up) to continue their conversation.

Think-Pair-Square

For example, in Hector Espinoza's second-grade class, students were focused on the following problem:

> Annaleah measured a piece of string for a game she was playing in her backyard. She thought that it was too long, so she cut off 42 inches. Then her string was 44 inches. How many inches was Annaleah's string before she cut it?

The students in Mr. Espinoza's class were used to think-pair-square and started talking about the problem with their partners. In one group, Paul said, "Why did she cut it? Now it's just two inches." His partner Jessie responded, "Why do you think it's two inches? Show me the way you got that." Paul picked up his dry-erase pen and wrote 44 – 42, saying, "You take away forty-two because she cut that off. So forty-four minus forty-two is two. See?"

Jessie, looking confused, said, "But that's too little to use. That doesn't make sense. Let's read it again." They read the problem together. Jessie says, "It says *then*, so it was after that it was forty-four. So it was bigger before, right?" Paul, studying the words, says, "Maybe if we draw a picture of what is going on, it will help." Jessie responds, saying, "First it says she had a long string. So let's start with a long line for the string." Paul adds, "Then the problem says she cut off forty-two inches. So let's put that we cut off forty-two inches."

Their picture looked like the following:

————————	————————————————————
? inches	42 inches

Paul notices and comments, "But it says she had forty-four inches left, and the amount we cut off is more than what's left. Forty-four is more than forty-two so it should be longer." Jessie excitedly says, "Wait! I think I got it. Since what is left is forty-four inches, our picture should look like this."

————————————————————	————————————————
44 inches	42 inches

"That's it! Now all we have to do is add forty-four and forty-two to find out how long it was before she cut it," adds Paul.

As they finish their conversation, Mr. Espinoza invites each partnership to meet with another partnership, saying, "Let's square up, but please don't start with telling the other team your answer. Please tell them *how* you went about solving the problem. We'll get to the answer in a bit." Jessie and Paul joined Arturo and Brian, engaging in a conversation about their respective problem solving. In collaborative tasks like these, students see the value in their voice and in listening to the voices of others.

Writing Rules

When individual accountability is warranted, the first (and possibly easiest) layer of accountability you can offer students is to ensure that if anyone writes, everyone writes. While having everyone in a group record the group's thinking won't guarantee they all learn, it does increase the likelihood of positive outcomes. One technique we use is collaborative posters during which time we assign each student a different colored marker. At a glance, you can see who contributed ideas, to what extent, and whether they need more guidance. Students are likely to be thinking about what they're writing and to critique or accept one another's reasoning as they're writing it down, and are less likely to tune out if they have to produce something. Something about writing helps to focus the mind.

CONVERSATION ROUNDTABLE

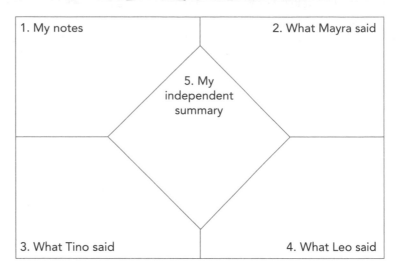

1. My notes	2. What Mayra said
5. My independent summary	
3. What Tino said	4. What Leo said

Figure 5.11

Rich problems often include performance-based tasks. These tasks involve more than just solving an equation to reach an answer. Students must go through several steps and often use multiple strategies such as making a model and finding a pattern, or making a table and generalizing. In these situations, writing helps students not only to make sense of a given situation, but also to think about how to show their work and explain how they reached the solution. Writing increases opportunities for students to think about their thinking (metacognition), which contributes to the phase of deep learning.

Conversation Roundtable

Another method we rely on is conversation roundtable. Students fold a sheet of paper into four quadrants, and then fold down the inner corner of the folded paper to form a rhombus. They unfold the paper and outline each section on the folds. The top left quadrant is reserved for their thinking, while the other three quadrants are reserved for recording the contributions of each group member. The rhombus in the middle is reserved for their own thinking at the end of the task. Each member hands in his or her own conversation roundtable, making all students individually accountable for the task. A sample can be found in Figure 5.11.

Individual Exploration

We have also seen teachers get better results by giving their students time to wrestle with a task individually before engaging with their teammates. In these cases, the teacher can structure students' think time so that they can answer four questions for themselves:

1. What is the question asking?
2. What useful information is given?
3. What other information would be helpful?
4. What might an answer look like?

Whether or not students are able to answer all four questions, the time spent reflecting on these questions increases the likelihood that they'll be able to bring something to the table when they join their teammates. Students may respond to the questions in writing or by creating models, charts, or diagrams. This access to multiple representations gives more ready access to each learner and encourages later conversation about how various representations relate to one another. This individual exploration time sets the stage for individual accountability by ensuring each group member has ideas to share.

Whole Class Collaboration and Discourse Strategies

Too often, whole group classroom discussion quickly slides back into a lecture, with the teacher occasionally posing a question and allowing a few students to respond before once again returning to his or her monologue.

When Is Whole Class Discourse Appropriate?

Discourse is not about brief interjections of students' voices. It should be designed to promote and extend mathematical thinking. Your guiding questions, prompts, and cues can either foster this or shut it down.

EFFECT SIZE
FOR
QUESTIONING
= 0.48

Remember the difference between a funneling question and a focusing question? You will want to stick with focusing questions for your class discussions, just like you do with small groups. You want your students to own the cognitive work, to figure things out as they reason with one another. In particular, you want students to ask questions about their work that they do not know the answer to. Sadly, students are rarely invited to ask these types of questions. John notes that the mode is about two questions per class per day, and that driving up the number of these questions underlies one of the most effective practices we know.

One of the differences between guided instruction with a small group and with the whole class is that discourse in a whole class should have students assume as much of the question *posing* as they can. This is the nature of true discourse; student learning becomes visible to them as they witness their own thinking and that of their peers. Students need encouragement from the teacher to question one another's thinking, to ask others how they arrived at a solution or why they chose one representation over another. You're looking for those times when the conversation soars, and you can step back for a few minutes as students engage with one another and carry the conversation themselves. The teacher can step to the side, waiting for students to clarify each other's thinking and question each other's thinking. Through these types of interactions, students come to see themselves as shaping the thinking of their peers, and learn to accept the same support from others (Hufferd-Ackles, Fuson, & Gamoran Sherin, 2004). But in order to do so, students need to be carefully taught. The following actions and guidelines will help build productive classroom discussions.

What Does Accountable Talk Look and Sound Like in Whole Class Discourse?

As with the example of Mrs. Rayos's class earlier in the chapter, accountable talk during whole class discussion should focus on having students ask questions of one another and press for clarification and explanations from each other. The teacher's role is to initiate the discussion with an engaging task or prompt. This might be a question or an invitation for one group to share a discussion with the entire class, allowing everyone to listen and join in the conversation. Students should be talking with one another while the teacher serves as a guide. As in small group work, student discourse should dominate whole class discussions; the teacher is just a facilitator.

> One of the differences between guided instruction with a small group and with the whole class is that discourse in a whole class should have students assume as much of the question *posing* as they can.

Supports for Whole Class Discourse

Have you attended a meeting in a room that wasn't suited for the conversation? Perhaps you couldn't see the speaker because of a pillar in a large meeting hall or were trying to talk with someone seated behind you on an airplane. The physical space where we work impacts the quality of the work we do. For whole class discourse to occur, the teacher must set the stage by creating an environment that supports the work.

Physical Layout

The physical layout of a classroom can foster or inhibit discussion across the entire group. Some teachers have desks attached to chairs; others have tables. Sometimes the furniture is in fixed locations, and other times it can be moved around. We can't change the reality of the furniture, and really, the type of furniture a teacher has should not limit students' interactions. Think creatively about ways to use the classroom environment, irrespective of the type of furniture provided.

Inside-Outside Circles

Inside-outside circles promote listening, because only a subset of students is engaged in active discussion while the rest of the group is observing the conversation. The easiest way to accomplish this is to have students arrange their chairs (or stand) in two concentric circles, with approximately half of the class in the inner talking circle and the other half of the class observing. Make sure the outer group has a task, such as cataloging when a particular mathematical concept is being utilized. After facilitating the discussion with the inner circle for five to ten minutes, ask the members of the outer circle to share their observations. This is an effective way to address worked examples, especially those that are incorrect.

Strategy Selection

Develop and deepen argumentation and reasoning by starting a discussion with a problem to be solved; then ask students to gather in areas of the classroom based on their chosen strategy for solving it. After allowing time for similarly minded students to discuss their approach, invite the groups into a larger discussion about the merits of each.

Jazmine Green uses this technique when posing questions about math concepts that her fifth-grade students are still learning, but have not completely mastered. "Multiplying fractions is a really tough concept because they have a hard time getting their heads wrapped around the fact that it's going to yield a smaller number, not a bigger one," she said. "Unfortunately, many students have been taught that multiplying makes everything bigger." She posed the following word problem.

There is $\frac{3}{4}$ of a pan of brownies sitting on the counter. You decided to eat $\frac{1}{3}$ of the brownies in the pan. What part of the whole pan of brownies did you eat?

Then she invited students to make a prediction about the answer given three possibilities: $1\frac{1}{12}$, $\frac{3}{12}$, and $\frac{5}{12}$. "No pencils and paper. I don't want you calculating. Just look at the three possible solutions; then stand near the sign on the wall that has your best choice. When you get there, talk with the other people who chose that answer about why you think that answer is correct." Ms. Green gave them three minutes of discussion time, and then brought their attention back as a whole group. "Now let's talk about this. Let's hear the reasoning for each possible answer, and I want you to listen to these opinions. If you change your mind, you can vote with your feet and join a new group." The teacher used accountable talk conversational moves to facilitate thinking, posing focusing questions and prompting justifications. Most of the students went to the corner with $1\frac{1}{12}$ as the product because they thought the product should be bigger than the factors. However, as they dove into the problem, they realized that if they ate $\frac{1}{3}$ of $\frac{3}{4}$, it just didn't make sense that they ate more than a whole pan of brownies when there was only $\frac{3}{4}$ of the pan to begin with. Now, they were working to make sense of the situation! As students were swayed by different arguments, they crossed the room to join a new group. As a student moved, Ms. Green asked him or her to state why he or she was changing the answer. Within several minutes, the entire class had arrived at the correct answer and, more importantly, a rationale for why multiplying fractions yields a smaller number. "I've taught this concept for many years, but many of them never really get it. Hearing the thinking of their classmates makes a world of difference. They get to consider errors and listen to faulty and accurate reasoning. The concepts behind this seem to stick so much better because students really made sense of the situation rather than trying to work with the numbers."

IMPORTANT CONNECTIONS AMONG MATHEMATICAL REPRESENTATIONS

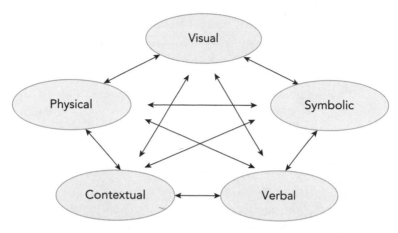

Source: National Council of Teachers of Mathematics (2014, p. 25).

Figure 5.12

Using Multiple Representations to Promote Deep Learning

Deep learning is about making connections. In mathematics, one of the powerful forms of connection is noticing how different representations are related or similar. Students demonstrate stronger problem-solving abilities and deeper mathematical understanding when they have experience representing mathematics in a variety of ways and showing the connections they see across those representations (Fuson, Kalchman, & Bransford, 2005; Lesh, Post, & Behr, 1987). Depth of understanding in mathematics, the connections that are central to deep learning, comes from the process of students internalizing various representations and connections among them (Pape & Tchoshanov, 2001; Webb, Boswinkel, & Dekker, 2008). Five types of mathematical representations are shown in Figure 5.12.

Physical representations are tangible objects, both formal manipulatives and objects from everyday life, used to represent mathematics. Visual representations are pictures and sketches, sometimes based on a physical representation. Symbolic representations, such as numerals and operation signs, are the abstract form of mathematics that we see and use most often as adults. For students, these symbols often appear as "squiggles on the page" until they are able to connect the symbols to representations that have more meaning. Deep learning is further enriched by the addition of contextual and verbal representations. Contextual representations situate the mathematics in a realistic scenario so students can see how the mathematics describes what is happening in the situation. Verbal representations are the language we use to talk about a physical model, describe a visual sketch, or speak to symbolic notation. For example, if a young learner is thinking about the number sentence 5 − 3 = 2, a contextual representation might be a simple story.

> Lorenzo saw five tortoises in the field. After three walked into the woods, two were left in the field.

The verbal representation might be "five subtract three is the same as two" or "three less than five is equal to two."

Strategic Use of Manipulatives for Deep Learning

The use of manipulatives can be as instructive at the deep phase of learning as it is at the surface phase. Employing these physical tools shouldn't be limited to building the initial understanding of a concept, but teachers and students can and should use them to make concepts concrete and visible, look for patterns, make connections, and form generalizations. They can likewise be used when constructing viable arguments and critiquing others' reasoning. To extend that thought, much research suggests that the instructional sequence of moving from physical representations *through* visual representations *to* symbolic representations leads to significant gains in mathematics learning and understanding, particularly for students struggling in mathematics (Gersten et al., 2009). As with surface learning, the deep learning phase benefits from having physical, verbal, and contextual representations incorporated as students engage in discourse about their thinking and make sense of the mathematics they see. In the deep phase of learning, teachers should select mathematical tasks and tools that allow students to see the progression from physical representations (e.g., building a model with base ten blocks to represent the notion that 8 times 14 is the same as 112) to visual representations of the same problem (e.g., drawing an area model), to the symbolic representation of the partial products (e.g., the algorithm $8 \times 14 = 112$). This multiplication task might have arisen from an exploration of area, and the teacher and students will employ the language of multiplication and place value throughout their discussion.

Conclusion

In this chapter, we have focused on developing deep learning through rich tasks and accountable talk. This phase of learning particularly helps students to leverage their surface learning to more deeply see patterns, look for and express regularity in repeated reasoning, make generalizations, and engage in discourse to help them construct viable arguments and critique the reasoning of others. Responsibility for accountable talk is shared by teachers and students. Meaningful mathematical discourse happens when students work on engaging tasks in thoughtfully selected small groups, so they can push each other to be accountable for deep learning about the mathematics at hand. Whole class discourse provides opportunities for students to share and debate both misconceptions and solution strategies. In this chapter, we shared a variety of strategies that promote student-to-student interaction in small groups and in whole class discussion. In the next chapter, we will discuss transfer learning, the application of surface and deep learning to new situations.

Reflection and Discussion Questions

1. Recall that discourse reaches beyond discussion to include ways of representing, thinking, talking, agreeing, and disagreeing; the way ideas are exchanged. Consider the mathematical discourse in your classroom. What opportunities do students have to share, explain, and justify their thinking? What questioning strategies could you use to provide additional opportunities for students to show their deep learning through explanation and justification?

2. Consider the grouping practices in your classroom. What strategies do you use to form mixed-ability groups and to ensure both group and individual accountability? What new ideas from this chapter could you use to ensure more rich and rigorous collaborative work in your mathematics classroom?

3. How do you use manipulatives in your mathematics instruction? Are students encouraged to use multiple representations as they work on mathematics collaboratively? Mathematical practice 5 calls for students using appropriate tools strategically. How do you allow students to make decisions about the tools they use in their work? What strategies can you use to make these tools more available to your students?

MAKING MATHEMATICS LEARNING VISIBLE THROUGH TRANSFER LEARNING

6

M ost of us have rented a car at one time or another. Rarely is the one we rent the same make and model as the one we drive at home. Yet after a few minutes of orienting ourselves to operating the mirrors, adjusting the seat, and figuring out how to turn the headlights and windshield wipers on, we pull out of the parking lot and set forth. How are we able to operate a complicated piece of machinery in an unfamiliar location? Because we were able to transfer what we know about cars and driving to a new situation. Sousa (2011) uses this as an example of transfer of learning in action. The driving example works for you because you engaged in a bit of transfer as you read this.

There are several reasons why this example works, and they have everything to do with methods for promoting transfer of learning. The first reason this works for you is because it is a situation nearly every adult has experienced, and it is therefore immediately relatable. Even if you have not rented a car, you are probably able to relate this to borrowing a friend's car. As we mentioned earlier, close association between a previously learned task and a new situation is necessary for promoting transfer of learning. A second reason this works is because there is an analogy at play here, in this case comparing driving a car to complex learning. But this falls apart if we use this example with someone who has never operated a car. A limiting factor in fostering transfer is in pairing the experience with the knowledge base of the learner. In the case of a non-driver, we would need to find a different example. That brings us to the third reason: knowing the learner developmentally and experientially is essential when promoting transfer of learning.

> A close association between a previously learned task and a new situation is necessary for promoting transfer of learning.

But there's one more factor, and perhaps the most critical one: we have the skills to detect the similarities and differences from one situation to another. In our car analogy, we know the key differences up front are the mirrors, seats, and headlights, and we know the key similarities are the brakes and accelerator. Having the skills to detect similarities and differences is key to transfer—without this, we may transfer the wrong ideas from our old car. Whoops, an accident waiting to happen!

In mathematics, much of transfer learning is the movement from learning the mathematics itself to learning to use the mathematics to describe information and situations in other disciplines and solve problems within those contexts. Algebra students learn about a variety of functions, including linear or exponential functions. Students can then transfer this learning about functions to describe and model situations that occur in science. How fast is this population of bacteria growing? How does the velocity of the ball change as it falls from the roof of a building? In Chapter 5, we shared an example of using slope to recognize that a variety of cell phone plans all have the same fee rate for the data usage portion of the plan. In that task, the context the teacher created gave the students a framework for thinking about creating a model. In chemistry class, studying the relationship between the pressure and volume of a gas in a balloon, students may have to create the tables and make the connections more independently.

The Nature of Transfer Learning

All of the work we do as teachers is for naught if students fail to transfer their learning appropriately by applying what they have learned in new situations. Generally speaking, John (Hattie, 2009) explains that transfer learning is about the ways in which students construct knowledge and reality for themselves as a consequence of surface and deep knowing and understanding. The distinctions are not clear-cut, as at all three levels we often learn in a haphazard manner. He argues that so much teaching is aimed at surface learning in the broader world of ideas and knowledge, and there is also much discussion about the importance of deep knowledge and thinking skills. But the task of teaching and learning best comes together when we attend to all three levels: ideas, thinking, and constructing.

Video 6.1
Teaching for
Transfer Learning

*http://resources.corwin.com/
VL-mathematics*

One concern is that mathematics instruction too often stops at the surface level of learning, and students (particularly struggling students) either fail to go deep and transfer, or they transfer *without* detecting similarities and differences between phenomena. When this happens, the transfer does not make sense, and too often students see this as evidence that they can't do mathematics.

As we mentioned in Chapter 1, in mathematics, **transfer** is both a goal of learning and also a mechanism for propelling learning to the next level. Transfer as a goal means that teachers want students to begin to take the reins of their own learning, think metacognitively, and apply what they know to a variety of real-world contexts. It also prepares them to move through the progression of mathematical understanding as ideas build on each other across grade levels. It's when students reach into their toolbox and decide what tools to employ to solve new and complex problems on their own. When students reach this phase, learning has been accomplished.

Transfer is the phase of learning in which students take the reins of their own learning and are able to apply their thinking to new contexts and situations.

Linda was a straight-A mathematics student in elementary and middle school. She understood the hows and the whys of mathematical computation. She could even (and still can) explain why the "invert and multiply" rule for division of fractions works. She understood the mechanics, surface learning (how) mixed with a little deep learning (why). Yet given a page of applications in which fractions were used in a variety of multiplication and division situations, she had no clue which operation to use. She had surface learning, and she had some deep learning to go along with it, but not being able to apply that knowledge in real-world contexts left her short of transfer learning. And quite frankly, knowing the how and the why without being able to apply that knowledge leads kids to ask a valid question: "When are we ever going to use this?"

We believe the true purpose of getting an education is to apprentice students into becoming their own teachers. We want them to be self-directed, lifelong learners, and to have curiosity about the world. We want them to have the tools they need to formulate their own questions, pursue meaningful answers, and, through metacognition, be aware of their own learning in the process. In other words, as their own learning becomes visible to them, we want the entire process to become the catalyst for ongoing learning, whether the teacher is present or not. However, we cannot leave these things to chance. Therefore, we must teach with intention, making sure that students acquire and consolidate the needed skills, processes, and metacognitive awareness that make self-directed learning possible. Recall John's definition of learning from Chapter 1:

> The process of developing sufficient surface knowledge
> to then move to deeper understanding such that one
> can appropriately transfer this learning to new tasks and
> situations.

In mathematics, this phase of transfer learning happens when students can *make connections among* mathematical understandings and then *use those understandings to solve problems* in unfamiliar situations, at the same time being intentionally aware of what they are doing. This often comes in the form of students asking themselves clarifying questions, and they can do this because in the deep learning phase, they had teachers who modeled how to ask those questions.

Chemistry students studying pressure and volume must deliberately think about what information to use in a data chart and what mathematical tools to use (equations? tables? graphs?) to identify the type of relationship (linear? exponential?) between the variables of pressure and volume. Students planting the school garden have to apply their knowledge of volume and some standard measures to determine how much mulch to buy to cover the garden plot. Using examples that relate to real-life situations not only provides students with opportunities to develop transfer learning; it also helps them to see the usefulness of mathematics.

In the next sections of this chapter, we will turn our attention to transfer mechanisms that help students go through this process. When we have a clear understanding of how transfer occurs, we can better establish the conditions for ensuring that students meet transfer goals.

Types of Transfer: Near and Far

Because learning is cyclical, not linear, transfer is actually happening all the time, not just at the end of a lesson or unit. In fact, the goal of *all* learning is eventual transfer (Bransford et al., 2000). By this we mean that the goals of instruction are not to leave students at the surface or even deep levels, but rather to ensure that they can take what they have learned and use it in the next unit, not to mention the next year and beyond. To help accomplish these goals, it helps to understand that transfer actually happens across two dimensions: near transfer and far transfer (Perkins & Salomon, 1992).

Near transfer occurs when the new situation is paired closely with a context students have experienced. For example, helping students become fluent with basic facts is one of the biggest challenges elementary teachers face. We know from experience that simply asking students to memorize their "times 8s" isn't very effective. If we begin by providing students with situational contexts for multiplication, it provides them with the opportunity to make sense out of what multiplication means and to use different representations to work toward understanding each situation.

Let's go back and visit Kate Franklin's class from Chapter 4. Students used the *In the Doghouse* activity to understand physical models of equal groups. They recognized how to write that using symbolic notation, and they talked about their understanding. Students needed ample time to become comfortable with the equal-groups model. But it didn't stop there. A few weeks later, Ms. Franklin continued to develop the concept of multiplication using situations that call for array models. Students connected that physical representation to real-life situations such as egg cartons (a 2 × 6 array) or cupcake tins (a 3 × 4 array). Again, surface learning and deep learning were closely aligned throughout all of these lessons.

Later in the year, as students began to explore area measurement, students could transfer understanding by extending their previous experiences to a new context. That is not all that was happening. Class and small group activities that supported deep understanding of multiplication went on throughout the year. Discourse, both in small groups and in the whole class, focused on looking for patterns that led students to recognize that changing the order of the factors in a multiplication example did not change the product. But they also learned that a 2 × 3 array would look different from a 3 × 2 array. Moving back and forth among surface, deep, and transfer learning helped students to become more fluent with multiplication facts as opposed to students who were told to simply memorize their multiplication tables.

The size of the leap is larger in *far transfer,* as the learner is able to make connections between more seemingly remote situations. For example, as Ms. Franklin began the study of division with her students, planning lessons that focused on connections between multiplication models and division models helped students move toward a deep understanding of division and recognize when a problem situation called for either multiplication or division. Fast forward to Grade 5 as students are beginning to multiply and divide fractions. Simply telling students to multiply numerators and multiply denominators provides no understanding of what it means to multiply fractions, not to mention why the product of two fractions is smaller than at least one of them. Perhaps an even better example is division of fractions. How many of us learned to flip one of the numbers and multiply, and how many of us quickly forgot or confused that rule because it made no sense? Worse yet, problems that called for one of those operations provided little context for understanding because all we had was a rule to depend on. Let's look at an example.

> A gasoline tank holds $16\frac{1}{2}$ gallons. If the pump delivers $3\frac{1}{4}$ gallons a minute, how long will it take to fill the tank, assuming it is empty at the start?

Many students would read this problem and ask themselves (or the teacher) what to do. However, those who have been taught the meaning of division and have the capacity for far transfer would be able to think about the situation and ask themselves how many $3\frac{1}{4}$ gallons fit into $16\frac{1}{2}$ gallons, and they would recognize this as a division problem. This is the same question they asked themselves with whole number division! Others might think $3\frac{1}{4}$ gallons times how many minutes would fill up a $16\frac{1}{2}$ gallon tank. This would be a missing factor problem, which still calls for division. This is an example of transferring understanding of whole number division to a new situation—fractions. Simply teaching students to invert and multiply develops no conceptual understanding and often leads to many misconceptions. Early experiences with division of whole numbers that included surface and deep learning at the third-grade level provides students far transfer opportunities as they later apply those understandings to fractional number situations.

Although this provides us powerful opportunities in mathematics instruction, it also calls for careful thinking about how mathematical ideas connect to each other as lessons are planned and concepts unfold.

The Paths for Transfer: Low-Road Hugging and High-Road Bridging

So far we have discussed transfer across a continuum from near to far. Now let's introduce mechanisms, or paths, for transfer: low-road and high-road transfer (Perkins & Salomon, 1992). In this case, the contrastive element is the extent to which the thinking involved is under the learner's conscious direction. In the left column, the teacher provides structure to support students in transfer. In the right column, the students are using their own strategies and learning to lead the work of transfer. Figure 6.1 summarizes each of these mechanisms.

Let's go back to the multiplication fact example. Developing fluency with facts helps to build automaticity—that is, as students continue to use those facts in a variety of situations, they will reach the point where they no longer have to think about a strategy or what the fact means. They just know it. And because they have learned it by building on conceptual understanding, they not only know those facts; they know when to apply them.

Applications in the real world such as the gas tank problem require higher level thinking. Without deeper understanding of the structure of mathematics—in this case, division—students would not be able to

HUGGING AND BRIDGING METHODS FOR LOW-ROAD AND HIGH-ROAD TRANSFER

Hugging to Promote Low-Road Transfer	Bridging to Promote High-Road Transfer
Students are learning to apply skills and knowledge.	Students are learning to make links across concepts.
Students can apply what they know about volume to various rectangular solids.	*Students apply what they know about volume of rectangular solids to cylinders.*
Teacher is associating prior knowledge to new knowledge.	Student is using multiple representations to illustrate connections across disciplines or content.
The teacher reminds students they can use a tool or strategy they already know in this new situation.	*A student creates equations to model two different situations (e.g., radioactive decay and growth of bacteria populations) and realizes that both are the same type of function.*
Students are categorizing information.	Students are deriving rules and principles based on examples.
Students categorize quadrilaterals into subgroups to think about how to find the area of each type of quadrilateral.	*Students can decompose a trapezoid into smaller parts to determine its area.*
Teacher asks purposeful questions.	Students use metacognition to reflectively plan and organize.
The teacher asks students about various strategies they might use to solve a problem.	*On their own, students try various strategies to solve a problem and use what has worked and not worked in the past to help select effective strategies.*
Students are summarizing and rehearsing knowledge.	Students are creating new and original content.
Students solve a variety of problems applying a familiar concept and justify their thinking.	*Students write their own problems using a variety of personal contexts to apply their understanding in new situations.*
Teacher creates modeling and simulation opportunities for students to apply new knowledge to parallel situations.	Students are applying new knowledge to dissimilar situations.
Students make scale drawings of the classroom to share ideas on arranging classroom furniture.	*Students compare two pizza shop promotions using cost and size of the pizza to find which is the best deal.*

Figure 6.1

transfer learning to this new situation. Many students struggle with algebraic ideas because they have not developed the conceptual understanding of ideas such as the distributive property, and they do not have the deep learning to apply these ideas to new and more abstract situations.

It is important to recognize that transfer as a mechanism (1) occurs even among the youngest learners and (2) changes in appearance as the learner progresses developmentally. While our example is from the upper elementary grades, learners of all ages transfer their learning as they become more independent learners.

Selecting Mathematical Tasks That Promote Transfer Learning

When providing learners with opportunity and support for transfer, teachers should select tasks that encourage connections. As with deep learning tasks, these will be higher complexity tasks with higher difficulty. They may not have a clear entry point—in fact, they could have multiple entry points and multiple steps. They may have no one correct solution, but rather call for students to make some judgment about the best solution and be able to use evidence to justify their thinking. They could be tasks in which mathematical ideas are to be applied in another discipline; for example, the mathematics of algebra will be used to think about a geometry problem, or the mathematics of calculus will be applied to physics. Tasks that are meant for transfer learning may take more than one lesson to solve. Teachers must select tasks that provide opportunities for near transfer and far transfer. For some learners, near transfer might be a familiar problem in a new context.

Let's look at an example from high school. Mr. Assof gives his eleventh graders a three-part task on exponential and logarithmic functions to work on in small groups. In this task—designed to take several class periods—student groups are asked to be a team of financial advisers who must help clients decide how to spend, save, and invest their money. All three clients are seeking advice on their upcoming vehicle purchases and want to know if they should pay cash for a new car, or finance the car and invest their cash. Part 1 of the task focuses on discussions about how auto loans and investment accounts operate, and students work to

Video 6.2
Transferring Learning to Real-World Situations

http://resources.corwin.com/ VL-mathematics

determine how their clients qualify for different interest rates and what down payment requirements they will have based on their credit scores. Mr. Assof has assigned each of the three fictitious clients a different profile that includes the price of the car they want to buy, their credit score, the length of the loan they want, and whether they are members of a credit union. Students must calculate each client's car payment based on these factors, using a table they've been given that compares the interest rates banks and credit unions offer for different time spans at different tiers of credit scores.

Once students have determined how much each client will pay in a monthly car payment if he or she chooses to finance the purchase, they can move into Part 2. This is where they will determine if each client should pay cash for the car, or if the client should finance the car and invest the cash in a mutual fund called the Bond, James Total Return Bond. This fund offers between a 5.8 percent and 6.2 percent per-year return (compounded monthly) to those investing their money between three and five years, respectively. Here students need to use what they have previously learned about exponential and logarithmic functions to determine how much money each client would make if he or she invested in the mutual fund, and if this amount is more or less than the total amount paid for the financed vehicle purchase, and then make a recommendation about what the client should do. In all cases, they needed to use specific evidence from their calculations to justify their response.

Part 3 of this task asks students to generalize their thinking by answering two questions: (1) Given the statement *Car salespeople use the rule "Your payment will increase by $200 for every $10,000 you finance,"* determine if this is accurate and explain why or why not using specific examples, and (2) Do you agree or disagree with the statement *"It is always better to pay cash for a car instead of finance"*? Justify your position by giving specific mathematical examples.

This task is a great illustration of transfer in that it requires leverage of prior surface and deep learning about exponential and logarithmic functions; it is a high-complexity, high-difficulty task with real-world application that will be a scenario many students will face in the near future. It requires students to think about the strategies in their tool belt that they need to utilize to solve a problem that may have no right or wrong answer, but requires some judgment on their part. It also requires them to engage deeply with many of the mathematical practices.

Conditions Necessary for Transfer Learning

It should come as no surprise that relevancy is a major condition for transfer learning. Learning becomes more meaningful when learners see what they're learning as being meaningful in their own lives. Relevancy doesn't have to be at the world peace level, but it does need to have implications that are developmentally appropriate and are seen as being useful in their learning lives. Also, the learning intentions and success criteria that we discussed at length in Chapter 2 are just as important for promoting transfer as they are for fostering initial learning. Although students are engaged in more self-directed learning during this transfer period, they need goals and ways to measure their own progress.

One of the problems for many students is that they rush to apply their learning to a new situation. It is time well spent to require that they pause and consider the similarities and differences between the new and a recently completed problem. Considering the specifics of the problem in front of them, the nature of the question, and any additional details are all worth attention. Too many students, especially struggling students, jump into a new problem without thinking about how it is different from or similar to a previous problem.

EFFECT SIZE
FOR COMPARE
AND CONTRAST
NEW WITH
OLD PROBLEMS
= 1.23

A team of middle school teachers used an engineering design challenge to provide an opportunity for students to transfer their learning from math and science class to solving a real-world problem. These teachers had heard conversations among their students about the amount of food thrown away in the school cafeteria, so they opened the unit with a discussion of the problem and how students might help to solve it. By beginning with a challenge they knew was relevant to the students, the teachers were creating good conditions for transfer learning. The teachers' instructional intentions were to teach their students about using design thinking (Crismond & Adams, 2012) to solve a real-world problem that required application of their math and science learning. They established small groups of students to work as design teams across all classes and taught the students about working as a team to communicate effectively, establish goals, develop a timeline, and set deadlines. These team collaboration skills are essential for transfer learning and for much of real-world problem solving.

While the teachers did not teach the students *how* to solve this problem, they intentionally selected a problem that highlighted concepts students had been studying in math and science and building on their prior knowledge in developmentally appropriate ways. The teachers knew that the students had learned to collect, organize, and analyze data. They understood about food webs and decomposition and how living things depend on one another in an ecosystem. The students were able to measure and calculate using those measurements. Students were ready to transfer this learning to a problem in their own school, managing cafeteria waste.

As student teams began to work, they approached the problem in different ways. One team wanted to collect data from students in the school about how serious they thought the problem was and what ideas they had to solve it. Another team decided that building a compost bin was the way to go and set about collecting information about the volume of food waste collected each day and using that to figure out the dimensions of the compost bin. A third team decided to focus on encouraging the cafeteria to serve meals that more students were likely to finish so there would be less waste in the first place. While each team had a different approach, all of them had to use their collaboration and problem-solving knowledge, along with their math and science learning, to design a solution to a real problem in their school.

The students used problem solving and reasoning to propose and test possible solutions. The practical criteria and constraints on a workable solution (for example, limits of space and budget and the fast turnover of students moving through the cafeteria at lunchtime) provided immediate and relevant feedback on potential solutions. Teachers circulated among the groups, asking questions about their strategies and helping them find effective ways to manage their sometimes conflicting data. Seeing the mathematics and science in this context provided opportunities for re-teaching in a new way if they found students were missing requisite surface or deep knowledge.

The conditions created by these middle school teachers allowed for teams to think conceptually, especially to identify problems and propose solutions, testing their proposals, making adjustments, and thinking of alternatives, all dispositions identified by Bereiter (2002) as evidence of transfer of learning. The teachers found a relevant and appropriate problem that built on students' prior learning. They deliberately taught teamwork skills so students could use their reasoning skills in collaborative ways. The teachers and the problem provided feedback, and teachers were close at hand to reteach when necessary.

Metacognition Promotes Transfer Learning

Having students practice self-reflection on their level of understanding, as it relates to a target, has been shown to be a powerful strategy to increase both understanding and motivation (National Research Council, 2005). This is a form of self-talk that promotes transfer learning. **Metacognition** is the ability to think about our thinking, and it is vital to the learning process. It first appeared in the education literature in the 1970s (e.g., Flavell, 1979), and it has become more of a buzzword ever since. The hype is well deserved: metacognitive processes have been shown quite clearly to boost student achievement. Marzano (1998, p. 106) called metacognition the "engine" that drives thinking. Garofalo and Lester (1985) went so far as to suggest that mathematics instruction without metacognitive instruction is inadequate. Palincsar (2013) describes metacognitive awareness as consisting of three parts:

1. Knowledge about our learning selves

2. An understanding of what the task demands and necessary strategies to complete it

3. The means to monitor learning and self-regulate

In other words, it describes our ability to observe and monitor our own thinking. But students need guidance in how to become more metacognitively aware. To develop their metacognitive skills, students need to learn the art of self-questioning.

Self-Questioning

As learners complete an assignment or work through a rich mathematical task, they will be most successful if they think about their thinking as they work. They may realize that they've reached a dead end with their strategy or that they are missing an important piece of information. These realizations come from a background series of questions we continually ask ourselves: "Does this make sense?" "Am I making progress finding a solution?" This **self-questioning** is a critical element of our metacognition as it allows us to track our understanding and catch ourselves when we realize we are off target.

How can you get students to think about their own thinking? Hastie (2011) found success by having teachers administer quick pre-lesson and post-lesson questions that encouraged metacognition. Not only did

Metacognition is the ability to think about our own thinking.

EFFECT SIZE FOR METACOGNITIVE STRATEGIES = **0.69**

EFFECT SIZE FOR SELF-VERBALIZATION AND SELF-QUESTIONING = **0.64**

Self-questioning is a metacognitive strategy that allows us to track our understanding and catch ourselves when we are off target.

PRE-LESSON QUESTIONS FOR SELF-VERBALIZATION AND SELF-QUESTIONING

- What are today's goals?
- How much do I already know about today's goals? ("Nothing" to "A great deal")
- I think today's goal will be . . . ("Very hard" to "Very easy")

At the end of a lesson, students would answer questions such as the following:

- What was today's goal?
- Did I achieve this goal? ("Not at all" to "Fully")
- How much effort did I put in? ("Not much" to "A great deal")

Then the students had a chance to think about why they may or may not have achieved their goals. They could tick off the reasons from options like the following:

- I wanted to learn about today's lesson.
- I wanted to achieve today's goal.
- I paid attention, etc.

Or . . .

- I gave up.
- It was too hard.
- I didn't understand what I was supposed to be doing, etc.

Figure 6.2

the students learn more math, they also showed higher levels of motivation and attention. Pre-lesson questions included those in Figure 6.2.

Hastie's results were quite impressive, though you may want to alter the checklist options based on your students and your lesson. Or you could have your students help generate the questions that will go on their checklists. Using a checklist is compelling because students can make check marks on a list pretty quickly, so you can bank more time for collaborative learning and rich class discussions.

There is also something about writing that clarifies students' understanding, though. It also makes them better writers. At the beginning of a lesson, middle school teacher Nate Hernandez uses prompts to have students write in their math journal.

- How much do I already know about today's learning intention? What makes me say that?

- How difficult do I think this lesson will be? Why do I think that?

- How do I rate my desire to be successful in this lesson? Why do I want to be successful?

- How much effort will I put into today's lesson?

- What strategies do I think will be helpful for me in meeting my learning objective today?

Mr. Hernandez decides which questions will be the most useful based on his ongoing evaluation of student cognition, metacognition, and attitudes toward learning. He also thinks about how much class time he wants to spend on this part of the lesson. At several points during Mr. Hernandez's lessons, he pauses from the mathematics instruction to have students rate their understanding of the learning intention again, and have them explain why they gave themselves their ratings. This leads to some interesting student writing, as they reflect, analyze, and clarify for themselves their levels of understanding. It also helps to keep Mr. Hernandez's kids focused on the learning objective as they note their progress.

Self-Reflection

Successful learners not only question themselves; they also think about the answers to those questions and change their strategies and routines based on what most leads them to success. **Self-reflection** is a follow-up technique once a lesson has occurred that helps students understand where they were and where they are now. This self-reflection allows learners to develop expertise and avoid making the same errors multiple times when solving similar problems. Once Mr. Hernandez's students are done with the majority of his lesson, he has them reflect on their experience. Figure 6.3 includes some of his go-to prompts for facilitating his students' reflections and metacognitive awareness.

> **Teaching Takeaway**
>
> Develop a checklist of questions that encourage metacognition and reinforce learning.

> **Self-reflection** helps students understand where they were and where they are now.

PROMPTS FOR FACILITATING STUDENTS' SELF-REFLECTION AND METACOGNITIVE AWARENESS

- How well do I think I understand _____ now?
- Why do I think that?
- How has my understanding increased as a result of today's lesson?
- What questions do I still have about the math I learned today?
- What do I still need to work on? How do I know?
- How do I rate my effort during today's lesson? Why?
- How do I rate my teamwork today? Why?
- Did I ask for help? Did I offer to help others? Did I encourage my teammates?
- How did I contribute to my group's efforts?
- If I could do _____ over again, what would I do differently? Why?
- What advice would I have for another student who was about to start this same lesson?

Figure 6.3

Mr. Hernandez does not count students' answers to these questions alone as evidence of mastery. Sometimes, he has students write these post-lesson reflections on the same paper as their exit tickets. This is interesting and useful for him, because when he collects the exit tickets he can gauge how accurately or thoughtfully students rate their own learning, effort, and social skills.

Mathematical Talk That Promotes Transfer Learning

The tasks discussed in this chapter that can be used for this ultimate level of transfer are fueled by the discourse that occurs because of rich class discussions. We've shared throughout this book the importance of intentional math talk, and nowhere is the language, thinking, and reasoning that happen when extended discussion happens more powerful than in the transfer of learning. Research and experience both point to the benefits of being able to speak coherently and thoughtfully during meetings and discussions, and in settings that are larger than four or five people. Furthermore, class discussions have been shown to help students learn content. These discussions provide students a chance to shine, to help each other, to hear ideas and make connections, and to make sense of mathematics. But not all class discussions are helpful. Some of them devolve into unrelated storytelling; random opinion sharing; or too commonly, as mentioned in Chapter 5, the teacher doing the majority of the talking.

EFFECT SIZE FOR CLASSROOM DISCUSSION = 0.82

Classroom discussion, especially for the purposes of transfer, should be so much more, and it is definitely not the time to play the "guess what's in the teacher's brain" game that researchers call I-R-E. Discourse is an essential part of the mathematics classroom, so much so that NCTM has featured it in its standards since 1991. Mathematics students are expected to be able to represent their thinking to others, pose questions, and engage in disagreements without being disagreeable. You're looking for mathematical discourse, not chatter about mathematics. But these practices can't be realized without significant changes in how discourse is fostered, taught, and supported. This doesn't mean that the teacher stands back and lets her students do all the talking. The teacher needs to be an active facilitator who uses questioning moves that elevate students' thinking, presses them for evidence, and requires them to link to concepts. These talk moves are an extension of the accountable talk techniques we discussed previously in this book.

Helping Students Connect Mathematical Understandings

During the transfer phase of learning, students take ownership of their work. Learners are in the driver's seat about what they want to learn and what tools they will use. This requires learners to have a sense of how the mathematics that they know is organized. The process of creating an organizational structure for their knowledge—in terms of both conceptual understandings and procedural skills—is a powerful tool.

EFFECT SIZE FOR ORGANIZING CONCEPTUAL KNOWLEDGE = 0.85

Peer Tutoring in Mathematics

A number of meta-analyses have been performed on the effects of peer tutoring programs on the achievement, self-concepts, and attitudes of tutors and tutees (e.g., Ginsburg-Block, Rohrbeck, & Fantuzzo, 2006). Peer tutoring programs work best when the following occur:

- The programs are structured.
- Tutors have received training.
- The tutor and tutee are of different ages.

EFFECT SIZE
FOR PEER
TUTORING = 0.55

Interestingly, under these conditions, the effect is as high on the person doing the tutoring as on the person being tutored. This is because the tutors must transfer their learning to the tutoring situation.

In order to help others understand mathematics more effectively, a peer tutor (indeed, any teacher) must be able to connect what we want the learner to master with what the learner already knows and understands. When students serve as peer tutors, they must understand how their own knowledge is organized well enough to create a path between what is already understood, or misunderstood, and the mathematics the person being tutored is learning.

The local high school has a tutoring club, where students who volunteer to be tutors are matched with students at nearby elementary and middle schools for tutoring. Ian is an Algebra II student and a math tutor; he is working with Maria, a seventh grader. Maria is having trouble mastering operations with integers, and Ian is working to help her. Guided by the teacher who leads the tutoring program, Ian has a set of six problems about adding and subtracting integers for Maria to solve at their first meeting. After introducing themselves, Ian asks Maria to solve the problems he brought so he can see how she thinks about adding and subtracting integers. As Maria works, she talks out loud about what she is doing. "7 – ⁻3 . . . I'm subtracting so I find seven minus three, that's four, and the sign is from the big number so it's positive. That one is positive four."

Ian listens and realizes Maria is mixing together several shortcuts for adding and subtracting integers. This means she gets some problems right and some problems wrong. After talking with the teacher who leads the tutoring program, Ian decides to take algebra tiles to their next session and model the math using this manipulative and making connections to addition as joining groups of objects and subtraction as separating groups of objects. Maria and Ian work through a number of problems together, and Maria builds understanding of what is actually happening rather than trying to follow shortcuts blindly.

This tutoring experience has helped Ian solidify his own understanding of adding and subtracting integers. He has to recognize the shortcuts Maria is using and find a path to help her make sense of the disconnected "rules" she has tried to learn. He begins to select problems for Maria to solve without the assistance of his advising teacher; this requires him to predict how Maria might solve the problem and what errors he might see and help her with. Not only has Maria's learning improved, but Ian's own understanding is stronger because he had this transfer learning experience.

Connected Learning

As students claim ownership of their learning and build their network of connections between their school learning and life during transfer learning, many learners are inspired to wonder about new problems. One strategy for providing opportunities for transfer is to create time and space for learners to explore their own ways of using what they have learned. "Connected learning is realized when a young person is able to pursue a personal interest or passion with the support of friends and caring adults, and is in turn able to link this learning and interest to academic achievement, career success or civic engagement" (Ito et al., 2013, p. 4). It is the connection of personal passions and academic achievement that makes this idea powerful for transfer.

Students are not going to benefit from opportunities to research and investigate their own problems and questions if they don't have a solid foundation of knowledge to use as a springboard for their investigations. Notably, Google's lauded investment in creativity, the Genius Hour, is directed at its highly accomplished engineering staff who already possess deep wells of knowledge to draw from. It's not likely that you'll get the same effect from simply announcing that every Thursday afternoon is dedicated to an hour of being a genius. Structure, of course, is essential. You can't just turn students loose without some procedures in place and expect that everything will be fine. On the other hand, we shudder at the bloom of "Genius Hour worksheets" that seem to be gaining popularity.

Opportunities for, and expectations of, transfer of knowledge should be woven into classroom life. We understand that setting aside sacred time to devote to this is both appealing and plausible. However, nothing magical happens at 1:30 p.m. if there hasn't been preparation. Students should be continually challenged to develop projects and investigations across the learning day. Asking students, "How could you use this?" near the end of a lesson can spur the kind of metacognitive thinking essential to learning. "How will you know you are successful?" reminds students (and ourselves) that one's internal measure is as important as an external evaluation.

Helping Students Transform Mathematical Understandings

Problem-Solving Teaching

Earlier in this book, we noted that our challenge as educators is not just to identify what works, as almost everything works for some students at some time, especially when zero growth is expected. Rather, we need to match what works to *accelerate* student learning, and then implement it at the right time (Hattie, 2009). Problem-based learning (PBL) is one such practice. The evidence is that when PBL is used too early in the learning cycle, before students have had sufficient experience with learning the declarative and procedural knowledge needed, the effect size is very low: 0.15. This is surface-level knowledge, and they just aren't equipped with enough knowledge to pursue inquiry. But when problem-solving teaching is employed, the effect size skyrockets. Unlike conventional PBL, where the problem is presented to students in advance of knowledge acquisition, problem-solving teaching is deployed when students are already deepening their knowledge.

EFFECT SIZE FOR PROBLEM-SOLVING TEACHING = 0.61

Problem-solving teaching is distinct from the problem-solving process we teach as part of mathematics instruction, although you will see some similarities. Problem solving in this broad sense involves

- Defining or determining the cause of the problem;
- Using multiple perspectives to uncover issues related to a particular problem;
- Identifying, prioritizing, and selecting alternatives for a solution;
- Designing an intervention plan; and
- Evaluating the outcome. (Hattie, 2009, p. 210)

STEM activities, in the form of engineering design challenges (Hester & Cunningham, 2007), are one form of problem-solving teaching that can encourage transfer of mathematics learning. In an engineering design challenge, students are asked to craft a solution to a problem within a set of criteria (the way we measure success) and constraints (limitations on the resources we can use). This requires learners to make connections between the elements of the design challenge (problem) and the mathematics and other disciplinary knowledge they bring to finding an optimal solution.

The engineering design process is an iterative process with several components. Notice the similarities to problem-solving teaching above.

1. Define the problem by asking questions about the situation.

2. Explore the elements of the problem, imagine potential solutions, and develop a plan.

3. Make and test a model or prototype.

4. Reflect on the testing and identify improvements to your solution. Revise/retest the plan.

This is an iterative process that can continue as long as time and resources permit. As the middle school students working on a solution to the problem of cafeteria waste learned, even in the real world, engineers do not typically find the perfect solution to a problem; they find the best solution given the available time and resources—the optimal solution.

Teachers can often identify design challenges for their students by listening thoughtfully to their wondering about the world around them. Preschool children might wonder about how they can go faster or slower down the slide. An elementary classroom might wonder about how to use their limited classroom storage space more effectively or the best way to design a school garden. By high school, student wonderings are often connected to the problems they will solve as adults in their careers.

Reciprocal Teaching

A common complaint among mathematics teachers is that the students cannot comprehend word problems well enough to solve them. Reciprocal teaching (Palincsar & Brown, 1984) is a literacy strategy used

> **Problem-solving teaching** helps students engage in the process of determining the cause of a problem; using multiple perspectives to uncover issues; identifying, prioritizing, and selecting alternatives for a solution; designing an intervention plan; and evaluating the outcome.

to build reading comprehension by having students work in structured collaborative groups to build their understanding of texts. Mathematics education researchers have adapted the strategy (e.g., Reilly, Parsons, & Bartolot, 2009; van Garderen, 2004) for use in the mathematics classroom to help students understand word problems.

As we have discussed, transfer learning is about working with difficult and complex tasks. If students do not comprehend the task, they cannot begin to solve it. In one study, Reilly et al. (2009) adapted the four phases of reciprocal teaching to mathematics as predicting, clarifying, solving, and summarizing. In the predicting phase, students use their knowledge of mathematics and the information provided in the problem to make predictions about what is happening in the problem and what mathematics they will need to solve the problem. In the clarifying stage, students make lists of information they need to solve the problem: unfamiliar vocabulary, known facts, and information they will need to determine to solve the problem. While the first two lists are fairly straightforward, the last requires some inference and more abstract mathematical thinking. Students are encouraged to work through this process in collaborative groups and to reread the problem once they have clarified the items on their lists.

During the solving phase, students use their problem-solving strategies to find one or more solutions to the problem. With the foundation laid by the predicting and clarifying stages, they are more successful in this process. Learners are encouraged to use multiple representations as they find solutions to the problem. Finally, the summarizing stage serves as individual self-reflection. For learners, this includes justifying the solution, reflecting on the effectiveness of the strategies selected, and evaluating their participation in the work of the group. Throughout the process, students keep a record of their thinking and work.

Too often, teachers jump straight to solving problems before ensuring students really understand the problem. When students are unsuccessful, it can be difficult to know if this is the result of not understanding the problem or not understanding/applying the mathematics correctly. With a strategy like reciprocal teaching, mathematics teachers can support students in understanding the problem well so they have the best opportunity to use their mathematics to solve the problem.

Conclusion

This chapter has focused on transfer, the application of what has been learned in mathematics to unfamiliar situations. It's nearly impossible for students to transfer if they don't also have surface and deep knowledge. In other words, it's hard to apply knowledge to unknown situations if you don't understand the ideas, procedures, or strategies. In many ways, transfer is all about answering the age-old question "When am I ever going to need this?" Transfer learning represents a leap from one context to another; these leaps can be smaller or larger. Tasks are generally both difficult and complex when they are selected to facilitate transfer learning. And, importantly, transfer allows students to develop and use their metacognitive skills.

Transfer also allows students to assume responsibility and ownership of their learning, essentially putting them in the driver's seat. From this perspective, self-reflection and self-questioning are critical elements of transfer learning. We shared several strategies for building comprehension of tasks, making learning engaging and relevant, and providing structured opportunities for learners to make sense of what they themselves know and can do. Like surface and deep learning, transfer learning should not be left to chance. Rather, it is up to caring teachers to deliberately design these opportunities by using effective strategies and an understanding of their students. But when transfer learning becomes visible, teachers can have no doubt whether they are making an impact.

Reflection and Discussion Questions

1. Think about the strategies you use to help learners make connections in their learning. What is the mix of near and far transfer opportunities you provide your students? How do you think about scaffolding these opportunities for learners?

2. What are your favorite or most powerful problem-based tasks for learners? Are you using them for maximum transfer impact? How could you refine your implementation of these tasks to make learning most visible?

3. What are your students' passions? How can you create space for your students to connect those passions to the important mathematics they are learning in your classroom?

ASSESSMENT, FEEDBACK, AND MEETING THE NEEDS OF ALL LEARNERS

7

Kirk Carlson teaches sixth-grade mathematics. He uses many of the teaching moves we have mentioned earlier, including rich tasks and collaborative grouping, and he balances his curriculum among conceptual understanding, procedural skills, and applications. Surface, deep, and transfer learning are always front and center in his mind as he plans units so that he knows his students are experiencing these phases of learning as they master a mathematical topic. He uses purposeful questions and prompts throughout his student-centered lessons. He and his students use accountable talk to share ideas and make connections. His students know the learning intention and success criteria for each lesson. What helps Kirk with all of this is that he knows his students and their level of understanding at just about any point in time. He does this by intentionally evaluating with both formative and summative assessments, using the information he gets from these assessments to diagnose students' understandings and misconceptions, and adjusting his instruction based on this information. At the same time, he regularly provides feedback to his students so they are aware of what they need to learn and how they can best accomplish that.

Mr. Carlson often ends his class with an exit ticket designed to quickly assess where students are in their understanding of the topic of the day. They are working on developing conceptual understanding of multiplication of fractions. Today's exit ticket has two problems and looks like the one in Figure 7.1.

Mr. Carlson collects the tickets as students leave class. He then sits down to quickly sort answers. While all of the students had the correct product for 6×5, a few were not clear with their explanations. Some explained that the problem meant 6 groups of 5. Bob and Marty wrote that the problem meant 5 groups of 6. Others skip counted by 5. One skip counted by 6. Work on the second problem varied more. Answers included $\frac{6}{5}$, $1\frac{1}{5}$, $\frac{6}{30}$, and $\frac{1}{5}$. Many students struggled with explanations or pictures. The final question gave Mr. Carlson information on whether students saw the relationship between multiplication of whole numbers and the fraction example. Mr. Carlson made brief notes about student misconceptions on a class record sheet that he used to keep track of student progress.

The half piece of paper he collected from each student provided Mr. Carlson with valuable feedback about each student's understanding or misconceptions, and it also provided information that would help

EXAMPLE EXIT TICKET

Name: _____ Date: _____

Solve each example. Use pictures, numbers, and words to show your thinking.

$$6 \times 5 = \underline{\hspace{2cm}}$$

$$6 \times \frac{1}{5} = \underline{\hspace{2cm}}$$

Explain how these two examples are alike and how they are different.

Figure 7.1

him design tomorrow's instruction and know which students would need extra support. This is an example of the power of assessment.

In this chapter, we will share our thoughts on the critical role of ongoing assessment and feedback to and from your students, which is so essential to helping students move through the phases of learning toward true mastery of mathematical content. We will begin with how to productively evaluate both your daily assessment of student understanding and summative assessments of student learning in ways that can inform your instruction and offer students feedback. We will also look at ways to differentiate instruction to meet individual needs through thoughtfully planned lessons. We will address intervention by looking at the research on Response to Intervention for students who need extra support and exploring options for students who show advanced ability in doing mathematics. We will address some of the things that we know from research *don't* work when it comes to instruction . . . things that have very low impact and you can stop spending time and energy on. Finally, we'll close with what John has identified as ten teacher mind frames that together summarize a great deal of the "what works" literature in an effort to inspire you to sharpen your tools and have the greatest possible impact on your students' learning.

Assessing Learning and Providing Feedback

Assessment needs to be a prominent feature of the classroom; unfortunately, it is too often left to the end-of-unit test that informs the teacher and the student very little about what they understand, nor does it allow the teacher an opportunity to adjust his or her instruction to meet students' needs. As we will discuss, formative and summative assessment are both important and should not be used simply to grade students' work, but rather to measure progress and compare it with the teaching that has occurred.

Formative Evaluation Embedded in Instruction

Formative evaluation is the process of gathering evidence to inform instruction. In other words, it is a way of thinking about measuring progress in learning and responding to it in teaching. Many teachers may be familiar with this activity by another name—formative assessment. Throughout this book, we prefer to use the terms *formative* and *summative evaluation* to describe this process. We argue that any assessment you give may be interpreted formatively or summatively, but when the teacher as the evaluator decides how to interpret where a student is during and after a lesson, and how to improve his or her teaching in response, it is the evaluation of the assessment that matters. Gathering real-time data about where students are in the learning process is critical to making good decisions about the next lesson or teaching move. Mr. Carlson's exit ticket is a formative assessment. He planned within his instruction to pause at this stage and find out where his students are in their learning. He not only gathered the data, but will use it in his own planning for teaching and will share it with students to inform their learning.

The formative evaluation process has several key elements (Leahy, Lyon, Thompson, & Wiliam, 2005), many of which will be familiar to you by now:

- Clarifying, sharing, and understanding learning intentions and criteria for success
- Engineering effective classroom discussions, activities, and learning tasks that elicit evidence of learning

Video 7.1
Continual Assessment for Precision Teaching

http://resources.corwin.com/ VL-mathematics

Formative evaluation is the process of gathering assessment evidence to inform instruction.

- Providing feedback that moves learning forward
- Activating learners as instructional resources for one another
- Activating learners as the owners of their own learning

In this section, we will focus on the role of feedback as a tool for moving learning forward. The evidence gathered in the process of formative evaluation serves as feedback to the teacher on the effectiveness of instruction. Teachers, in turn, provide feedback to students and support students in providing feedback to themselves and each other; this feedback moves the learning process forward.

Feedback for the Teacher: Adjusting Instruction

Daily formative evaluation is a chief way for teachers to make instructional decisions about what will occur next. In Chapter 3, we discussed questioning techniques to check for understanding. Other ways to check for understanding are listed in Figure 7.2.

These kinds of activities—when done routinely—offer teachers and students a lot of insight into student understanding. But these remain moment-in-time snapshots if not further contextualized through the administration and analysis of pre- and postassessments and regularly paced progress monitoring. In other words, it's what we do with it that counts. If assessment is used for nothing more than sorting students, we will continue to achieve the results we have always gotten.

John (Hattie, 2012) speaks of several internal questions that drive learners:

- Where am I going? What are my goals?
- How am I going there? What progress is being made toward the goal?
- Where to next? What activities need to be undertaken next to make better progress? (p. 116)

These are the same three questions teachers must ask about instruction as they make adjustments based on the data they gather from students. When Mr. Carlson realized that students were struggling to explain their reasoning about multiplying 6 times $\frac{1}{5}$, he decided to modify his lesson for the next day to include a fraction multiplication word

> ### Teaching Takeaway
>
> Formative evaluation is about gathering real-time data about where students are in the learning process, and it is critical to making good decisions about instruction.

> If assessment is used for nothing more than sorting students, we will continue to achieve the results we have always gotten.

Numbered Heads Together	Students in each group get a number, for example, from 1 to 4. In turn, every table group is also numbered. Let students know that after they discuss a problem with their group, you will call on a number (for example, number 3). Then direct each group to make sure that all team members are adequately prepared to answer, should they be selected. Listen in at each table as they do so, since this will give you an idea of how much your students know. After they have worked collaboratively in their groups, select a table number and student number to answer (many teachers do this with a spinner). In the meantime, you've created an opportunity for every student to be engaged, not just the single child who provides the answer.
Response Cards	Every student can write on a dry-erase board and hold it up at the same time for the teacher to see. This allows you to rapidly assess who comprehends concepts in the lesson and who needs more help.
Purposeful Sampling	As students chat with each other, listen to what they're saying. This may give you a smaller sample size, since you won't be able to listen to every student at once. There are several reasons to select a student to share. Choosing a typically high-performing student, a typically low-performing student, and a typically mid-performing student can give you a comparative sample. Choosing a student who represented the solution in a unique way can foster dialogue. Selecting a student who can link his or her ideas to a previous student can facilitate dialogue. Inviting a student with low social status and with strong work can build that student's efficacy and change the way the class views him or her.
Exit Tickets	Have all students write answers to a question, or a handful of questions, before they leave at the end of class. Then, after the children leave, read through their answers to see who knows what. Seventh-grade prealgebra teacher Allie Robinson does this a lot. The day after she gives an exit ticket, she often meets with a small group of the students who didn't understand what she had taught, and she teaches it to them in a different way. She can do this because her exit tickets showed her who needs additional instruction. A principal that Will knows didn't ask her teachers to submit lesson plans, but rather had them hand in their exit tickets. This school realized big gains in both student achievement and teacher morale.

Figure 7.2

problem so that students could be reminded of the meaning of multiplication and the language used to describe situations as they move toward multiplying fractions.

Feedback for the Student: Adjusting Learning

Through frequent assessment, teachers discover when students need additional support to continue their learning. The feedback that we as teachers then provide in return can inform them about errors and misconceptions that need to be addressed. We should know our students well and teach to their strengths while closely monitoring learning gaps. Feedback has a powerful impact on student learning, with an effect size of 0.75, placing it in the top ten influences on achievement. When students are engaged in appropriately challenging tasks, they are more likely to respond to feedback because they need feedback to continue growing and learning. Feedback then is designed to close the gap between students' current level of understanding or performance and the expected level of performance, which we call the success criteria. For feedback to work, teachers have to understand

> EFFECT SIZE FOR
> FEEDBACK = **0.75**

- students' current level of performance,
- students' expected level of performance, and
- actions they can take to close the gap.

It is important to note that grades may not serve as feedback. Studies such as Elawar and Corno (1985) along with Butler (1988) tell us that "the effect of giving both scores and comments [is] the same as the effect of giving scores alone" (Wiliam, 2011, p. 109). Giving scores alone, or scores and comments, does not necessarily lead to the visible learning effect provided by feedback. "To be effective, feedback needs to direct attention to what's next" (Wiliam, 2011, p. 128). As Brookhart (2008) describes it, feedback needs to be "just-in-time, just-for-me information delivered when and where it can do the most good" (p. 1), and receiving it strengthens students' metacognitive and self-regulatory skills. When feedback is delivered such that it is timely, specific, understandable, and actionable, students assimilate the language used by the teacher into their own self-talk. In other words, what we say to students, as well as how we say it, contributes to their identity and sense of agency, as well as to their success. Figure 7.3 includes information about the ways in which feedback can vary in terms of timing, amount, mode, and audience.

> When feedback is delivered such that it is timely, specific, understandable, and actionable, students assimilate the language used by the teacher into their own self-talk.

FEEDBACK STRATEGIES

Feedback Strategies Can Vary in . . .	In These Ways . . .	Recommendations for Good Feedback
Timing	• When given • How often	• Provide immediate feedback for knowledge of facts (right/wrong). • Delay feedback slightly for more comprehensive reviews of student thinking and processing. • Never delay feedback beyond when it would make a difference to students. • Provide feedback as often as is practical, for all major assignments.
Amount	• How many topics addressed • How much about each topic	• Prioritize—pick the most important topics. • Choose topics that relate to major learning goals. • Consider the student's developmental level.
Mode	• Oral • Written • Visual/ demonstration	• Select the best mode for the message. Would a comment in passing the student's desk suffice? Is a conference needed? • Interactive feedback (talking with the student) is best when possible. • Give written feedback on written work or on assignment cover sheets. • Use demonstration if "how to do something" is an issue or if the student needs an example.
Audience	• Individual • Group/class	• Individual feedback says, "The teacher values my learning." • Group/class feedback works if most of the class missed the same concept on an assignment, which presents an opportunity for reteaching.

Source: Brookhart (2008). Used with permission.

Figure 7.3

The feedback we give students at any point in their learning falls into four levels, not all of which are considered optimal (Hattie, 2012):

1. Feedback about the task:

   How well has the task been performed; is it correct or incorrect? For example, when reviewing student work on word problems, the teacher noticed that students often gave solutions as numbers without contexts. They would respond "3" rather than "3 cups of flour are needed to bake the cake." Feedback might include a note about remembering to include units of measure because "naked numbers" don't always make sense.

2. Feedback about the process:

   What are the strategies needed to perform the task; are there alternative strategies that can be used? For instance, there are often multiple approaches to solving rich mathematical tasks. Students provide feedback to one another about the strategies they use when they share their approaches to solving the problem.

3. Self-regulatory feedback:

   What is the conditional knowledge and understanding needed to know what you're doing? This can include self-monitoring, directing the processes and tasks, and strategic thinking. For example, the teacher might provide a broad timeline for completing a large project. One element of feedback to students becomes questions or comments asking them to relate their progress on their specific project to the general timeline. Based on this, students will be reassured that they are making good progress or reminded of necessary steps they have missed.

4. Feedback about self:

   Evaluation and affect about the person. For example, "Excellent job! You are so smart!"

Video 7.2
Feedback That
Fosters Learning

http://resources.corwin.com/
VL-mathematics

The first two levels, task and process, are more commonly used in classrooms, and we witness teachers using these on a frequent basis. This form of feedback can be most effective when students are working at the task or process level, but if you want to move them toward self-regulation, then more feedback at this level is critical. Effective teachers look for opportunities to give feedback to students by playing back what occurred.

Saying to a student, "I can see you had trouble with this part of the task, but then you solved it. What did you do that led to this success?" alerts him to think reflectively about the strategic thinking and action he took to get himself over a hurdle. It also acknowledges to the student that you are listening to what he is doing—and such respect is typically welcomed, builds trust, and leads to students realizing that the feedback is just for them. In doing so, we give students the internal scripts they need to become increasingly self-directed learners.

The third level of feedback—self-regulatory feedback—is one that plays such a prominent role during deep consolidation and transfer of learning. All of these methods offer critical opportunities for teachers to dialogue with students as they delve into increasingly self-directed learning. Consider the power of the self-regulatory feedback that eighth-grade teacher Mr. Bintz from Chapter 5 gave to a student who was having difficulty with the complex problem comparing cell phone plans.

Mr. Bintz: It looks like you're stuck about how to get started on solving this problem. What strategies have you tried to get moving?

Clemensia: I've underlined the important information in the problem and started a list of other things I need to know. I'm just not sure what they're asking me to do with it.

Mr. Bintz: What do you think an answer to this question would look like? What form would it take?

Clemensia: I think it's looking for a recommendation about the best cell phone plan. I don't know what the right evidence is to support my idea.

Mr. Bintz: Let's think about that. What are some important things to consider when selecting a plan?

Clemensia: I'm not sure.

Mr. Bintz: Then that's a good thing for you to think about next. Take a look at the information you've marked as important, think about how you use your phone, and consider talking with a classmate to help clarify your thinking. I admire how you're being persistent in working to figure out what this problem is asking and what evidence you'll need. Let's talk again tomorrow. You can share what you've figured out and the next steps you've decided on to help you solve the problem.

Notice that throughout the conversation, the teacher keeps his tone warm and encouraging, yet the focus is on feedback about the task and the process, emphasizing the student's ability to take action and change the outcomes. To be sure, the discussion took a few minutes to conduct. But the time is well worth it and is critical as students move from deepening their learning to moving into transfer.

The fourth level—feedback about self—is employed too often by well-meaning teachers. Although meant to bolster self-esteem, it appears to have a zero to negative impact on learning, especially in discouraging students from engaging in any further revision of their work (Hyland & Hyland, 2001). We want students to think positively about themselves, and praise is a tool that can contribute to positive teacher-student relationships. The message should not be interpreted as "do not give praise"; instead, the message is to separate the praise about a person's traits from the effort put into a task and into learning.

It's important that adults don't withhold their unconditional positive regard for students, but praise that masquerades as feedback can undermine efforts to motivate and encourage. Dweck (2006) has written extensively on the damage that praise about the individual can do in reinforcing a fixed mindset, rather than a growth mindset. Students with a fixed mindset have been conditioned to believe that innate qualities such as intelligence and talent are the keys to success, and they discount the role of effort or their own agency. Although we don't mean to, too often we communicate our own beliefs in a fixed mindset when we tell students, "You're so good at math!" instead of saying, "Your problem solving has really improved this quarter. Look at the difference in your scores since the last quarter." Highlighting progress further builds learners' sense of agency as they see the relationship between their success and their actions.

Furthermore, feedback focused on something that you already know does little to change understanding. Feedback thrives on errors, which we believe should be expected and celebrated because they are opportunities for learning. If students are not making errors, they have likely previously mastered the learning intention and are not stretching themselves. That said, if they make too many, they may need more help or to start in a different place. Unfortunately, in too many classrooms, students who already know the content are privileged and students who make errors feel shame. In those situations, learning isn't occurring for students who already know the content; they've already learned it. But

Video 7.3
Feedback That
Fosters Perseverance

*http://resources.corwin.com/
VL-mathematics*

learning also isn't occurring for the students who make errors because they hide their errors and avoid feedback. Classrooms have to be safe places for errors to be recognized.

It's only when the feedback is received and absorbed that it works. The messages that students receive externally become the messages they give themselves. We must make sure that we not only commend learners when and specifically on what they are doing well, but also help them to identify the actions they need to take in order to get back on the path. Asking a learner, "What can you do next to find that answer?" sends an underlying message that she has agency and can take steps. In contrast, telling a learner, "The answer is on page 37," without giving her an opportunity to resolve what's blocking her, tells her that you don't believe she is capable of doing so. Asking students, "What did you understand by the feedback I just gave you?" can reinforce that their interpretation of the feedback is much more critical than just having the teacher give the feedback. Indeed, feedback not listened to is not worth much, which is why so many grades alone have little value—they are not interpreted by the student other than "the work is over!"

Summative Evaluation

Summative evaluation is when we use broader assessments with the purpose of determining what students know and are able to do at a given point in time. In the case of mathematics, they indicate what students know about mathematics content and problem solving. Some types of summative assessment include the following:

- State assessments or standardized tests are used to provide data about student performance in relation to other students. They are usually administered under the same conditions and scored in the same manner for all students. Although they may include a few open-ended tasks, most questions usually have one correct answer and are often in multiple-choice format. These tests allow comparisons to be made among all students taking the test. The scores can also help schools and districts see patterns and make changes to improve student achievement over time. Data returned to teachers and parents are often quite general, reporting student achievement by general topics.

- District benchmark or interim assessments are commercially available or can be written by a group of teachers within a district. They are given at certain points over the course of the academic year. Because these tests are administered under district guidelines, they can vary greatly in how and when they are administered and the format they take. Benchmark assessments are usually used to (1) evaluate where students are in their learning progress and (2) determine whether they are on track to performing well on future assessments, such as standardized or state tests.

- Higher level mathematics courses such as algebra, geometry, statistics, or calculus often include end-of-course summative assessments that are cumulative. A certain percentage of a student's grade is made up of this test result.

- Unit or chapter tests can come from the mathematics program being used or written by a classroom teacher or group of teachers teaching the grade or course. These tests can take the form of computational examples, application problems, open response, or performance tasks.

Video 7.4
Growth Mindset: The Students' Perspective

http://resources.corwin.com/ VL-mathematics

Assessments such as unit quizzes and tests can be used for evaluation purposes in that they may provide information to support student learning and guiding instruction. We believe that a fundamental part of understanding mathematics is to realize how concepts grow and expand over time. For example, over the past twenty years, the mathematics education community has recognized the importance of developing early algebraic thinking in the elementary grades to build a good foundation as students enter formal algebra courses. Students need to understand the meaning of multiplication in order to really understand division and the idea of inverse operations. There are many examples of these connections based on important concepts that begin as early as kindergarten.

Now consider a second-grade student who is struggling to understand place value and regrouping in subtraction. His teacher gives him extra help in the form of more concrete experiences, and although he is starting to catch on, most of his classmates are progressing and this young boy fails the chapter test. Let's stop for a minute and consider the impact on this child's mathematical mindset. He begins to believe he cannot do mathematics, and his parents' disappointment exacerbates that belief.

Is there a way to use the results of the summative assessment, in this case the chapter test, to determine next steps for instruction and for the student?

How can the process of summative evaluation help a teacher determine next steps for instruction? When a student does poorly (even a student who "passes" with a low grade) on a chapter test, we have several choices. We can move him on to the next topic and hope he catches up. The problem with this approach is that the lack of foundational understanding in mathematics compounds. Too often, by the time a student is in middle school, the chances of getting caught up are slim and he likely hates mathematics. Another possibility is to analyze error patterns and misconceptions that a student has and look for extra time to fill in gaps and continue to address misconceptions. This is a good time to share specifics with parents or support personnel within the school so that any opportunity for extra help can focus on exactly what that student needs rather than waste time on nonessential instruction. The third option is to recommend a student for intervention (RTI) support, where a mathematics specialist can address the gaps in depth and the student is given additional time to get this support.

How can the process of summative evaluation help a teacher determine next steps for a student? While diagnosis and remediation are certainly not the main purposes of summative assessment, we should take advantage of any opportunity to provide feedback to students, both their strengths as well as areas that need additional work. Formative evaluation opportunities provide consistent feedback, yet at times, a chapter test can provide a clearer picture for all students (not just struggling students) of areas that may still need some attention.

There are several different ways you can address feedback for students using information that you gather from summative assessments. In general, if the class did well, you might take some time to discuss test items that several students missed. You may want to set up a time to meet individually with students to go over the test. One practice Linda used was to have all students correct any errors on their tests in a pen or pencil of a different color. We all have experienced giving a test that just about everyone in the class botched. That was a sign to us and to our students that we needed to spend more time on those concepts before we moved on. It helped us to know where students still had misconceptions or needed more practice, and it helped the students know where to focus their efforts.

Did you ever take a mathematics test and have to wait a week for it to be graded and returned? That is not fair to students and doesn't support providing immediate feedback on what students know and don't know. The point here is that even though a test is a form of summative assessment, students still deserve and should receive timely feedback on what they know or need to learn to be prepared for the next unit of study.

Meeting Individual Needs Through Differentiation

As we all discover in our first years in the classroom, a lesson that works wonderfully for some students is not a good choice for others. Just as "one-size-fits-all" T-shirts don't fit many people very well, one-size-fits-all instruction tends not to respond to the needs of all learners well. Our challenge as teachers is to differentiate instruction, to provide a thoughtful range of options that make teaching and learning more responsive to individual needs. Differentiation is about finding a balancing point between the need to respond to individual differences among students and the need to keep lessons manageable by not trying to individualize instruction for every learner in the classroom.

Tomlinson (1995) defines **differentiated instruction** as "the consistent use of a variety of instructional approaches to modify content, process, and/or products in response to the learning readiness and interest of academically diverse students" (p. 80). In this section, we will discuss structures and strategies for differentiation in the regular classroom.

Classroom Structures for Differentiation

A classroom that is structured for differentiation has two key attributes: a wide range of learning resources available to students and a flexible classroom environment. The wide range of learning resources available in a mathematics classroom includes a range of manipulative tools; a range of problem-solving strategies; and, particularly for secondary students, a range of reference/resource materials available to help students solve problems. By having many strategies and tools available, both teachers and students can draw on different tools at different times. In the primary grades, this may mean some students are still working with counters and tally marks for addition and subtraction while others are working with base ten blocks and sketches. By middle school, students

> Even though a test is a form of summative assessment, students still deserve and should receive timely feedback on what they know or need to learn to be prepared for the next unit of study.

> **Differentiated instruction** is the "use of a variety of instructional approaches to modify content, process, and/or products in response to the learning readiness and interest of academically diverse students" (Tomlinson, 1995, p. 80).

should be comfortable with a wide range of problem-solving strategies. These can range from the simple (act it out or make an organized list) to the more complex (generalize or change your point of view). Teachers should deliberately cultivate a classroom environment where a wide range of strategies and tools is available and valued.

As we discussed in Chapter 5, students can be grouped for learning in a variety of ways. Differentiation works most smoothly when the classroom norm is that groups change often and they change based on the learning task at hand; students are used to working collaboratively and they are used to working with different students in their groups. As the teacher develops a menu of instructional options, the flexibility of grouping students in a variety of ways makes implementing the menu a more straightforward task.

Adjusting Instruction to Differentiate

Teachers can differentiate instruction by making adjustments in one or more of three areas: content, process, and product. For teachers just starting to differentiate, we recommend selecting one area for adjustment at a time. Remember, our goal is to be sure each learner is making progress mastering the grade-level standards at an appropriate degree of challenge, working in what Vygotsky (1978) calls the "zone of proximal development." When students are working on tasks they already know how to do, they may build fluency, but they are likely not learning much that is new. The zone of proximal development is that area where students are challenged, but with adult or peer support can be successful. This area of stretching is where learning happens. Differentiation of instruction is about making sure all students are working within their own zone of proximal development.

When teachers adjust content, they are modifying the mathematics students are working on. Adjusting content does not mean that students are moving more quickly through the standards or are working on standards for a grade level ahead of where they are. Rather, adjusting content means working within grade-level standards to provide different levels of difficulty and complexity that match where students are in the learning process. This may mean using larger or "less friendly" numbers in the word problems students are solving or adjusting the complexity of the problem. Compare these two examples from a third-grade class:

> Pablo is getting new carpet for his bedroom, and he needs to know the area of the room. Pablo's room is 10' wide and 8' long. How many square feet of carpet will Pablo need in his room?
>
> Pablo is getting new carpet for his bedroom and he needs to know the area of the room. Pablo's room is 9' wide and 8' long. There is also an alcove by the window that is a 5' square. How many square feet of carpet will Pablo need in his room?

Both problems involve multiplication of whole numbers in the context of area, and the numbers are similar in magnitude, within the parameters for third-grade students. For learners who are ready to work in more complex situations, the second problem, with two parts to the room, is more challenging.

When teachers adjust process, they are making adjustments to the strategies students use to access information. Process differentiation in mathematics might mean emphasizing different representations for different groups of students. It is spring in Ms. Corral's kindergarten class, and the children are working to find a solution to this problem: Juan had four tennis balls and DaShaun had five more. How many tennis balls do the boys have together? For a young child who is still focusing on counting all as a strategy for addition, the teacher provides counters and encourages the child to draw a picture to help the student move to a more visual representation. For another group of students, the teacher might guide the students to use the counting on strategy with a number line to find a solution. Rich mathematical tasks with multiple entry points, such as those discussed in Chapter 3, have great power, in part because they make process differentiation easier. The entire class is working on the same task but using different tools and strategies to find solutions.

Teachers adjust product when they ask students to complete different tasks to show what they have learned. One student might build models of various geometric shapes while another shares pieces of art that include the shapes as components. For students still mastering the attributes of shapes, the challenge of creating models on their own that have the correct attributes is sufficient to move them forward with learning. For a student who already knows the basics about the shapes, recognizing them in the context of art or architecture provides a more difficult task at a more appropriate level of challenge.

Differentiation is often presented as a strategy for meeting the needs of academically and intellectually gifted students, or in the context of this book, those who are top performers in mathematics. These same differentiation strategies can be used to reach back and reinforce a fundamental idea from a previous grade for students who are struggling, while allowing those students who are working at grade level to continue their own progress. The key idea is that the teacher has a practical structure for adapting instruction to meet the needs of the wide range of learners in the classroom.

Intervention

When you hear the term *intervention*, it is likely you think of models of support for struggling students, and the **RTI (Response to Intervention)** model is probably the best known model. RTI focuses on providing high-quality instruction and interventions matched to student need, monitoring progress frequently to make decisions about changes in instruction or goals, and applying child response data to important educational decisions. However, we often forget students at the other end of the spectrum, those who have a unique ability or talent in mathematics and intrinsic motivation to explore ideas in mathematics beyond the usual school curriculum. In the next section, we will discuss research-based RTI strategies for mathematics that support visible teaching and learning as well as strategies for meeting the needs of students who show a special aptitude for doing mathematics.

As we have noted before, there is no one right way to teach, and there are a lot of things that teachers do that are effective. Teaching is about making adjustments and trying to determine what will work for a particular group of students. Designing learning opportunities, monitoring for impact, and then making adjustments are the hallmarks of effective teachers. But there are more formal ways to monitor impact.

Response to Intervention (RTI)

The evidence for Response to Intervention is significant; it's one of the top influences studied thus far, with an effect size of 1.07. In other words, it works (e.g., VanDerHeyden, McLaughlin, Algina, & Snyder, 2012).

> RTI focuses on providing high-quality instruction and interventions matched to student need, monitoring progress frequently to make decisions about changes in instruction or goals, and applying child response data to important educational decisions.

EFFECT SIZE FOR RESPONSE TO INTERVENTION = 1.07

There are several components of an effective RTI effort that combine to produce the impact seen in the studies. These include universal screening, quality core instruction, progress monitoring, and supplemental and intensive interventions (Lembke, Hampton, & Beyers, 2012). We know that the earlier students who need support are identified and attended to, the greater the success rate for those students. Entire books have been written on RTI (Gersten & Newman-Gonchar, 2011), so this section will highlight only the key components necessary for teachers to understand.

RTI focuses efforts on providing evidence-based interventions for students who do not respond to quality core instruction (also known as Tier 1). This quality core instruction includes differentiated experiences discussed earlier. In the language of RTI, students can receive Tier 2 or Tier 3 interventions, or a combination of both. This multitiered system of support can result in improved student learning. It requires that teachers notice when students do not respond (when the impact is insufficient) and then change the instruction or intervention to reach the desired outcome. The two levels of response are as follows:

- Tier 2: Also known as supplemental interventions
- Tier 3: Also known as intensive interventions

The following questions posed by Gresham and Little (2012) offer guidance on what to consider when implementing RTI at the district, school, or classroom level.

1. What are the critical mathematical concepts and skills to be learned by *all* students?

2. How do the current resources in my classroom address the selected lesson's mathematical concepts and skills of the standard I am to teach?

3. What prior mathematical knowledge do students need or have to master to reach the content standard?

4. What may be sources of difficulty and confusion for the students?

5. How can this lesson build on students' prior mathematical knowledge and experiences?

6. What will students think and do in response to the instructional lesson?

7. What scaffolding and support can I provide to meet the needs of *all* learners through differentiating instruction and accommodating individuals?

8. Which questions, resources, strategies, activities, examples, and so on will clarify and/or extend conceptual learning by students?

9. Which grouping arrangements, accommodations, adaptations, use of levels of learning, cognitive/metacognitive strategies, and/or technology are needed for whole/small groups of students?

10. How can I make the mathematical learning task less complex without changing the goal?

11. What kinds of data are available and will help us assess students' mathematics progress toward the set mathematical goals?

12. How will I check for mathematical conceptual understanding and depth of mathematical knowledge?

In the IES Practice Guide, *Assisting Students Struggling With Mathematics: Response to Intervention (RtI) for Elementary and Middle Schools* (Gersten et al., 2009), a committee of mathematics researchers and practitioners with expertise on this topic proposed eight recommendations based on the best available research evidence. A brief summary of each recommendation follows.

Recommendation 1: Screen all students to identify those at risk for potential mathematics difficulties and provide interventions to students identified as at risk. For RTI efforts to be most effective, school staff members have to screen students at the outset of the year. These screening tools are typically quick checks to identify students who may need additional intervention.

- Screening time may range from five minutes to twenty minutes.

- Number sense is critical at the elementary level. Assess various aspects of knowledge of whole numbers—properties, basic arithmetic operations, understanding of magnitude, and application of mathematical knowledge to word problems.

- Upper elementary and middle grades screening measures (usually ten minutes) should cover a proportional sampling of grade-level objectives.

Screening tools can focus on basic (e.g., sums to 12, subtraction 0–20, fact families) or advanced (e.g., multiplying multidigit numbers with regrouping, converting numbers to percentages, solving equations) computation skills. Both have empirical evidence for their ability to screen for students who may need supplemental or intensive intervention (VanDerHeyden & Witt, 2005). A more comprehensive list of screening tools can be found at http://www.rti4success.org/resources/tools-charts/screening-tools-chart.

Recommendation 2: Instructional materials for students receiving interventions should focus intensely on in-depth treatment of whole numbers in kindergarten through Grade 5 and on rational numbers in Grades 4 through 8. With the adoption of recent standards, conceptual understanding of whole number operations should be a focus in Grades K through 5. While other topics are important parts of the curriculum, we know that if students progress through the grades without appropriate surface and deep learning, they run the risk of failing upper-level courses. The same is true for the topics of rational numbers (fractions and decimals) in Grades 4 through 8. Again, focusing on conceptual understanding through the use of concrete and pictorial representations and explicitly making connections to procedural skills and applications is critical here. Just focusing on drill and kill will not provide the support these students need.

Recommendation 3: Instruction during the intervention should be explicit and systematic. This includes providing models of proficient problem solving, verbalizing thought processes, guided practice, corrective feedback, and frequent cumulative review. The final report of the National Mathematics Advisory Panel (2008) describes characteristics of explicit instruction:

- Clear models provided by teachers for solving a problem using an array of examples

- Extensive student practice of newly learned strategies and skills

- Think-aloud opportunities for students to verbalize decisions and steps
- Extensive feedback for students

Notice how these strategies are those we have been discussing throughout this book. Let's look in on an intense intervention session. Mrs. Jensen is working with a group of fifth graders who are working with addition of fractions. While the standards call for adding and subtracting fractions with unlike denominators in Grade 5, Mrs. Jensen knows from screening data that these students are still struggling with equivalent fractions and addition of fractions with like denominators. Since these two concepts are essential for working with unlike denominators, she decides to begin her session focusing on building sets of equivalent fractions. She gathers a set of fraction bars for each student. (Fraction bars are physical models of shaded bars to represent various fractions. Additionally, the bars are color coded according to the denominator. Halves are green, thirds are yellow, fourths are blue, etc.) Mrs. Jensen also decides that she will limit the student work to related fractions, so she pulls the halves, fourths, eighths, and twelfths from the deck for the first activity, which is a memory game. As the students enter, she has the fraction bars set out in a rectangular array face down on the table. She explains and models the rules of the game to the students. They take turns turning over two bars. If the shaded amounts are the same, they keep the bars, and if not, they turn them back over and the next student takes a turn.

When the game is over, students place their pairs of matching bars face up. Mrs. Jensen reviews how to write fractions for each bar—the number of shaded parts is the numerator, and the total number of parts is the denominator. She works together with the students to practice writing several fractions. The last part of the lesson is for the students to record the fractional numbers for each matching pair they found. As students are recording their pairs, Mrs. Jensen is writing some of their equations on the board. She also invites students to add other pairs they may have found.

$$\frac{1}{2} = \frac{2}{4} \qquad \frac{1}{4} = \frac{3}{12} \qquad \frac{3}{4} = \frac{9}{12}$$

Mrs. Jensen works with the students to review the vocabulary (numerator, denominator, equivalent fractions, equation) for this concept. She also has these words on her word wall. This gives the students the language they need to have a discussion about what they notice.

Mrs. Jensen guides the discussion with questions that will focus students on looking for patterns. Her learning intention for this lesson is for students to see the relationships among equivalent fractions. By the time students leave, they have demonstrated a conceptual understanding that equivalent fractions are built on multiplying the numerator and the denominator by the same factor. Even more deeply, they are beginning to see that in doing so, they have actually multiplied the fraction by a name for one. She has taken forty-five minutes to develop this concept, and when students return in a few days, she will increase the set of fractions to include thirds, fifths, sixths, and tenths. Students will continue to work on recognizing equivalent fractions using concrete and pictorial representations and making explicit connections to symbolic representations.

Notice that Mrs. Jensen has a very clear understanding of the progression of topics that is necessary before students can even begin to reach the final goal of adding fractions with unlike denominators. She carefully plans the sequence of her lessons, making certain that she is spending enough time to ensure that students have a conceptual understanding of the topic before moving to procedural rules and skills. While this takes more time than what might be spent in the regular class's mathematics instruction, students are getting the support they need through lessons that are more explicit and systematic.

Recommendation 4: Interventions should include instruction on solving word problems that is based on common underlying structures. Word problems provide a context for understanding what happens when I am operating on numbers. How do I know what operation to perform in a given situation? Did you know there are fifteen different situations that call for addition or subtraction (National Governors Association Center for Best Practices & Council of Chief State School Officers, 2010)? Too often, teachers give students a variety of addition or subtraction word problems with a mix of these contexts before students have had the chance to explore, model, and understand each one. Research shows that the use of key words, a strategy often used by teachers, is ineffective (van de Walle, Karp, & Bay-Williams, 2013). Another strategy may be to have students come up with their own strategies for solving problems. A group of fourth graders was asked how they determined what operation to use when solving a problem. The overall response was, "When the problem has more than two numbers in it, you add because that is the only operation that you can do with more than two numbers. If it has two numbers and they are close together, you subtract. If they are far apart, you divide, but if you get a remainder, then that is wrong so you multiply the numbers instead." Many of us have seen similarly strange approaches to solving word problems! Providing students with explicit instruction on problem-solving situations such as those in Figures 7.4 and 7.5 will provide experience through modeling and making connections that help them not only to solve problems but also to see the underlying structure and meaning for each operation.

Recommendation 5: Intervention materials should include opportunities for students to work with visual representations of mathematical ideas, and interventionists should be proficient in the use of visual representations of mathematical ideas. Students need many opportunities to work with physical and then pictorial representations of mathematical ideas. Early learning of number and place value and operation concepts should incorporate the use of linking cubes or bundling straws. Fraction work should include fraction bars, rectangles, or circles. It is important for students to be able to physically manipulate materials to help them see the structure of what is happening when they do a particular mathematics operation. After ample time to work with concrete materials, explicit connections should be made to pictorial representations. Too often, we give students some time to work with materials and we expect them to make the transfer to pictures with little instruction. Following many opportunities to work with visual representations, explicit connections to the symbolic (numerals) representation should be made. In making that transition to mathematical notation, it is helpful for the teacher to model how to write an expression or equation using numbers while students are working with physical or pictorial representations. When students are ready, they can begin to make the connection to symbolic notation.

Recommendation 6: Interventions at all grade levels should devote about ten minutes in each session to building fluent retrieval of basic arithmetic facts. Expecting students to become fluent is more than "go home and memorize the plus sixes tonight." Fluency means that students think about facts flexibly, efficiently, and

ADDITION AND SUBTRACTION SITUATIONS

	Result Unknown	Change Unknown	Start Unknown
Add to	Two bunnies sat on the grass. Three more bunnies hopped there. How many bunnies are on the grass now? $2 + 3 = ?$	Two bunnies were sitting on the grass. Some more bunnies hopped there. Then there were five bunnies. How many bunnies hopped over to the first two? $2 + ? = 5$	Some bunnies were sitting on the grass. Three more bunnies hopped there. Then there were five bunnies. How many bunnies were on the grass before? $? + 3 = 5$
Take From	Five apples were on the table. I ate two apples. How many apples are on the table now? $5 - 2 = ?$	Five apples were on the table. I ate some apples. Then there were three apples. How many apples did I eat? $5 - ? = 3$	Some apples were on the table. I ate two apples. Then there were three apples. How many apples were on the table before? $? - 2 = 3$
	Total Unknown	**Addend Unknown**	**Both Addends Unknown**[1]
Put Together/ Take Apart[2]	Three red apples and two green apples are on the table. How many apples are on the table? $3 + 2 = ?$	Five apples are on the table. Three are red and the rest are green. How many apples are green? $3 + ? = 5, 5 - 3 = ?$	Grandma has five flowers. How many can she put in her red vase and how many in her blue vase? $5 = 0 + 5, 5 = 5 + 0$ $5 = 1 + 4, 5 = 4 + 1$ $5 = 2 + 3, 5 = 3 + 2$
	Difference Unknown	**Bigger Unknown**	**Smaller Unknown**
Compare[3]	("How many more?" version): Lucy has two apples. Julie has five apples. How many more apples does Julie have than Lucy? ("How many fewer?" version): Lucy has two apples. Julie has five apples. How many fewer apples does Lucy have than Julie? $2 + ? = 5, 5 - 2 = ?$	(Version with "more"): Julie has three more apples than Lucy. Lucy has two apples. How many apples does Julie have? (Version with "fewer"): Lucy has three fewer apples than Julie. Lucy has two apples. How many apples does Julie have? $2 + 3 = ?, 3 + 2 = ?$	(Version with "more"): Julie has three more apples than Lucy. Julie has five apples. How many apples does Lucy have? (Version with "fewer"): Lucy has three fewer apples than Julie. Julie has five apples. How many apples does Lucy have? $5 - 3 = ?, ? + 3 = 5$

Source: National Governors Association Center for Best Practices & Council of Chief State School Officers (2010). Adapted from Box 2-4 of *Mathematics Learning in Early Childhood*, National Research Council (2009), pp. 32, 33.

[1] These take apart situations can be used to show all the decompositions of a given number. The associated equations, which have the total on the left of the equal sign, help children understand that the equal sign does not always mean "makes" or "results in" but always does mean "is the same amount as."

[2] Either addend can be unknown, so there are three variations of these problem situations. Both Addends Unknown is a productive extension of this basic situation, especially for numbers less than or equal to ten.

[3] For the Bigger Unknown or Smaller Unknown situations, one version directs the correct operation (the version using more for the bigger unknown and using fewer for the smaller unknown). The other versions are more difficult.

Figure 7.4

MULTIPLICATION AND DIVISION SITUATIONS

	Unknown Product $3 \times 6 = ?$	Group Size Unknown ("How many in each group?" Division) $3 \times ? = 18$, and $18 \div 3 = ?$	Number of Groups Unknown ("How many groups?" Division) $? \times 6 = 18$, and $18 \div 6 = ?$
Equal Groups	There are 3 bags with 6 plums in each bag. How many plums are there in all?	If 18 plums are shared equally into 3 bags, then how many plums will be in each bag?	If 18 plums are to be packed 6 to a bag, then how many bags are needed?
	Measurement example. You need 3 lengths of string, each 6 inches long. How much string will you need altogether?	*Measurement example.* You have 18 inches of string, which you will cut into 3 equal pieces. How long will each piece of string be?	*Measurement example.* You have 18 inches of string, which you will cut into pieces that are 6 inches long. How many pieces of string will you have?
Arrays,[1] **Area**[2]	There are 3 rows of apples with 6 apples in each row. How many apples are there?	If 18 apples are arranged into 3 equal rows, how many apples will be in each row?	If 18 apples are arranged into equal rows of 6 apples, how many rows will there be?
	Area example. What is the area of a 3 cm by 6 cm rectangle?	*Area example.* A rectangle has area 18 square centimeters. If one side is 3 cm long, how long is a side next to it?	*Area example.* A rectangle has area 18 square centimeters. If one side is 6 cm long, how long is a side next to it?
Compare	A blue hat costs $6. A red hat costs 3 times as much as the blue hat. How much does the red hat cost?	A red hat costs $18, and that is 3 times as much as a blue hat costs. How much does a blue hat cost?	A red hat costs $18 and a blue hat costs $6. How many times as much does the red hat cost as the blue hat?
	Measurement example. A rubber band is 6 cm long. How long will the rubber band be when it is stretched to be 3 times as long?	*Measurement example.* A rubber band is stretched to be 18 cm long, and that is 3 times as long as it was at first. How long was the rubber band at first?	*Measurement example.* A rubber band was 6 cm long at first. Now it is stretched to be 18 cm long. How many times as long is the rubber band now as it was at first?
General	$a \times b = ?$	$a \times ? = p$, and $p \div a = ?$	$? \times b = p$, and $p \div b = ?$

Source: National Governors Association Center for Best Practices & Council of Chief State School Officers (2010).

Note: The first examples in each cell are examples of discrete things. These are easier for students and should be given before the measurement examples.

[1] The language in the array examples shows the easiest form of array problems. A harder form is to use the terms *rows* and *columns*: *The apples in the grocery window are in 3 rows and 6 columns. How many apples are in there?* Both forms are valuable.

[2] Area involves arrays of squares that have been pushed together so that there are no gaps or overlaps, so array problems include these especially important measurement situations.

Figure 7.5

accurately (Bay-Williams & Kling, 2014). Young children need carefully planned and sequenced instruction to develop strategies that support all of the components of fluency. This is built on using models, finding patterns, and making connections.

Recommendation 7: Monitor the progress of students receiving supplemental instruction and other students who are at risk. Progress monitoring is a scientifically based practice that is used to assess students' academic performance and evaluate the effectiveness of instruction. Progress monitoring can be implemented with individual students or an entire class.

Both formative and summative evaluations can be used to monitor progress. What is important is that there is a specific plan for tracking and following the data that show student growth and progress so that further instruction can be based on individual student needs.

- Assessment tools for monitoring progress are available from multiple sources (such as the National Center on Student Progress Monitoring, www.studentprogress.org). It is essential that assessments are capable of identifying growth.

- Curriculum-embedded assessments might be commercially, researcher, or district/school developed. Unit tests, mastery tests, daily probes, and other assessments can be used to base decisions on which concepts need to be reviewed, which need to be retaught, and which have been mastered.

Recommendation 8: Include motivational strategies in Tier 2 and Tier 3 interventions. Let's face it, mathematics taught poorly can be boring. On the other hand, when taught well using a variety of teaching techniques (group work, rich tasks, games), it can be one of the most exciting subjects in the school curriculum! Constant drill and kill, use of worksheets, and textbook pages with nothing but computational exercises can be lethal to motivating all students, but especially those who struggle with mathematics. Thinking about how to make a topic interesting and tapping into the curiosity of students can make all the difference in student success but also in encouraging students to develop a growth mindset. Who doesn't like a good mystery or a game? Think of the mathematical tasks you provide for your students as potentially a good mystery to solve or a game that is fun to play but also provides opportunity to learn or practice a particular concept or skill.

Basic fact fluency means that students think about facts flexibly, efficiently, and accurately.

There are many good resources available on the Internet, but beware—for every good website with great activities, rich problems, or games, there are likely ten times as many websites with poor examples or resources that do little to inspire, support, or motivate students.

In summary, RTI efforts are based on the expectation that students receive quality core instruction as part of their ongoing participation in school. Also known as good first teaching, quality core instruction comprises Tier 1 of the RTI efforts. It's unreasonable to expect that all students receive supplemental and intensive interventions—there isn't time or money for that. If the vast majority of students are not being impacted by the regular classroom environment, we would suggest that the tenets in this book are not in place. In school systems that implement high-quality instruction, based on the influences on achievement outlined in this book, and then monitor the impact of those actions, fewer and fewer students need the extensive support offered through RTI (Gersten et al., 2009). To our thinking, quality core instruction includes at least the following:

- Teacher clarity on, and communication about, the learning intentions and success criteria
- Student ownership of the expectations for learning
- Positive, humane, growth-producing teacher-student relationships
- Modeling and direct instruction of content
- Collaborative learning opportunities on a daily basis
- Small group learning based on instructional needs rather than perceived ability
- Spaced (rather than mass) independent practice and application of content

These are easy to write, and obvious to many, but not yet common in classrooms around the world. When these actions become the norm in classrooms, the need for additional interventions declines and students learn more and better mathematics.

Intervention for Advanced Students

While much of the research on intervention has a focus on struggling students, highly advanced students will benefit from intervention as well. These are students who need more than a differentiated class-room provides. They are students who can consistently find the correct answer but may struggle to explain why their answer is correct because "they just know it." These are students who begin the school year having already mastered many of the grade-level standards. Overall, they likely represent the top 3 to 5 percent of students at a given grade level.

Assessment is critical for these students because spending time with content they already know leads to boredom and misbehavior. These students can benefit from serving as peer tutors if they have the social/emotional development to do this successfully, as described in Chapter 6. It is also important, however, that these students continue to learn new mathematics and explore the mathematics they know in a variety of contexts and in increasingly rigorous settings. Researchers such as Sheffield (1999) and Lubinski and Benbow (2006) have a long history of work with these students and strategies that work effectively for them. These students can benefit from curriculum compacting (National Association for Gifted Children, n.d.), a strategy in which teachers replace content students have already mastered with new content, enrichment options, or other activities.

New content might mean that students explore mathematics beyond their grade-level standards. For example, the ideas and problems in *Mathematics, A Human Endeavor* (Jacobs, 1994) are an excellent beginning for extending student thinking (deeper understanding and transfer learning) in the upper elementary grades. In these tasks, students are looking at the uses of mathematics in everyday life and see how mathematics relates to reasoning. The tasks are rich and complex while remaining accessible without a great deal of formal mathematical instruction. Enrichment options could include more highly differentiated tasks such as projects with a larger scope. In order to work on these specialized assignments, students should be grouped with others who have similar learning needs.

From time to time, student success with this new content or more highly differentiated tasks may indicate that students are ready to move on to the next grade level's mathematics content. It is essential that this decision is made based on good evidence of visible learning—surface, deep, and transfer—of all grade-level standards. Too often, the decision to accelerate students, particularly to have students placed in Algebra 1 early, is made as a status marker for parents rather than a decision that

> **Teaching Takeaway**
>
> Interventions for high-performing students can help them explore mathematics they know in a variety of contexts in increasingly rigorous settings.

is driven by evidence of student mastery and learning needs. As we have said throughout this book, visible evidence of learning should guide instruction and help keep every student challenged.

Learning From What Doesn't Work

Thus far, we have focused our attention on influences that can positively impact students' learning. We explored surface, deep, and transfer levels of learning and noted that there are some instructional protocols that work better at each level. We also shared ways in which teachers could determine their impact on student learning and then respond when the impact was not as expected. Now, it's time to focus on some things that we know from John's research really don't work to build students' mathematical thinking. We don't want teachers to undo all of their hard work by engaging in practices that waste valuable learning time or may even be harmful to student understanding. Unfortunately, these are too often common in use. Even worse, many of these practices are the result of not focusing on the potential impact of effective teaching strategies, and instead spending time cataloging a student's shortcomings.

Grade-Level Retention

EFFECT SIZE FOR
RETENTION = –0.13

EFFECT SIZE FOR
RESPONSE TO
INTERVENTION = 1.07

Students are often retained in a grade level based on their achievement. The meta-analyses of this indicate that the practice is actually having the reverse effect, with an effect size of –0.13. As Frey (2005) and others have noted, grade-level retention is not a defensible practice. But schools and districts still hold on to the hope that another year of schooling will ensure that students learn to read and write at higher levels. Why would another year of the same curriculum, often the same type of teaching, and the same assessment tasks make a difference? What most students who struggle need is not more of the same, but demonstrably different and better instruction. Instead, they would be wise to consider Response to Intervention. In most RTI efforts, students receive supplemental and intensive interventions throughout the year, delivered by knowledgeable adults who can monitor and adjust as needed to reach a desired level of achievement.

Ability Grouping

We have lost count of the number of times we have talked with well-meaning educators who hope that the solution to their students' achievement lies in grouping students by their perceived ability. Taking a grade level of students and giving one teacher the lowest performing students, another teacher average performing students, and yet another the highest performing students may be popular, but the evidence is clear that it is not the answer. The two most common forms of ability grouping are

- *Within-class grouping*—putting students into collaborative groups based on the results of an assessment

- *Between-class grouping*—separating students into different classes, courses, or course sequences (curricular tracks) based on their previous academic achievement

The risk in writing this is that some readers will overgeneralize. Within-class and between-class ability grouping should be avoided. These sorts of rigid, long-term grouping are sometimes known as tracking and typically assume student learning needs and potential remain constant over time. This practice is not supported by research. But needs-based instruction, with flexible groups, should not be eliminated. Student-centered teaching, basing instructional actions on students' understanding, and then engaging students in small group learning can be very effective provided the grouping is flexible rather than fixed. The key to this approach is the condition that the groups change and the instruction must match the needs of the learner, including those needs based on ability. Let's look at the difference, occurring at the same school. In one sixth-grade classroom, the teacher administered a preassessment to determine student knowledge of measuring volume. She grouped her students based on their scores. The students with the lowest scores were in one group, slightly better performers formed a second group, and so on. She then met with groups over several weeks, providing instruction to each group. Sounds familiar and logical, right? It just didn't work. The postassessments were not much different from the original samples. The lowest performing students were still the lowest, but their scores inched up a barely perceptible amount. That was a lot of work for very little benefit.

Down the hall, another sixth-grade teacher administered the same assessment. She then analyzed the patterns of errors and misconceptions found in her students' work and continually regrouped students based on the original assessment but also on daily exit tickets to

EFFECT SIZE
FOR ABILITY
GROUPING = 0.12

EFFECT SIZE FOR
SMALL GROUP
LEARNING = 0.49

determine who was still having difficulty. On one day, she met with a group of students who needed more support generalizing the formula for finding the volume of a rectangular solid, and later with another group of students who needed the right questions to connect their understanding of volume of rectangular solids to the volume of cylinders. While she was working with small groups, she used many of the differentiation protocols mentioned earlier to reinforce and extend concepts for those students who were ready to move on.

In the same amount of time as was available to her colleague, she was able to address many of the instructional needs of her students using small groups. And the results speak for themselves. The average score increased a full performance level, and there wasn't a single student remaining who did not understand the concept and procedure of finding the volume of cylinders and applying this to a variety of applications. These may seem like subtle differences, but they are important. Small group instruction is effective, but not when the intervention for the students is solely the ability of the group. The groups have to be flexible so that the instruction each group receives aligns with its current performance and understanding.

Simply said, there is no evidence to suggest that rigid ability grouping over long periods of time will yield breakthrough results. The effect size of ability grouping is negligible in terms of impact, yet it remains common in many schools. As typically implemented, the greatest effects of ability grouping are to disrupt the learning community, socially ostracize some learners, and compromise social skills, to name a few (Sapon-Shevin, 1994). And the effects on minority groups is much more serious, with more minority students likely to be in lower ability classes destined to low performance based on low expectations, and often with the least effective teachers (Butler, 2008).

Matching Learning Styles With Instruction

Another practice that has become widespread, but for which there is no supporting evidence, is rigidly matching learning styles with instruction. It may very well be that there are differences in how we prefer to access and share information, and that preference may change in different situations with different groups of people, but teaching students in a way that is limited to our perception of their particular type of

EFFECT SIZE FOR MATCHING LEARNING STYLES = 0.17

intelligence is of very little value. Let's take for example a student named Musab. He loves music. He has earbuds in any time they're allowed. He quotes rap songs in response to questions and essay prompts. He sings quietly in the halls and performs in every talent show the school offers. He can listen to a tune and immediately replicate it on a piano. Some might say that he is gifted in the area of music. Others might say that his preferred learning style is musical. Does that mean he is excused from developing interpersonal skills? Should we excuse his errors in computation? Should his teachers be encouraged to sing their lessons and rap their instructions? And if he's in class with students who have other preferences, should we separate him? NO. Matching instruction with a perception of a learning style is not going to radically raise achievement in mathematics. Why condemn Musab to one form of learning (via music), when indeed he needs to be taught other ways to learn? Let's acknowledge that there are differences in learners, but let's not label students. Instead, let's focus on instructional routines and habits that will ensure all students learn at high levels. Teachers may need to use a variety of methods to capitalize on multiple ways of learning, but the mistake is to categorize students into one or more learning styles and consider that enough.

EFFECT SIZE FOR
NOT LABELING
STUDENTS = 0.61

Test Prep

Test prep, including teaching test-taking skills, is another area for which there is insufficient evidence to warrant continued use. We've all done it because there is an appeal to one's surface logic to teaching students generic test-taking skills. It just wastes a lot of precious time. The small effect we have noted is mainly related to short-term gains, but there is little long-term gain, the learning does not transfer, and more often than not, the material learned via test prep is forgotten soon after the test! Instead, teach learning and study skills as an integral part of every lesson (not as a separate subject). Focus on teaching students the content and how to learn this content, as this has been shown to be much more effective in increasing student achievement on external measures of success. That's not to say that students shouldn't understand the format of a test, but that only takes a short time. They should be taught about how to best prioritize time doing any task, as this can be a critical test-prep skill—but again, do this within the context of the regular lessons, not as a stand-alone skill. Test prep and teaching test-taking skills are consuming significant numbers of instructional minutes, despite the

EFFECT SIZE
FOR TEACHING
TEST-TAKING = 0.27

EFFECT SIZE FOR
STUDY SKILLS = 0.63

fact that we know there is no evidence that these measures are going to inherently improve instruction or learning (Hattie, 2015; Hattie & Donoghue, 2016).

Another aspect of test preparation to be considered is stopping all teaching before a high-stakes test. We have all been there, and in many states, teachers' performance is based on our students' results on these tests. We know that distributed practice over time has a much higher impact than stopping all new instruction several weeks before the test for the sake of doing a massive review. As one of our colleagues so accurately describes it, "The best test prep is ongoing, high-quality instruction."

Homework

EFFECT SIZE FOR
HOMEWORK = 0.29

The final lesson we offer with respect to learning from what doesn't work focuses on homework. Overall, homework has little impact on students' learning. In this case, it's worth it to examine the value of homework at different grade levels. At the elementary level, homework has a limited impact on student learning, with an effect size of 0.10. At the middle school level, the effect size is 0.30, whereas at the high school level, the effect size is 0.55. The major reason for these differences comes from the nature of homework. Homework that provides another chance to practice something already taught and the student has begun to master can be effective (and much high school homework is of this nature), but homework that involves new materials, projects, or work a student may struggle with when alone is least effective (and too much elementary homework is of this nature). Importantly, homework may not be the answer to increasing students' achievement, and efforts to raise the rigor of schooling by assigning more independent learning that students must complete at home is misguided and potentially harmful. Students can succeed just as much from what they do in school, so we should not ask them to create a school at home where many students need adult expertise. While nearly all parents want to help their students, some do not know how. Many parents can be poor teachers of school work!

This section has been focused on teacher actions that do not work. We could have also focused on the finger pointing common in some schools. Yes, mobility has a negative impact on students' learning, as does summer vacation. John (Hattie, 2012) noted that about 50 percent of the achievement variation found in schools is attributed to student characteristics and demographics. Unfortunately, in many schools, that 50 percent gets all the play. After the students themselves, teachers have the biggest impact on student achievement, followed by school effects, the principal, parents, and the home. This is really, really important: a significant amount of the variance in student achievement is attributed to teachers. What teachers do matters. How teachers think really matters. Making informed decisions about what actions to take, based on evidence, should be the focus of professional learning sessions and grade-level or department conversations rather than admiring problems and blaming students for the conditions in which they live.

Visible Mathematics Teaching and Visible Mathematics Learning

Students need to witness their own learning. To do so, they need a teacher who is clear in communicating the learning intentions and success criteria. They need lots of formative evaluation paired with feedback to measure their progress as they move toward transfer. In turn, teachers need a clear sense of their own impact on student learning. Only then do teaching and learning become visible to everyone in the room. Figure 7.6 summarizes the relationship between what we do as teachers and how those teaching behaviors create the conditions for transferring learning.

As we've said many times, teachers should focus on *learning*. It's a mindset that we all need if we are going to ensure that students develop. A major theme throughout this book is about how teachers think (and also how we want students to think). John (Hattie, 2012) suggests ten mind frames that can be used to guide decisions, from curriculum adoptions to lesson planning (Figure 7.7). Taken together, these mind frames summarize a great deal of the "what works" literature.

Conclusion

Measuring one's impact on student learning means that assessment is a prominent feature of the classroom. The purpose is not to grade students' work, but to measure progress and compare it with the teaching that has occurred. Daily assessment is a chief way for teachers to make instructional decisions about what will occur next. Ways to check for

> A significant amount of the variance in student achievement is attributed to teachers. What teachers do matters. How teachers think really matters.

THE RELATIONSHIP BETWEEN
VISIBLE TEACHING AND VISIBLE LEARNING

Highly effective teachers . . .	Such that students . . .
Communicate clear learning intentions	Understand the learning intentions
Have challenging success criteria	Are challenged by the success criteria
Teach a range of learning strategies	Develop a range of learning strategies
Know when students are not progressing	Know when they are not progressing
Provide feedback	Seek feedback
Visibly learn themselves	Visibly teach themselves

Source: Hattie (n.d.).

Figure 7.6

understanding include asking questions, using exit tickets, and giving students lots of opportunities to self-assess. But these remain moment-in-time snapshots if not further contextualized through the administration and analysis of pre- and postassessments and regularly paced progress monitoring. The assessments discussed in this book are a reminder of the many ways we have of tracking student progress. But it's what we do with them that counts. If assessment is used for nothing more than sorting students, we will continue to achieve the results we have always gotten. These assessments are measures of *our* progress, too, but only if we choose to look closely at our impact.

The risk to our students in failing to examine our impact is significant and damaging. The reliance on ineffective practices such as in-grade retention and ability grouping is the result of decisions by well-meaning but misguided adults who have focused their attention on the characteristics of students at the exclusion of the effectiveness of the instruction they have received. We should know our students well and teach to their strengths while closely monitoring learning gaps. But the evidence is clear. Although what the student brings to school in terms of his or her learning background is important, a significant percentage of achievement variance

MIND FRAMES FOR TEACHERS

1. I cooperate with other teachers.
2. I use dialogue, not monologue.
3. I set the challenge.
4. I talk about learning, not teaching.
5. I inform all about the language of learning.
6. I see learning as hard work.
7. Assessment is feedback to me about me.
8. I am a change agent.
9. I am an evaluator.
10. I develop positive relationships.

Source: Adapted from Hattie (2012). Used with permission.

Figure 7.7

lies within the teacher's influence (Hattie, 2009). Yet too often, the vigor with which teachers locate explanations that lie with the student have far outstripped their efforts to examine their impact on student learning and adjust accordingly.

"I am a change agent."

This isn't a platitude. In the hands of an effective teacher, visible teaching and learning center our practices. It's an essential mind frame, and one that is vital if one is going to foster transfer of learning. It's true that some students will engage in transfer learning without any of us paying much attention to it, but that signals a lost opportunity as well. The key word in the first sentence is *agent*. As teachers, we have the potential for tremendous agency—to make learning happen—if we'd only seize the chance to do so. Being a change agent means bearing witness to student learning, reflecting on it, and recognizing that student progress tells us something about ourselves. How will we ever know what students are truly capable of if we don't get deeply involved in their learning lives?

This book has been about empowering educators to do exactly that. The profession is filled with dedicated people who have devoted their professional careers to improving the lives of children and youth. Prowess in mathematics matters. And the good news is that teachers matter. We mean this not as coffee-cup sentimentality, but rather as an empowering sentiment. What teachers do matters when they scale learning to move from surface, to deep, to transfer learning, and match approaches to their students' conceptual levels of knowledge. What teachers do matters when they monitor their impact and use that information to inform instruction and intervention. What teachers do matters when they reject institutional practices that harm learning. And best of all, what teachers do matters when they make mathematics learning visible to their students so students can become their own teachers.

Reflection and Discussion Questions

1. In what ways is the formative evaluation process a part of your classroom routine? In particular, think about the situations in which you provide feedback *without* grades. How can you do this more effectively and/or more often as part of your instructional practice?

2. Consider the framework for differentiated instruction discussed in this chapter. Thinking back over the recent units of study you have taught, what forms of differentiation do you use most often? Which forms would your students benefit from your using more often? How can you accomplish this?

3. This chapter discussed intervention as a tool for supporting learners where differentiation does not provide enough support or challenge. What does intervention look like in your school or classroom? How can you use what you've learned in this chapter (and this book) to strengthen your intervention program for both advanced and struggling learners?

4. What mind frames (Figure 7.7) resonate most for you? How does this impact your practice?

APPENDIX A. EFFECT SIZES

Rank	Influence	ES
1	Self-reported grades/student expectations	1.44
2	Piagetian programs	1.28
*3	Response to intervention	1.07
*4	Teacher credibility	0.90
5	Providing formative evaluation	0.90
6	Micro-teaching	0.88
*7	Classroom discussion	0.82
8	Comprehensive interventions for students who are learning disabled	0.77
9	Teacher clarity	0.75
10	Feedback	0.75
11	Reciprocal teaching	0.74
12	Teacher–student relationships	0.72
13	Spaced versus mass practice	0.71
14	Metacognitive strategies	0.69
15	Acceleration	0.68
16	Classroom behavioral	0.68
17	Vocabulary programs	0.67
18	Repeated reading programs	0.67
19	Creativity programs on achievement	0.65
20	Prior achievement	0.65
21	Self-verbalization and self-questioning	0.64
22	Study skills	0.63
23	Teaching strategies	0.62
24	Problem-solving teaching	0.61
25	Not labeling students	0.61
26	Comprehension programs	0.60
27	Concept mapping	0.60
28	Cooperative versus individualistic learning	0.59
29	Direct instruction	0.59
30	Tactile stimulation programs	0.58
31	Mastery learning	0.58

(Continued)

Rank	Influence	ES
32	Worked examples	0.57
33	Visual perception programs	0.55
34	Peer tutoring	0.55
35	Cooperative versus competitive learning	0.54
36	Phonics instruction	0.54
*37	Student-centered teaching	0.54
38	Classroom cohesion	0.53
39	Pre-term birth weight	0.53
40	Keller's Master Learning	0.53
41	Peer influences	0.53
42	Classroom management	0.52
43	Outdoor/adventure programs	0.52
44	Home environment	0.52
45	Socio-economic status	0.52
46	Interactive video methods	0.52
47	Professional development	0.51
48	Goals	0.50
49	Play programs	0.50
50	Second/third chance programs	0.50
51	Parental involvement	0.49
52	Small group learning	0.49
53	Questioning	0.48
54	Concentration/persistence/engagement	0.48
55	School effects	0.48
56	Motivation	0.48
57	Student ratings of quality of teaching	0.48
58	Early interventions	0.47
59	Self-concept	0.47
60	Preschool programs	0.45
61	Writing programs	0.44
62	Expectations	0.43
63	School size	0.43
64	Science programs	0.42

Rank	Influence	ES
65	Cooperative learning	0.42
66	Exposure to reading	0.42
67	Behavioral organizers/adjunct questions	0.41
68	Mathematics programs	0.40
69	Reducing anxiety	0.40
70	Social skills programs	0.39
71	Integrated curricula programs	0.39
72	Enrichment	0.39
73	Principals/school leaders	0.39
74	Career interventions	0.38
75	Time on task	0.38
*76	Psychotherapy programs	0.38
77	Computer-assisted instruction	0.37
78	Adjunct aids	0.37
79	Bilingual programs	0.37
80	Drama/arts programs	0.35
81	Creativity related to achievement	0.35
82	Attitude to mathematics/science	0.35
83	Frequent/effects of testing	0.34
84	Decreasing disruptive behavior	0.34
*85	Various teaching on creativity	0.34
86	Simulations	0.33
87	Inductive teaching	0.33
88	Ethnicity	0.32
89	Teacher effects	0.32
90	Drugs	0.32
91	Inquiry-based teaching	0.31
*92	Systems accountability	0.31
93	Ability grouping for gifted students	0.30
94	Homework	0.29
95	Home visiting	0.29
96	Exercise/relaxation	0.28

(Continued)

Rank	Influence	ES
97	Desegregation	0.28
98	Teaching test-taking	0.27
99	Use of calculators	0.27
*100	Volunteer tutors	0.26
101	Lack of illness	0.25
102	Mainstreaming	0.24
103	Values/moral education programs	0.24
104	Competitive versus individualistic learning	0.24
105	Programmed instruction	0.23
106	Summer school	0.23
107	Finances	0.23
108	Religious schools	0.23
109	Individualized instruction	0.22
110	Visual/audio-visual methods	0.22
111	Comprehensive teaching reforms	0.22
*112	Teacher verbal ability	0.22
113	Class size	0.21
114	Charter schools	0.20
115	Aptitude/treatment interactions	0.19
116	Extra-curricular programs	0.19
117	Learning hierarchies	0.19
118	Co-/team teaching	0.19
119	Personality	0.18
120	Within-class grouping	0.18
121	Special college programs	0.18
122	Family structure	0.18
*123	School counseling effects	0.18
124	Web-based learning	0.18
125	Matching learning styles	0.17
126	Teacher immediacy	0.16
127	Home-school programs	0.16
128	Problem-based learning	0.15

Rank	Influence	ES
129	Sentence-combining programs	0.15
130	Mentoring	0.15
131	Ability grouping	0.12
132	Diet	0.12
133	Gender	0.12
134	Teacher education	0.12
135	Distance education	0.11
136	Teacher subject matter knowledge	0.09
*137	Changing school calendar/timetable	0.09
138	Out-of-school curricular experiences	0.09
139	Perceptual motor programs	0.08
140	Whole language	0.06
*141	Diversity of students	0.05
142	College halls of residence	0.05
143	Multi-grade/age classes	0.04
144	Student control over learning	0.04
145	Open versus traditional learning spaces	0.01
146	Summer vacation	−0.02
147	Welfare policies	−0.12
148	Retention	−0.13
149	Television	−0.18
150	Mobility	−0.34

Source: Adapted from Hattie (2012). Reproduced with permission.

* Represents an effect that has been added to the original list since the publication of *Visible Learning: A Synthesis of Over 800 Meta-Analyses Relating to Achievement* (Hattie, 2009).

Notes: In-chapter references to effect size for ability grouping in elementary grades, compare and contrast new with old problems, goal setting, homework at the elementary, middle, and high school levels, manipulatives, mnemonics, organizing conceptual knowledge, and student self-monitoring are not listed here and are based on the ongoing synthesis of learning strategies research.

APPENDIX B. STANDARDS FOR MATHEMATICAL PRACTICE

Standard for Mathematical Practice	What the Teacher Does	What the Students Do

1. Make sense of problems and persevere in solving them.	• Provides students with rich tasks that focus on and promote student understanding of an important mathematical concept.
	• Provides time for and facilitates the discussion of problem solutions.
	  ○ What are you asked to find?
	  ○ Have you solved similar problems before?
	  ○ What is your plan for solving the problem?
	  ○ Can you explain how you solved the problem?
	  ○ Does your answer make sense?
	  ○ Did you use a different method to check your answer?
		• Actively engage in solving problems by working to understand the information that is in the problem and the question that is asked.
		• Choose appropriate manipulatives or drawings to help make sense of the actions in the problem.
		• Use a variety of strategies that make sense to solve the problem.
		• Ask themselves if their solution makes sense.

2. Reason abstractly and quantitatively.	• Provides a variety of concrete materials and encourages their use to help students develop mathematical ideas.
	• Gives students problem situations and encourages varied solution paths.
	• Helps students use mathematical reasoning by asking questions such as the following:
	  ○ Can you tell me what is happening here?
	  ○ How can you show what is happening in the problem using materials?
	  ○ Can you write a number sentence (equation) to match the story?
	  ○ What do the numbers in the number sentence mean?
		• Use varied strategies, models, and drawings to think about the mathematics of a task or example.
		• Demonstrate mathematical understanding about the "numberness" of a given situation (quantitative reasoning).
		• Connect concrete examples with pictorial and symbolic representations as developmentally appropriate.

3. Construct viable arguments and critique the reasoning of others.	• Provides tasks that encourage students to construct mathematical arguments.
	• Expects students to explain their strategies and mathematical thinking to others.
	• Expects students to listen to the reasoning of others.
	• Helps students to compare strategies and methods by asking questions such as the following:
	  ○ How can you prove that your answer is correct?
	  ○ What do you think about _____'s strategy?
	  ○ How is your method different from _____'s? How is it similar?
	  ○ What questions do you have for _____?
		• Explain their strategies and thinking orally or in writing using concrete models, drawings, actions, or numbers.
		• Use number sense to determine whether a solution is reasonable.
		• Listen to the thinking of others in the class.
		• Ask questions of one another and the teacher to clarify their understanding.
		• Look for similarities among different ways to solve problems.

4. Model with mathematics.	• Provides a variety of materials for students to use as they work to make sense of mathematical ideas and solve problems.
	• Poses real-world tasks that are developmentally appropriate for students.
	• Uses the progression of developing conceptual understanding through the use of concrete models; pictorial models; and, when students are ready, symbolic representations.
	• Encourages students to use models as they create mathematical arguments and explain their thinking to others.
	• Asks students questions such as the following:
	  ○ Can you show me how you solved this using a _____?
	  ○ Can you draw a picture or act out what is happening in the problem?
	  ○ Is this working, or do you need to change your model?
		• Put the problem or situation in their own words.
		• Model the situation using concrete materials and an appropriate strategy (e.g., arrays, area models, fraction bars, number lines, decimal models).
		• Describe what they do with the models and how it relates to the problem situation.
		• Check to see if an answer makes sense and changes a model when necessary.

Standard for Mathematical Practice	What the Teacher Does	What the Students Do
5. Use appropriate tools strategically.	• Encourages students to use models in constructing mathematical arguments. • Provides a variety of concrete materials and encourages their use to help students develop mathematical ideas. • Helps students to link concrete to pictorial to numerical representations as developmentally appropriate.	• Select concrete materials that will help to develop conceptual understanding. • Begin to make the transition from concrete to pictorial representations **when conceptual understanding is apparent.** • Determine if mental computation, concrete models, or paper and pencil is the most efficient way to solve a problem or task.

6. Attend to precision.	• Supports students in developing an understanding of mathematical vocabulary by explicitly introducing terms and having them available for students to use (for example, by using a word wall).
	
	• Repeats a student's explanation using accurate vocabulary when necessary.
	
	• Supports students' precision by asking the following questions:
	  ○ What does _____ mean?
	  ○ What labels could you use with your answer?
	  ○ What unit of measure would you use when you are measuring _____?
		• Communicate precisely using grade-level-appropriate vocabulary.
		
		• Work to carefully formulate clear explanations.
		
		• State the meaning of symbols, and calculate accurately and efficiently.
		
		• Choose appropriate units of measure.
		
		• Label accurately when measuring.

7. Look for and make use of structure.	• Provides explicit situations in which students can use a strategy to develop understanding of a concept.
	
	• Supports student thinking by providing materials that are appropriate to the concept (for example, using area models and arrays to learn multiplication and division facts).
	
	• Asks questions that help students to see the structure of the mathematics and make generalizations, such as the following:
	  ○ What happens when you multiply a number by one? By zero?
	  ○ What do you notice when a number is ten times as great as another number?
	  ○ What do you notice when you divide a number by ten?
	  ○ How can you use what you know to explain why this works?
	  ○ What patterns do you see?
		• Look for patterns when developing conceptual understanding of place value, whole number operations, and rational numbers.
		
		• Recognize patterns related to properties of addition and subtraction.
		
		• Identify efficient strategies to use in a variety of situations using concrete materials and then generalizing to any similar situation.
		
		• Develop conceptual understanding by working to determine why numbers work the way they do.

8. Look for and express regularity in repeated reasoning.	• Provides a variety of examples that explicitly focus on patterns and repeated reasoning.
	
	• Asks students to fine-tune their mathematical arguments with questions such as the following:
	  ○ What do you notice about the products of 5 × 3 and 3 × 5?
	  ○ If you think about the value of the numbers, can you find an easier way to think about the problem?
	  ○ How could this problem help you solve another problem?
		• Notice repeated calculations and make generalizations.
		
		• Continually evaluate the reasonableness of their answers and their thinking.
		
		• Make generalizations by seeing patterns based on properties, models, or patterns, and use these generalizations to develop conceptual understanding.

Source: National Governors Association Center for Best Practices & Council of Chief State School Officers (2010).

APPENDIX C. A SELECTION OF INTERNATIONAL MATHEMATICAL PRACTICE OR PROCESS STANDARDS*

USA Common Core State Standards 8 Mathematical Practices[a]	USA Texas Essential Knowledge and Skills TEKS 7 Mathematical Practice Standards[b]	USA Virginia Mathematics 5 Standards of Learning[c]	International Baccalaureate 6 Assessment Objectives[d]	Hong Kong Key Learning Area 7 Generic Skills[e]	Singapore Mathematical Problem-Solving Processes[f]	Australian F-10 Mathematics Curriculum Key Ideas[g]
1. Make sense of problems and persevere in solving them.	A. Apply mathematics to problems arising in everyday life, society, and the workplace.	Mathematical problem solving	Knowledge and understanding	Collaboration skills	Reasoning, communications, and connections	Understanding
2. Reason abstractly and quantitatively.	B. Use a problem-solving model that incorporates analyzing given information, formulating a plan or strategy, determining a solution, justifying the solution, and evaluating the problem-solving process and the reasonableness of the solution.	Mathematical communication	Problem solving	Communication skills	Applications and modeling	Fluency
3. Construct viable arguments and critique the reasoning of others.	C. Select tools, including real objects, manipulatives, paper and pencil, and technology as appropriate.	Mathematical reasoning	Communication and interpretation	Creativity	Thinking skills and heuristics	Problem solving
4. Use appropriate tools strategically.	D. Communicate mathematical ideas, reasoning, and their implications using multiple representations, including symbols, diagrams, graphs, and language as appropriate.	Mathematical connections	Technology	Critical thinking skills		Reasoning
5. Attend to precision.	E. Create and use representations to organize, record, and communicate mathematical ideas.	Mathematical representations	Reasoning	Information technology skills		
6. Look for and make use of structure.			Inquiry approaches	Numeracy skills		
				Problem-solving skills		

USA Common Core Standards 8 Mathematical Practices[a]	USA Texas Essential Knowledge and Skills TEKS 7 Mathematical Practice Standards[b]	USA Virginia Mathematics 5 Standards of Learning[c]	International Baccalaureate 6 Assessment Objectives[d]	Hong Kong Key Learning Area 7 Generic Skills[e]	Singapore Mathematical Problem-Solving Processes[f]	Australian F-10 Mathematics Curriculum Key Ideas[g]
7. Look for and express regularity in repeated reasoning. 8. Model with mathematics.	F. Analyze mathematical relationships to connect and communicate mathematical ideas. G. Display, explain, and justify mathematical ideas and arguments using precise mathematical language in written or oral communication.					

*Note that this is a non-exhaustive list of international mathematical practice/process standards as of June 2016. Because standards are often under review, you can look to your own state or country's individual documents to find the most up-to-date practice/process standards.

[a]Retrieved June 22, 2016, from http://www.corestandards.org/Math/Practice/.

[b]Retrieved June 22, 2016, from http://ritter.tea.state.tx.us/rules/tac/chapter111/ch111a.html.

[c]Retrieved June 22, 2016, from http://www.doe.virginia.gov/testing/sol/standards_docs/mathematics/2009/stds_math.pdf.

[d]Retrieved June 22, 2016, from http://www.ibo.org/globalassets/publications/recognition/5_mathsl.pdf.

[e]Retrieved June 22, 2016, from http://www.edb.gov.hk/attachment/en/curriculum-development/kla/ma/curr/Math_CAGuide_e_2015.pdf.

[f]Retrieved June 22, 2016, from https://www.moe.gov.sg/docs/default-source/document/education/syllabuses/sciences/files/mathematics-syllabus-(primary-1-to-4).pdf.

[g]Retrieved June 22, 2016, from http://www.australiancurriculum.edu.au/mathematics/curriculum/f-10?layout=1.

APPENDIX D. EIGHT EFFECTIVE MATHEMATICS TEACHING PRACTICES

Teaching Practice	Purpose	What the Teacher Does	What the Students Do
1. Establish mathematics goals to focus learning.	• Set the stage to guide instructional decisions. • Expect students to understand the purpose of a lesson beyond simply repeating the standard.	Considers broad goals as well as the goals of the unit and the actual lesson, including the following: • What is to be learned? • Why is the goal important? • Where do students need to go? • How can learning be extended?	• Make sense of new concepts and skills, including connections to concepts learned in previous grades. • Experience connections among the standards and across domains. • Deepen their understanding and expect mathematics to make sense.
2. Implement tasks that promote reasoning and problem solving.	• Provide opportunities for students to engage in exploration and make sense of important mathematics. • Encourage students to use procedures in ways that are connected to understanding.	Chooses tasks that • are built on current student understandings. • have various entry points with multiple ways for the problems to be solved. • are interesting to students.	• Work to make sense out of the task and persevere in solving problems. • Use a variety of models and materials to make sense of the mathematics in the task. • Convince themselves and others the answer is reasonable.
3. Use and connect mathematical representations.	• Provide concrete representations that lead students to develop conceptual understanding and later connect that understanding to procedural skills. • Provide a variety of representations that range from using physical models to using abstract notations.	• Uses tasks that allow students to use a variety of representations. • Encourages the use of different representations, including concrete models, pictures, words, and numbers, that support students in explaining their thinking and reasoning.	• Use materials to make sense out of problem situations. • Connect representations to mathematical ideas and the structure of big ideas, including operational sense with whole numbers, fractions, and decimals.
4. Facilitate meaningful mathematical discourse.	• Provide students with opportunities to share ideas, clarify their understanding, and develop convincing arguments. • Advance the mathematical thinking of the whole class by talking and sharing aloud.	• Engages students in explaining their mathematical reasoning in small group and classroom situations. • Facilitates discussions among students that support making sense of a variety of strategies and approaches. • Scaffolds classroom discussions so that connections between representations and mathematical ideas take place.	• Explain their ideas and reasoning in small groups and with the entire class. • Listen to the reasoning of others. • Ask questions of others to make sense of their ideas.

Teaching Practice	Purpose	What the Teacher Does	What the Students Do
5. Pose purposeful questions.	• Reveal students' current understanding of a concept. • Encourage students to explain, elaborate, and clarify their thinking. • Make the learning of mathematics more visible and accessible for students.	• Asks questions that build on and extend student thinking. • Is intentional about the kinds of questions asked to make the mathematics more visible to students. • Uses wait time to provide students with time to think and examine their ideas.	• Think more deeply about the process of the mathematics rather than simply focusing on the answer. • Listen to and comment on the explanations of others in the class.
6. Build procedural fluency from conceptual understanding.	• Provide experiences with concrete materials that allow students to make sense of important mathematics and flexibly choose from a variety of methods to solve problems.	• Provides opportunities for students to reason about mathematical ideas. • Expects students to explain why their strategies work. • Connects student methods to efficient procedures as appropriate.	• Understand and explain the procedures they are using and why they work. • Use a variety of strategies to solve problems and make sense of mathematical ideas. • Do not rely on shortcuts or tricks to do mathematics.
7. Support productive struggle in learning mathematics.	• Provide opportunities for productive struggle, which is significant and essential to learning mathematics with understanding. • Allow students to grapple with ideas and relationships. • Give students ample time to work with and make sense of new ideas, which is critical to their learning with understanding.	• Supports student struggle without showing and telling a procedure but rather focusing on the important mathematical ideas. • Asks questions that scaffold and advance student thinking. • Builds questions and plans lessons based on important student misconceptions rather than focusing on the correct answer. • Recognizes the importance of effort as students work to make sense of new ideas.	• Stick to a task and recognize that struggle is part of making sense. • Ask questions that will help them to better understand the task. • Support each other with ideas rather than telling others the answer or how to solve a problem.
8. Elicit and use evidence of student thinking.	• Elicit and use evidence of student thinking, which helps teachers access learning progress and can be used to make instructional decisions during the lessons as well as help to prepare what will occur in the next lesson. • Assess student thinking and understanding by using formative assessment through student written and oral ideas.	• Determines what to look for in gathering evidence of student learning. • Poses questions and answers student questions that provide information about student understanding, strategies, and reasoning. • Uses evidence to determine next steps of instruction.	• Accept that reasoning and understanding are as important as the answer to a problem. • Use mistakes and misconceptions to rethink their understanding. • Ask questions of the teacher and peers to clarify confusion or misunderstanding. • Assess progress toward developing mathematical understanding.

Source: Adapted from National Council of Teachers of Mathematics (2014).

APPENDIX E. WEBSITES TO HELP MAKE MATHEMATICS LEARNING VISIBLE

http://illuminations.nctm.org

Illuminations works to serve you by increasing access to quality standards-based resources for teaching and learning mathematics, including interactive tools for students and instructional support for teachers.

http://www.illustrativemathematics.org

This site provides rich instructional and assessment tasks, lesson plans, and other resources for teachers, assessment writers, and curriculum developers.

http://www.insidemathematics.org

This site provides rich tasks, videos, performance assessment tasks, tools for teachers, and information and resources on the content and practice standards.

http://mathforum.org

The Math Forum provides resources, materials, activities, person-to-person interactions, and educational products and services that enrich and support teaching and learning in an increasingly technological world.

http://www.nctm.org

This is the website of the National Council of Teachers of Mathematics, the national professional organization for PreK–16 teachers of mathematics. Find information on current research-based initiatives in mathematics education, publications, journals, and support materials.

https://nrich.maths.org

The NRICH project aims to enrich the experience of the mathematics curriculum for all learners, offer challenging and engaging activities, develop mathematical thinking and problem-solving skills, and show rich mathematics in meaningful contexts.

http://www.teachingchannel.org

A nonprofit video showcase—on the Internet and TV—of inspiring, high-quality, and effective teaching practices.

http://visible-learning.org

The aim of this website is to bring together the freely available online resources related to John Hattie's Visible Learning research (videos, research papers, books, and news articles) and to enable a deeper understanding of the underlying concepts.

References

Ainsworth, L., & Viegut, D. (2006). *Common formative assessments: How to connect standards-based instruction and assessment.* Thousand Oaks, CA: Corwin.

Atkinson, R. K., Derry, S. J., Renkl, A., & Wortham, D. W. (2000). Learning from examples: Instructional principles from the worked examples research. *Review of Educational Research, 70,* 181–214.

Bahekar, A. A., Singh, S., Saha, S., Molnar, J., & Arora, R. (2007). The prevalence and incidence of coronary heart disease is significantly increased in periodontitis: A meta-analysis. *American Heart Journal, 154*(5), 830–837.

Bahrick, H. P., & Hall, L. K. (1991). Lifetime maintenance of high school mathematics content. *Journal of Educational Psychology, 120,* 20–33.

Bandura, A. (1997). *Self-efficacy: The exercise of control.* New York: Freeman.

Bay-Williams, J. M., & Kling, G. (2014). Enriching addition and subtraction fact mastery through games. *Teaching Children Mathematics, 21*(4), 238–247.

Bay-Williams, J. M., & Livers, S. (2009). Supporting math vocabulary acquisition. *Teaching Children Mathematics, 16*(4), 238–245.

Beck, I. L., McKeown, M. G., & Kucan, L. (2013). *Bringing words to life: Robust vocabulary instruction* (2nd ed.). New York: Guilford.

Bennett, N., & Cass, A. (1989). The effects of group composition on group interactive processes and pupil understanding. *British Educational Research Journal, 15*(1), 19–32.

Bereiter, C. (2002). *Education and mind in the knowledge age.* Mahwah, NJ: Lawrence Erlbaum.

Biddle, M. (2007). When opportunity knocks: Integrating language arts and the daily calendar. *Reading Teacher, 60*(5), 488–491.

Biggs, J., & Collis, K. (1982). *Evaluating the quality of learning: The SOLO taxonomy.* New York: Academic Press.

Black, P. J., & Wiliam, D. (1998). Inside the black box: Raising standards through classroom assessment. *Phi Delta Kappan, 80*(2), 139.

Boaler, J. (1997). Setting, social class and survival of the quickest. *British Educational Research Journal, 23*(5), 575–595.

Boaler, J. (2015). *What's math got to do with it? How teachers and parents can transform mathematics learning and inspire success* (Rev. ed.). New York: Penguin.

Boaler, J. (2016). *Mathematical mindsets.* New York: Jossey-Bass.

Bransford, J., Brown, A. L., & Cocking, R. R. (2000). *How people learn: Brain, mind, experience, and school* (Expanded ed.). Washington, DC: National Academy Press.

Brookhart, S. M. (2008). *How to give effective feedback to your students.* Alexandria, VA: ASCD.

Butler, R. (1988). Enhancing and undermining intrinsic motivation: The effects of task-involving and ego-involving evaluation on interest and performance. *British Journal of Educational Psychology, 58*, 1–14.

Butler, R. (2008). Ego-involving and frame of reference effects of tracking on elementary school students' motivational orientations and help seeking in math class. *Social Psychology of Education, 11*(1), 5–34.

Carmody, G., & Wood, L. (2009). Peer tutoring in mathematics for university students. *Mathematics & Computer Education, 43*(1), 18–28.

Carpenter, T., Fennema, E., Franke, M. L., Levi, L., & Empson, S. B. (2014). *Children's mathematics: Cognitively guided instruction* (2nd ed.). Portsmouth, NH: Heinemann.

Center on Disability & Community Inclusion. (2014). Core concepts. Retrieved from http://www.uvm.edu/~wfox/CoreConcepts.html

Chapin, S., O'Connor, C., & Anderson, N. (2009). *Classroom discussions: Using math talk to help students learn* (2nd ed.). Sausalito, CA: Math Solutions.

Clarke, S., Timperley, H., & Hattie, J. A. C. (2003). *Unlocking formative assessment: Practical strategies for enhancing students' learning in the primary and intermediate classroom* (1st New Zealand ed.). Auckland: Hodder Moa Beckett.

Crismond, D. P., & Adams, R. S. (2012). The Informed Design Teaching and Learning Matrix. *Journal of Engineering Education, 101*(4), 738–797.

Cronbach, L. J. (1942). Measuring knowledge of precise word meaning. *Journal of Educational Research, 36*(7), 528–534.

Cunningham, P. M. (2000). *Classrooms that work: They can all read and write.* New York: Addison-Wesley.

DeLashmutt, K. (2007). *A study of the role of mnemonics in learning mathematics* (Summative Projects for MA Degree). Retrieved July 12, 2012, from http://digitalcommons.unl.edu/mathmidsummative/19

Domino, J. (2010). *The effects of physical manipulatives on achievement in mathematics in Grades K–6: A meta-analysis.* Unpublished doctoral dissertation, State University of New York at Buffalo.

Dweck, C. S. (2006). *Mindset: The new psychology of success.* New York: Random House.

Elawar, M. C., & Corno, L. (1985). A factorial experiment in teachers' written feedback on student homework: Changing teacher behaviour a little rather than a lot. *Journal of Educational Psychology, 77*(2), 162–173.

Elliot, A., & Harackiewicz, J. (1994). Goal setting, achievement orientation, and intrinsic motivation: A meditational analysis. *Journal of Personality and Social Psychology, 66*(5), 968–980.

Ellis, J. A., Semb, G. B., & Cole, B. (1998). Very long-term memory for information taught in school. *Contemporary Educational Psychology, 23,* 419–433.

Fendick, F. (1990). *The correlation between teacher clarity of communication and student achievement gain: A meta-analysis.* Unpublished doctoral dissertation, University of Florida, Gainesville.

Fisher, D., & Frey, N. (2014). *Better learning through structured teaching: A framework for the gradual release of responsibility* (2nd ed.). Alexandria, VA: ASCD.

Flavell, J. H. (1979). Metacognition and cognitive monitoring: A new area of cognitive-developmental inquiry. *American Psychologist, 34,* 906–911.

Flores, M. M., & Kaylor, M. (2007). The effects of a direct instruction program on the fraction performance of middle school students at-risk for failure in mathematics. *Journal of Instructional Psychology, 34*(2), 84–94.

Foundation—Year 10 Australian Curriculum. (2015). Retrieved from http://www.australiancurriculum.edu.au/mathematics/curriculum/f-10?layout=1

Frayer, D., Frederick, W. C., & Klausmeier, H. J. (1969). *A schema for testing the level of cognitive mastery.* Madison: Wisconsin Center for Education Research.

Frey, N. (2005). Retention, social promotion, and academic redshirting: What do we know and need to know? *Remedial and Special Education, 26*(6), 332–346.

Frey, N., & Fisher, D. (2013). *Rigorous reading: 5 access points for comprehending complex texts.* Thousand Oaks, CA: Corwin.

Fuson, K. C., Kalchman, M., & Bransford, J. D. (2005). Mathematical understanding: An introduction. In M. S. Donovan & J. D. Bransford (Eds.), *How students learn: History, mathematics, and science in the classroom* (pp. 217–256). Washington, DC: National Academies Press.

Garofalo, J., & Lester, F. K., Jr. (1985). Metacognition, cognitive monitoring, and mathematical performance. *Journal for Research in Mathematics Education, 16*(3), 163–176.

Gentry, M., & Owen, S. (1999). An investigation of the effects of total school flexible cluster grouping on identification, achievement, and classroom practices. *Gifted Child Quarterly, 43*(4), 224–243.

Gersten, R., Beckmann, S., Clarke, B., Foegen, A., Marsh, L., Star, J. R., & Witzel, B. (2009). *Assisting students struggling with mathematics: Response to Intervention (RtI) for elementary and middle schools* (NCEE 2009-4060). Washington, DC: National Center for Education Evaluation and Regional Assistance, Institute of Education Sciences, U.S. Department of Education. Retrieved from http://ies.ed.gov/ncee/wwc/publications/practiceguides/

Gersten, R., & Newman-Gonchar, R. (Eds.). (2011). *Understanding RTI in mathematics: Proven methods and applications.* Baltimore: Brookes.

Ginsburg-Block, M. D., Rohrbeck, C. A., & Fantuzzo, J. W. (2006). A meta-analytic review of social, self-concept, and behavioral outcomes of peer-assisted learning. *Journal of Educational Psychology, 98*(4), 732–749.

Graves, M. F. (1986). Vocabulary learning and instruction. *Review of Research in Education, 13,* 49–89.

Graves, M. F. (2006). *The vocabulary book: Learning & instruction*. New York: Teachers College Press.

Gresham, G., & Little, M. (2012). RtI in math class. *Teaching Children Mathematics, 19*(1), 20–29.

Hastie, S. (2011). *Teaching students to set goals: Strategies, commitment, and monitoring*. Unpublished doctoral dissertation, University of Auckland, New Zealand.

Hattie, J. (2009). *Visible learning: A synthesis of over 800 meta-analyses relating to achievement*. New York: Routledge.

Hattie, J. (2012). *Visible learning for teachers: Maximizing impact on learning*. New York: Routledge.

Hattie, J. (2015). The applicability of visible learning to higher education. *Scholarship of Teaching and Learning in Psychology, 1*(1), 79–91.

Hattie, J. (n.d.). Visible Learning that makes the difference in education [PowerPoint Presentation]. Visible Learning Laboratories, University of Auckland, New Zealand.

Hattie, J., & Donoghue, G. (2016). Learning strategies: A synthesis and conceptual model. *Nature Partner Journals, 1*. doi:10.1038/npjscilearn.2016.13

Hattie, J., & Yates, G. (2014). *Visible learning and the science of how we learn*. New York: Routledge.

Herbel-Eisenmann, B. A., & Breyfogle, M. L. (2005). Questioning our patterns of questioning. *Mathematics Teaching in the Middle School, 10*(9), 484–489.

Hester, K., & Cunningham, C. (2007, June). *Engineering is elementary: An engineering and technology curriculum for children*. Paper presented at the 2007 Annual Conference & Exposition, Honolulu, Hawaii. https://peer.asee.org/1469

Hufferd-Ackles, K., Fuson, K., & Gamoran Sherin, M. (2004). Describing levels and components of a math-talk learning community. *Journal for Research in Mathematics Education, 35*(2), 81–116.

Humphreys, C., & Parker, R. (2015). *Making number talks matter: Developing mathematical practices and deepening understanding, Grades 4–10*. Portland, ME: Stenhouse.

Hyland, F., & Hyland, K. (2001). Sugaring the pill: Praise and criticism in written feedback. *Journal of Second Language Writing, 10*(3), 185–212.

Iacoboni, M., Molnar-Szakacs, I., Gallese, V., Buccino, G., Mazziotta, J. C., & Rizzolatti, G. (2005). Grasping the intentions of others with one's own mirror neuron system. *PLoS Biology, 3*(3), e79.

Ingersoll, R. M. (2011). Do we produce enough mathematics and science teachers? *Kappan Magazine, 92*(6), 37–41.

Ito, M., Gutiérrez, K., Livingstone, S., Penuel, B., Rhodes, J., Salen, K., Schor, J., Sefton-Green, J., & Watkins, S. C. (2013). *Connected learning: An agenda for research and design*. Irvine, CA: Digital Media and Learning Research Hub.

Jackson, R. (2015). *10 promises worth keeping to your students*. Retrieved from https://mindstepsinc.com/2015/08/10-promises-worth-keeping-to-your-students/

Jacobs, H. R. (1994). *Mathematics: A human endeavor* (3rd ed.). New York: Freeman.

Jensen, E. (2005). *Teaching with the brain in mind* (2nd ed.). Alexandria, VA: ASCD.

Jeon, K. (2012). Reflecting on PEMDAS. *Teaching Children Mathematics, 18*(6), 370–377.

Kapur, M. (2008). Productive failure. *Cognition and Instruction, 26*(3), 379–424.

Kapur, M. (2012). Productive failure in learning the concept of variance. *Instructional Science, 40*(4), 651–672.

Karp, K. S., Bush, S. B., & Dougherty, B. J. (2014). 13 rules that expire. *Teaching Children Mathematics, 21*(1), 18–25.

Knight, J., & van Nieuwerburgh, C. (2012). Instructional coaching: A focus on practice. *Coaching: An International Journal of Theory, Research and Practice, 5*(2), 100–112.

Kolb, D. A. (1984). *Experiential learning: Experience as the source of learning and development.* Englewood Cliffs, NJ: Prentice Hall.

Kulik, J. A., & Kulik, J. C. (1992). Meta-analytic findings on grouping programs. *Gifted Child Quarterly, 3,* 72–76.

Leahy, S., Lyon, C., Thompson, M., & Wiliam, D. (2005). Classroom assessment: Minute-by-minute and day-by-day. *Educational Leadership, 63*(3), 18–24.

Lembke, E. S., Hampton, D., & Beyers, S. J. (2012). Response to intervention in mathematics: Critical elements. *Psychology in the Schools, 49*(3), 257–272.

Leinwand, S. (2016). *Thoughts on revising how we do math homework.* Personal communication.

Lesh, R., Post, T., & Behr, M. (1987). Representations and translations among representations in mathematics learning and problem solving. In C. Janvier (Ed.), *Problems of representation in the teaching and learning of mathematics* (pp. 33–40). Hillsdale, NJ: Lawrence Erlbaum.

Levasseur, K., & Cuoco, A. (2003). Mathematical habits of mind. In H. L. Schoen (Ed.), *Teaching mathematics through problem solving: Grades 6–12* (pp. 23–37). Reston, VA: National Council of Teachers of Mathematics.

Lin-Siegler, X., Ahn, J. N., Chen, J., Fang, F. A., & Luna-Lucero, M. (2016). Even Einstein struggled: Effects of learning about great scientists' struggles on high school students' motivation to learn science. *Journal of Educational Psychology, 108*(3), 314–328.

Livers, S. D., & Bay-Williams, J. M. (2014). Vocabulary support: Constructing (not obstructing) meaning. *Mathematics Teaching in the Middle School, 10*(3), 153–159.

Lobato, J., Clarke, D., & Ellis, A. B. (2005). Initiating and eliciting in teaching: A reformulation of telling. *Journal for Research in Mathematics Education, 36*(2), 101–136.

Locke, E. A., & Latham, G. P. (1990). *A theory of goal setting and task performance.* Englewood Cliffs, NJ: Prentice Hall.

Loehr, A. M., Fyfe, E. R., & Rittle-Johnson, B. (2014). Wait for it . . . Delaying instruction improves mathematics problem solving: A classroom study. *Journal of Problem Solving, 7*(1), Article 5. Retrieved from http://docs.lib.purdue.edu/jps/vol7/iss1/5

Lubinski, D., & Benbow, C. P. (2006). Study of mathematically precocious youth after 35 years: Uncovering antecedents for the development of math-science expertise. *Perspectives on Psychological Science, 1*(4), 316–345.

Marzano, R. J. (1998). *A theory-based meta-analysis of research on instruction.* Aurora, CO: Mid-Continent Regional Education Lab.

McGinn, K., Lange, K., & Booth, J. (2015). A worked example for creating worked examples. *Mathematics Teaching in the Middle School, 21*(1), 26–33.

Munter, C., Stein, M. K., & Smith, M. S. (2015a). Dialogic and direct instruction: Two distinct models of mathematics instruction and the debate(s) surrounding them. *Teachers College Record, 117*(11), 1–32.

Munter, C., Stein, M. K., & Smith, M. S. (2015b). Is there a common pedagogical core? Examining instructional practices of competing models of mathematics teaching. *NCSM Journal of Mathematics Education Leadership, 16*(2), 3–13.

Nathan, M. J., & Petrosino, A. (2003). Expert blind spot among preservice teachers. *American Educational Research Journal, 40*(4), 905–928.

National Association for Gifted Children. (n.d.). *Curriculum compacting.* Retrieved June 4, 2016, from https://www.nagc.org/resources-publications/gifted-education-practices/curriculum-compacting

National Council of Teachers of Mathematics. (1991). *Professional standards for teaching mathematics.* Reston, VA: Author.

National Council of Teachers of Mathematics. (2000). *Principles & standards for school mathematics.* Reston, VA: Author.

National Council of Teachers of Mathematics. (2014). *Principles to actions: Ensuring mathematical success for all.* Reston, VA: Author.

National Governors Association Center for Best Practices & Council of Chief State School Officers. (2010). *Common core state standards for mathematics.* Washington, DC: Authors.

National Mathematics Advisory Panel. (2008). *Foundations for success: The final report of the National Mathematics Advisory Panel.* Washington, DC: U.S. Department of Education.

National Research Council. (2001). *Adding it up: Helping children learn mathematics.* Washington, DC: National Academies Press.

National Research Council. (2005). *How students learn: History, mathematics, and science in the classroom.* Washington, DC: National Academies Press.

National Research Council. (2009). *Mathematics learning in early childhood: Paths toward excellence and equity.* Washington, DC: National Academies Press.

National Research Council. (2012). *Education for life and work: Developing transferable knowledge and skills in the 21st century.* Washington, DC: National Academies Press.

Orlowski, M., Lorson, K., Lyon, A., & Minoughan, S. (2013). My classroom physical activity pyramid: A tool for integrating movement into the classroom. *Journal of Physical Education, Recreation & Dance, 84*(9), 47–51.

Palincsar, A. S. (2013). Reciprocal teaching. In J. Hattie & E. Anderman (Eds.), *International guide to student achievement* (pp. 369–371). New York: Routledge.

Palincsar, A. S., & Brown, A. L. (1984). Reciprocal teaching of comprehension-fostering and comprehension-monitoring activities. *Cognition and Instruction, 1*(2), 117–175.

Pape, S. J., & Tchoshanov, M. A. (2001). The role of representation(s) in developing mathematical understanding. *Theory Into Practice, 40*(2), 118–127.

Parks, M., Solmon, M., & Lee, A. (2007). Understanding classroom teachers' perceptions of integrating physical activity: A collective efficacy perspective. *Journal of Research in Childhood Education, 21*(3), 316–328.

Perkins, D. N., & Salomon, G. (1992). Transfer of learning. *Contribution to the International Encyclopedia of Education* (2nd ed.). Oxford, England: Pergamon Press.

Plato. (1996). *The republic* (R. W. Sterling & W. C. Scott, Trans.) (Paperback ed.). New York: Norton.

Purkey, W. W. (1992). An introduction to invitational theory. *Journal of Invitational Theory and Practice, 1*(1), 5–15.

Reilly, Y., Parsons, J., & Bortolot, E. (2009). Reciprocal teaching in mathematics. *Proceedings of the Mathematics of Prime Importance Conference, the 46th Conference of the Mathematical Association of Victoria* (pp. 182–189). Retrieved from http://www.mav.vic.edu.au/files/conferences/2009/13Reilly.pdf

Resnick, L. B., Michaels, S., & O'Connor, C. (2010). How (well structured) talk builds the mind. In R. Sternberg & D. Preiss (Eds.), *Innovations in educational psychology: Perspectives on learning, teaching and human development* (pp. 163–194). New York: Springer.

Rizzolatti, G., & Craighero, L. (2004). The mirror-neuron system. *Annual Review of Neuroscience, 27*(1), 169–192.

Rosenzweig, C., Krawec, J., & Montague, M. (2011). Metacognitive strategy use of eighth-grade students with and without learning disabilities during mathematical problem solving: A think-aloud analysis. *Journal of Learning Disabilities, 44*(6), 508–520.

Sapon-Shevin, M. (1994). *Playing favorites: Gifted education and the disruption of community.* Albany, NY: SUNY Press.

Schoenfeld, A. H. (1992). Learning to think mathematically: Problem solving, metacognition, and sense making in mathematics. In D. Grouws (Ed.), *Handbook of research on mathematics teaching and learning* (pp. 334–370). New York: Macmillan.

Schunk, D. H. (1996). Goal and self-evaluative influences during children's cognitive skill learning. *American Educational Research Journal, 33,* 359–382.

Scott, P. (2007). Successfully bringing parents into the classroom. *Education Digest: Essential Readings Condensed for Quick Review, 73*(2), 47–49.

Senko, C., & Hulleman, C. S. (2013). The role of goal attainment expectancies in achievement goal pursuit. *Journal of Educational Psychology, 105,* 504–521.

Sheffield, L. J. (Ed.). (1999). *Developing mathematically promising students.* Reston, VA: National Council of Teachers of Mathematics.

Short, D., & Fitzsimmons, S. (2007). *Double the work: Challenges and solutions to acquiring language and academic literacy for adolescent English language learners— A report to Carnegie Corporation of New York.* Washington, DC: Alliance for Excellent Education.

Sidney, P. G., & Alibali, M. W. (2015). Making connections in math: Activating a prior knowledge analogue matters for learning. *Journal of Cognition and Development, 16*(1), 160–185.

Simpson, A., & Cole, M. W. (2015). More than words: A literature review of the language of mathematics research. *Educational Review, 67*(3), 369–384.

Sloyer, C. W. (2004). The extension-reduction strategy: Activating prior knowledge. *Mathematics Teacher, 98*(1), 48–50.

Smith, M. S., & Stein, M. K. (1998). Selecting and creating mathematical tasks: From research to practice. *Mathematics Teaching in the Middle School, 3*(5), 344–350.

Smith, M. S., & Stein, M. K. (2011). *5 practices for orchestrating productive mathematics discussion.* Reston, VA: NCTM.

Sousa, D. (2011). *How the brain learns.* Thousand Oaks, CA: Corwin.

Stein, M. K., Smith, M. S., Henningsen, M., & Silver, E. A. (2000). *Implementing standards-based mathematics instruction: A casebook for professional development.* New York: Teachers College Press.

Stiggins, R. J. (2001). The unfulfilled promise of classroom assessment. *Educational Measurement: Issues and Practice, 20*(3), 5–15.

Stinson, D. W. (2004). Mathematics as "gate-keeper" (?): Three theoretical perspectives that aim at empowering all children with a key to the gate. *Mathematics Educator, 14*(1), 8–18.

Sweller, J. (2006). The worked example effect and human cognition. *Learning and Instruction, 16*(2), 165–169.

Texas Essential Knowledge and Skills for Mathematics. (2012). 19 TAC Chapter 111. Retrieved from http://ritter.tea.state.tx.us/rules/tac/chapter111/ch111a.html

Throndsen, I. (2011). Self-regulated learning of basic arithmetic skills: A longitudinal study. *British Journal of Educational Psychology, 81*(4), 558–578.

Tomlinson, C. A. (1995). Deciding to differentiate instruction in middle school: One school's journey. *Gifted Child Quarterly, 37*(2), 77–87.

VanDerHeyden, A., McLaughlin, T., Algina, J., & Snyder, P. (2012). Randomized evaluation of a supplemental grade-wide mathematics intervention. *American Educational Research Journal, 49,* 1251–1284.

VanDerHeyden, A. M., & Witt, J. C. (2005). Quantifying the context of assessment: Capturing the effect of base rates on teacher referral and a problem-solving model of identification. *School Psychology Review, 34,* 161–183.

Van de Walle, J. A., Karp, K. S., & Bay-Williams, J. M. (2013). *Elementary and middle school mathematics: Teaching developmentally* (8th ed.). Boston: Pearson.

Van Garderen, D. (2004). Reciprocal teaching as a comprehension strategy for understanding mathematical word problems. *Reading & Writing Quarterly, 20*(2), 225–229.

Van Loon, M. H., de Bruin, A. B. H., van Gog, T., & van Merriernboer, J. J. G. (2013). Activation of inaccurate prior knowledge affects primary-school students' metacognitive judgments and calibration. *Learning and Instruction,* *24,* 15–25.

Veenman, M. V., Van Hout-Wolters, B. H., & Afflerbach, P. (2006). Metacognition and learning: Conceptual and methodological considerations. *Metacognition and Learning, 1*(1), 3–14.

Vygotsky, L. S. (1962). *Thought and language.* Cambridge, MA: MIT Press.

Vygotsky, L. S. (1978). *Mind in society: The development of higher mental processes.* Cambridge, MA: Harvard University Press.

Webb, D. C., Boswinkel, N., & Dekker, T. (2008). Beneath the tip of the iceberg: Using representations to support student understanding. *Mathematics Teaching in the Middle School, 14*(2), 110–113.

Wiliam, D. (2011). *Embedded formative assessment.* Bloomington, IN: Solution Tree Press.

Willingham, D. T. (2009). *Why don't students like school? A cognitive scientist answers questions about how the mind works and what it means for the classroom.* San Francisco: Wiley.

Wood, T. (1998). Alternative patterns of communication in mathematics classes: Funneling or focusing? In H. Steinbring, M. G. Bartolini Bussi, & A. Sierpinska (Eds.), *Language and communication in the mathematics classroom* (pp. 167–178). Reston, VA: NCTM.

Yackel, E., & Cobb, P. (1996). Sociomathematical norms, argumentation, and autonomy in mathematics. *Journal for Research in Mathematics Education, 27*(4), 458–477.

Zevenbergen, R. (2005). The construction of a mathematical habitus: Implications of ability grouping in the middle years. *Journal of Curriculum Studies, 37*(5), 607–619.

Index

Notes

Notes

Notes

Notes

CM CORWIN MATHEMATICS

Why Corwin Mathematics?

We've all heard this—"either you are a math person, or you are not." At Corwin Mathematics, we believe ALL students should have the opportunity to be successful in math! Trusted experts in math education such as Linda Gojak, Ruth Harbin Miles, John SanGiovanni, Skip Fennell, Gary Martin, and many more offer clear and practical guidance to help all students move from surface to deep mathematical understanding, from favoring procedural knowledge over conceptual learning, and from rote memorization to true comprehension. **We deliver research-based, high quality content that is classroom-tested and ready to be used in your lessons**—today!

Through books, videos, consulting, and online tools, we offer a truly **blended learning experience that helps teachers demystify math for students.** The user-friendly design and format of our resources provides not only the best classroom-based professional guidance, but many activities, lesson plans, rubrics, and templates to help you implement changes at your own pace in order to sustain learning improvement over time. We are **committed to empowering every learner.** With our forward-thinking and practical offerings, Corwin Mathematics helps you enable all students to realize the power and beauty of math and its connection to everything they do.

Warm Regards,
The Corwin Mathematics Team

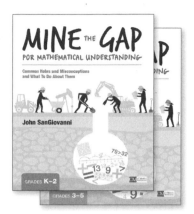
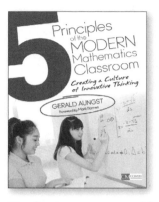
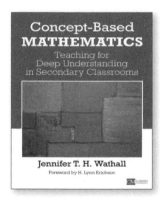

A SAGE Publishing Company

CORWIN HAS ONE MISSION: to enhance education through intentional professional learning.

We build long-term relationships with our authors, educators, clients, and associations who partner with us to develop and continuously improve the best evidence-based practices that establish and support lifelong learning.